LIMITLESS

LIVING THE LIFE OF AN *Overcomer*

Nancy Coen

Limited Edition
with BONUS CHAPTERS

REVELATION PARTNERS PUBLISHING
~ in association with ~
NANCY COEN MEDIA

Copyright © 2019 Nancy Coen and Revelation Partners.

Published by Revelation Partners (a subsidiary of Son of Thunder Publications, Ltd.), www.revelationpartners.org, in association with Nancy Coen Media.

All rights reserved. Short extracts, single chapters, activations and prayers may be copied for non-profit educational or devotional purposes only, without prior permission. Otherwise no part of this publication may be reproduced, stored in a retrieval system, or transmitted in any form or by any means, electronic, mechanical, photocopying, scanning or otherwise, without the prior written consent of the publisher.

Note: This author teaches that her audience is powerful enough to choose what they believe and want to follow. All statements in this book are the teachings of Nancy Coen. This publishing house, together with transcribers, editors and all other contributors and professionals, takes no legal, spiritual, religious or other responsibility for the teachings of the author as printed here or any actions taken by readers as a result.

Cover Design by Iain Gutteridge, I.G. Design, ig-graphic-design.co.uk
Edited and Interior Design by Rachel L. Hall

Scripture quotations marked "AMP" are taken from the Amplified® Bible, Copyright © 1954, 1958, 1962, 1964, 1965, 1987 by The Lockman Foundation. Used by permission. (www.Lockman.org). All rights reserved.

Scripture quotations marked "EXB" are taken from The Expanded Bible. Copyright ©2011 by Thomas Nelson. Used by permission. All rights reserved.

Scripture quotations marked "KJ21" are taken from the 21st Century King James Version®, copyright © 1994. Used by permission of Deuel Enterprises, Inc., Gary, SD 57237. All rights reserved.

Scripture quotations marked "MIR" are from The Mirror Bible, tranlated by Francis DuToit and published by Mirror Word Publishing. Copyright © 2014 by Mirror Word Publishing. Used by permission. All rights reserved.

The scripture quotations marked MSG are taken from *THE MESSAGE*, copyright © 1993, 2002, 2018 by Eugene H. Peterson. Used by permission of NavPress. All rights reserved. Represented by Tyndale House Publishers, Inc.

Scripture quotations marked (NIV) are taken from the Holy Bible, New International Version®, NIV®. Copyright © 1973, 1978, 1984, 2011 by Biblica, Inc.™ Used by permission of Zondervan. All rights reserved worldwide. www.zondervan.com The "NIV" and "New International Version" are trademarks registered in the United States Patent and Trademark Office by Biblica, Inc.™

Scripture quotations marked NKJV are taken from the New King James Version®. Copyright © 1982 by Thomas Nelson. Used by permission. All rights reserved.

Scripture quotations marked "TLB" are taken from The Living Bible. Copyright © 1971 by Tyndale House Foundation. Used by permission of Tyndale House Publishers Inc., Carol Stream, Illinois 60188. All rights reserved.

Scripture marked "TLV" is taken from the Holy Scriptures, Tree of Life Version. Copyright © 2014,2016 by the Tree of Life Bible Society. Used by permission o Tree of Life Bible Society.

Scripture quotations marked TPT are from The Passion Translation®. Copyright © 2017, 2018 by Passion & Fire Ministries, Inc. Used by permission. All rights reserved. ThePassionTranslation.com.

Each chapter in this book is an edited and updated transcript taken from messages given by Nancy Coen at different times over a period of years.

Limitless: Living the Life of an Overcomer/ Nancy Coen. —1st ed.

ISBN 978-1-911251-42-2   Hardback, Limited Edition with Bonus Chapters
ISBN 978-1-7321638-6-7   Paperback, Standard Edition
ISBN 978-1-911251-46-0   eBook, Standard Edition

Contents

A Note from the Publisher 7
Author's Acknowledgments 9
Introduction 11
All Creation Groaning 13
    Ascension Prayer 18
    Silent Prayer and the Kingdom Within 25
    Properties of Water 30
    All Things Work Together 32
Prophetic Sight in the Kingdom Age 36
    A Perspective Change 37
    Transfiguration from Old to New 40
    The Source and Foundation of Prophetic Vision 42
    The Gift vs. the Spirit of Prophecy 43
    Times and Seasons 45
    A Pattern from Revelation 48
    Prayer 57
Overcoming 59
    Jacob as Overcomer 59
    Wrestling with God / Wrestling with Brothers 60
    The Peter-Paul Principle 62
    Joshua as Overcomer 63
    Jesus as Overcomer 65
    The Time Has Come 66
    Glory Restored and Authority Granted 69
    Completing the Work 70
    In Him from Before the World Began 71
    Our Purpose: Revealing Him 72
    Understanding the Mystery of God 73
    Casting Down the Accuser of the Brethren 76
    Becoming Overcomers 78
Being an Overcomer 81
    Judgment to Ephesus 82
    Judgment to Smyrna 85
    Judgment to Pergamos 93

- Judgment of Thyatira 99
- Judgment of Sardis 102
- Judgment of Philadelphia 103
- Judgment to Laodicea 109

Revelation 119
- Pursuing End-Time Understanding 121
- The Record of the Coming King 122
- Seeing Revelation from the Kingdom Within 124
- A Blinding Ascension 128
- Seeing the Things Which Are 132
- On the Island of Patmos 137
- Becoming What We Behold 138
- Entering the Open Door 139
- From Decision to Decree 141
- The Prophets Saw 142
- The Simplicity of Seeing 144
- Believe in the Kingdom; Believe in Rapture Now 149
- Accessing Our Inheritance Through Love 151

Seventh Day Transfiguration 155
- Kingdom Gospel Revealed through Jesus' Pattern ... 156
- The Day of Glorious Revealing 157
- From the Thousands to the One 158
- Moses and Elijah at the Transfiguration 160
- Peter and the Age of the Church 163
- Falling in the Fear of Lord 163
- Arise and See Jesus Only 168
- The Spirit of Elijah Precedes Restoration 169
- Revelation Increases as Transfiguration Approaches ... 172

Restoration 175
- My Journey Towards Believing God Restores All 175
- Reconciling Eternal Judgment and Every Knee Bowed ... 179
- All Means All, So is Death the End? 182
- Creation of Body, Soul and Spirit 185
- Severing Flesh from Spirit, Frequency 186
- God's Permissive vs. Sovereign Will 192
- Death Row Testimony 203

Going on to Perfection 208
- Dominion in Healing 210

- Leaving the First Principles Behind 214
- Entering the Third Day/Coming Up to Perfection 216
- Take Off Religious Masks 217
- Confront Anger, Bitterness and Resentment 218
- Remove Confusion and Double-Mindedness 222
- Give Up the Right to be Right 225
- Cast Out Fear 225
- A Note on Suffering 228
- Prayer 229

The Power of Unlimited Vision 231
- Unlimited Knowledge 232
- Unlimited Anointing 235
- Unlimited Resources 236
- Unlimited Transportation (Teleportation) 236
- Unlimited Authority 238
- Unlimited Dominion 241
- Prayer 244

The New Mystical Move 245
- Being a Mystic 247
- Bodily Pain 249
- Manifestations of the Mystical Move 251
- Bi-Location: From Jesus' Pattern 259
- Telepathic experience 267
- Precognition 275

The Order of Melchizedek 279
- Prayer 302

About The Author 303

A Note From the Publisher

It has been an honour working with Nancy Coen to produce her first book. Nancy's teaching and testimonies give the reader a lift of faith and inspiration as her love for people and passion for the Lord shines through.

I'd like to thank Shannon Bates for her support and Wayne Holcomb for his input. There are also many volunteers who helped to make this book a reality, including Sheila Bunch, Mary Lynn Bushong, Melissa Tabor, Barbara Krueger, Rose Marie Gagnon, Elizabeth Jones, Kim Stephens, Sue Towne, Nina Hayden, Jeff Domansky, Timothy Whalen, and Paul Ferrante. But the biggest thanks goes to our editor Rachel Hall who diligently combed through every chapter.

Thank you: we love you all.

Heather Rayner
Revelation Partners
October 2019

Author's Acknowledgments

MY WHOLE LIFE has been one amazing adventure after another. First, I want to thank Yahweh, Yeshua, and Ruach for choosing me, empowering me, equipping me, and launching me into ministry in the nations. None of this would have been possible without their leading, guidance, and direction. Thank You, Holy Trinity. It is a blessing and privilege to serve you.

Second, I want to acknowledge that I owe all that I have been able to accomplish to my precious husband, Bob Coen. The extent of my travel times away from home have meant great sacrifice for us both. We love one another deeply, and truly enjoy our time together.

His patience with all of my years of spiritual gymnastics has been amazing! It is indeed a rare thing to find a husband who is willing and able to release his wife into sometimes dangerous and often compromising positions. I have only been able to fly as high as I have because he has indeed been the wind beneath my wings.

We will have been married for over fifty years by the time this book is released and I have been traveling into foreign nations for over half of that time, while he is committed to holding down the fort and keeping the home fires burning on his own.

I asked him once if he wouldn't be happier if I were a normal, everyday housewife who stayed home baking cookies for her family. He responded with tears in his eyes: "I would be lying if I said that perhaps sometimes I didn't wish you were home a little more. But, whenever I start to think that way, I just close my eyes and I see that little boy being raised from the dead, that little girl whose burned limbs were restored and whose badly scarred skin was returned to glorious perfection. I think about the Mullahs and the cannibals who have given their lives to Yeshua because of the depths of your love for them, and I have to ask myself: 'What is that worth, really?'"

Thank you, honey, for over fifty years of faithfulness and sacrifice. I am who I am today because of the depths of your selfless love.

I would also like to acknowledge my children, my grandchildren, and now my great-grandchildren for all their years of encouragement in the ministry. And to all my friends throughout the world who have made my journey such a total delight in Him, I praise God daily for you all, and am so thankful that you have been such a significant part of my journey, both in the natural and in the spiritual realms.

Thank you. Thank you all. THANK YOU!!!

INTRODUCTION

Limitless is a collection of updated teachings in which I invite you to consider our misunderstanding of what has happened from the beginning of creation, because we have only acknowledged a part of the truth. We have tried to bring the huge, magnificent, all-knowing, all-seeing, all-powerful, all-present, infinite mind of God down into the earth realm. To attempt to understand it all, we have tried to make our little, tiny, finite minds encompass His vast unlimited mind.

It does not work that way, because the *"wisdom of man is foolishness to God,"* and the wisdom of God is foolishness to man. Scripture teaches:

> *Where is the wise? Where is the scribe? Where is the disputer of this world? Has not God made foolish the wisdom of this world?* (1 Corinthians 1:20 NKJV)

> *For the wisdom of this world is foolishness with God. For it is written, "He catches the wise in their own craftiness."* (1 Corinthians 3:19)

We clearly cannot stay in the place of the wisdom of man. We need to learn how to ascend into the heavenly realms. We will see Him face-to-face so that we can be introduced to who we really are in the realms of the Spirit. Jesus came to be your pattern. If you are going to seek Him with all of your heart, soul, mind, strength and with everything that is in you, then your life will follow in the same pattern as His.

There will be days and years while you are young that you study to show yourself approved of God and man (2 Timothy 2:15). Then there will come a time when you will go down in the water one way and come up from the water another way. The heavens will open up and say, *"This is my beloved Son, in whom I am well-pleased"* (Matthew 3:17 KJV). When that happens, the Holy Spirit will immediately come to drive you into the wilderness to be tempted of the devil, but you will overcome. Jesus left the pattern that we are about ready to step into.

You will come out of the wilderness full of anointing and power, working signs, wonders and miracles. Then, there will come a time when that power will be set aside. You will be accused, defiled, defamed, slandered, betrayed, and made fun of. Many know exactly what I am talking about because you have gone through it.

But be encouraged, and get ready. God is doing some amazing things.

– Nancy Coen

Chapter 1

All Creation Groaning

AT THIS TIME, all creation is groaning for the manifestation of the sons of the living God. In response to this groaning, new technology is being ushered into the body of Christ for the advancement of the Kingdom and His righteousness in all the earth.

I want to start off by sharing how I was transformed by the groaning that the Lord is ushering into the earth at this hour. In 1997, I was doing a conference in Georgia. I took a walk one day out in the woods. Suddenly, I saw two old trees dripping with Spanish moss. In between them, a blue-white tube/chute from the throne of Heaven came and struck the earth. The Lord told me to step into it. As I did, I fell on the ground and went into a very deep groaning.

After I left the conference and got home, the groaning continued for seven days. For 24/7, around the clock without a break, I continued in a deep level of groaning. I had no idea what it was all about or what it was about to produce in my ministry, in my body, in my spirit or in any other thing. I simply yielded to what I felt the Holy Spirit doing.

For several years, I would go into this groaning at significant times in my ministry. I never really understood what was happening until the Lord revealed to me the technology of what it was producing. The groaning was a sound and frequency that would affect and impact all of the spiritual realm which was being originated in the high command positions of the powers of darkness.

As I began to investigate the different sounds, I went into the Word of God. (I always check and back everything up with the Word of God.) I found there are many different kinds of sounds and frequencies referred to in scripture. One is the sound of all creation groaning. There is the sound of the shedding of innocent blood, the sound of the trumpet, the sound of the shofar, the sound of the wind, the sound of waterspouts, the sound of deep calling unto deep—which is one of my favorite sounds of all. There is the sound of the abundance of rain, the sound of the armies of God, and the sound of man.

Let me draw your attention to Romans 8, and then I will share you a few testimonies about how all of this might operate in your life to bring you to a higher level of functionality. *"For as many as are led by the Spirit of God, these are sons of God"* (Romans 8:14 NKJV). I do not know how to tell you this, but women of the Kingdom are not daughters—women are sons. In the realms of the spirit, there is neither male nor female. So, if a husband can be part of the bride, a wife can be part of the sons. We are called the sons of God in many different locations in the Bible. Whenever scripture refers to sons of God, I want women to embrace that as a title which refers to them as well as to men.

We are adopted into God's family as sons:

> *For you did not receive the spirit of bondage again to fear, but you received the Spirit of adoption by whom we cry out, "Abba, Father."* (Romans 8:15 NKJV)

The Spirit of adoption is rarely taught. My daughter recently adopted two children. When they were adopted, their whole inheritance shifted and changed. First, their names changed. The word *name* in Hebrew (*Strong's* H8034) can also be used like the word *nature*, or character. When you are adopted in the Kingdom, you receive a new name: Yahweh breathes in you a new name, a new nature.[1] That new name is referred to in Revelation when you become an overcomer:

To him who overcomes I will give some of the hidden manna to eat. And I will give him a white stone, and on the stone a new name written which no one knows except him who receives it. (Revelation 2:17 **NKJV**)

After my daughter adopted her children, not only did their names change, their estates changed in that they became the legal inheritors of everything procured by their adopted father. When you receive the Spirit of adoption, everything the Father has is now transferable to you—it is a part of your inheritance. When the Word says that we are exalted to the right hand of God the Father Almighty, we are joint heirs to the Kingdom of Heaven with Jesus Christ, that means we are joint heirs, and we will begin to function as such when we truly understand the Spirit of adoption. We can be assured of this, as Paul states: *"The Spirit Himself bears witness with our spirit that we are children of God"* (Romans 8:16 **NKJV**).

In our natural state, we have the DNA which was passed down to us from our earthly parents. But we are entering into an era where we are going to transition out of being controlled and manipulated by our earthly-natured DNA and be transferred into the DNA of God's nature. When that happens, we will begin to totally function from the position of glory that the Lord has given us as sons of God.

If children, then heirs—heirs of God and joint heirs with Christ, if indeed we suffer with Him, that we may also be glorified together. (Romans 8:17 **NKJV**)

Some of you have suffered lately, especially those of the ten percent who are being called out to establish an entirely new foundation to be laid down for the Kingdom of God and His righteousness. Many of you have been falsely accused. You have been slandered and defiled. Your character has been insulted. Many of those insults have come

---

[1] See the article titled "Name" by Jeff A. Benner, available on the Ancient Hebrew Research Center website at https://www.ancient-hebrew.org/definition/name.htm

from the body of Christ and from well-meaning pastors who thought they were trying to protect the reputation of the church.

Many of you have seen a severance of relationships with people whom you love dearly who are not hearing the same things that you are hearing. When you begin to share with them the things that you are hearing, they say, "Be careful," because they fear you are going off the deep end. They want you to back what you're hearing and seeing up with the Word, but even when you do, they do not believe you because they do not have ears to hear the same things that you are hearing.

> *For I consider that the sufferings of this present time are not worthy to be compared with the glory which shall be revealed in us. For the earnest expectation of the creation eagerly waits for the revealing of the sons of God.* (Romans 8:18–19 NKJV)

There is a time coming soon when the Glory of God will be revealed in us. It has not yet been revealed, but it will soon be revealed. All of creation is waiting for the revealing of the sons of God, which will make its appearance in the seventh day transfiguration of the corporate Son of Man.[2]

I have much to say about the following verse, but much of it will be better held for another book: *"For the creation was subjected to vanity, not willingly, but because of Him who subjected it to the same in hope…"* (Romans 8:20 NKJV). Suffice it to say this for now: in the age of church, our doctrine said, "We believe in an All-Knowing, All-Present, All-Seeing, All Powerful God, so big, so powerful, so present in all things, that He is going to give away 90% of all that He made to the devil. God is so smart, but that old devil was so cunning, and so smart, that he just snuck into the Garden of Eden and snatched the promise of God right out from under his nose." What? I don't think so! Such false doctrine makes the devil infinitely more powerful than God, because

---

[2] For more information on this appearing, see the teaching by the same name from GlobalAscensionNetwork.net.

God only ended up with 10% and the devil ended up with 90%. How ludicrous is that?³

Paul teaches, *"... the creation itself also will be delivered from the bondage of corruption into the glorious liberty of the children of God"* (Romans 8 21 NKJV, emphasis mine). Please note he was writing in future tense. It is something that Paul recognized was still to come. The creation will be delivered (futuristically speaking) from the bondage of corruption and into the glorious liberty of the children of God.

He goes on to write: *"For we know that the whole creation groans and labors with birth pangs together until now"* (Romans 8:22 NKJV). The word *groans* comes from the Greek *sustenazo*. According to *Strong's* G4959, it means "together with one voice." All of creation is groaning together jointly, and labors with birth pangs together until now.

When I began to teach about groaning, many people, especially intercessory prayer warriors in the church, would come and say they had been groaning in intercession for years. However, I would explain they had not been groaning, they had been travailing.

Travailing is different than groaning. Travailing is the process we go through when we birth something out of the spiritual realm into the earthly realm. The thing that we have been travailing for for two thousand years is now born. It is here in the earth. It's called "The One New Man."

So what is the difference between travailing and groaning? Travailing is for birthing. Groaning is for the redemption of the body. Paul explains, *"Not only that, but we also who have the firstfruits of the Spirit, even we ourselves groan within ourselves, eagerly waiting for the adoption, the redemption of our body"* (Romans 8:23 NKJV).

Recognize here that Paul was still *"eagerly waiting for the **adoption**, the **redemption** of our body"* (emphasis mine). At the writing of this scripture, adoption and redemption were still to come in the future. Was Paul referring to the redemption of our physical body, the Body

---

³ More about this concept is available under the topic "Restoration of All Things" at GlobalAscensionNetwork.net.

of Christ, or "the Body," including all things ever created? That is a question that can be answered unilaterally with a YES! to all.[4]

ASCENSION PRAYER

Paul writes about our salvation and asks a question: *"For we were saved in this hope, but hope that is seen is not hope; for why does one still hope for what he sees?"* (Romans 8:24 NKJV)

Through ascension prayer, we are given access by God to be caught up in the moment, in the twinkling of an eye, to see as John did the things that were, the things that are, and the things that are yet to come.

> *Therefore, leaving the discussion of the elementary principles of Christ, let us go on to perfection, not laying again the foundation of repentance from dead works and of faith toward God, of the doctrine of baptisms, of laying on of hands, of resurrection of the dead, and of eternal judgment.* (Hebrews 6:1–2 NKJV)

What are the elementary principles of Christ and the repentance from dead works? The doctrine of baptisms, the laying on of hands, resurrection of the dead, and the doctrine of eternal judgment are the elementary principles. If we stay in only those, we operate in a low level of functionality. Repentance from dead works means we are not going to do any more dead works. The works that we are going to do are going to produce magnificent results. Therefore, there will be no future need for repentance from dead works.

When the Lord first enacted that verse inside of me and made it living and active, I called out to Him. I asked about the verse which reads, *"without faith it is impossible to please Him"* (Hebrews 11:6 NKJV). How can we set aside faith towards God, if without faith it is impossible to please God? The Lord just laughed at me. (He laughs at me all the time.) He asked me what I thought faith meant. I answered Him with the verse, *"Faith is the substance of things hoped for, the evidence of things*

---

[4] For more about the redemption of the body, "Release from Human Limitations" is available GlobalAscensionNetwork.net. You will be amazed to see how the Lord is using this groaning process to begin the magnificent redemption of our body.

not seen" (Hebrews 11:1 NKJV). Then He spoke into my heart this question: "Why do you still hope for the thing you have already seen?" (That is to say, what I have seen through ascension prayer.)

When we learn how to ascend and descend, when we continue to practice doing so, and when we are caught up in the moment to see Jesus Christ and all the magnificent, wonderful things that take place in the heavenly realms, our low level of faith is no longer necessary, because we will see the thing that we previously considered to be yet afar off.

In the Age of the Church, we thought we had to die to go to Heaven and see Jesus. But the truth of the matter is that to be caught up and carried away in the moment, in the twinkling of an eye, is to stand face-to-face with Him. This is a now-present and historically an everyday reality available to us at all times. Through ascension prayer, you will see Him. I promise that when you gaze into His eyes, touch His hair, feel His breath in your face and hear His whisper in your ears, the things of earth will grow strangely dim. You might be thinking, "Well, I need faith to be able to pay my mortgage." But many of the things on earth that seem so incredibly heavy and weighty for us will suddenly melt away to nothing.[5]

> *If we hope for what we do not see, we eagerly wait for it with perseverance. Likewise the Spirit also helps in our weaknesses.* (Romans 8:24–25 NKJV)

Perseverance is sadly lacking in the body of Christ. Many will go up and come down, go up and come down, two or three times even, but they do not persevere. Because they lack perseverance, the measure of change effected in their life is minimal.

Many claim that Romans 8:25 means that the Spirit of God helps us in sicknesses. No: that is not it! The *weaknesses* the Spirit helps us with are the weaknesses of the limitations the human mind operates with so long as we are under the gravitational pull of the earth. We

---

[5] To become a member of an ascension group, contact GlobalAscensionNetwork.net. The teaching "Ascending and Descending" will help you discover how you can begin to practice.

are weak because we have not yet seen the thing that the Lord is going to do.

When you learn to be caught up in the moment and carried away, you will learn that Jesus is multi-faceted. He is multi-frequencied, multi-colored, and multi-multi-dimensional. Every time you are caught up, He will reveal to you a different facet of His character. Once it is revealed to you, when you come back, you can manifest that facet of His character according to the dimension of Christ that He revealed to you.

I encourage you to not give up! Use the perseverance the Spirit of the Lord has given you as He woos and drives you into higher levels of functionality. The more intensely you desire union with the Divine nature, the more He meets your desire. He wants this level of communion even more than you do!

Paul makes an interesting statement: *"For we do not know what we should pray for as we ought, but the Spirit Himself makes intercession for us with groanings which cannot be uttered"* (Romans 8:26 NKJV). What does he mean, *"We do not know what we should pray for as we ought"*? In the Age of the Church, we prayed infantile prayers. Basically, our prayers focused on gaining everything we needed to make our life more comfortable. "Lord, I need more money. Lord, I need salvation for my children. Lord, I need a business. Lord, I need to be released into missions. Lord, I want. Lord, I need." Those are infantile prayers. In fact, if I went around the nation and listened in on the prayers of well-meaning, Jesus-loving, chandelier-swinging Christians, their prayers would almost always focus on how to maintain their comfort zone. Rather than being caught up to see the things that were, the things that are, and the things that are yet to come, and speaking and praying out of those things, they pray what they think the Lord wants for them.

I used to have a ministry in Washington, D.C. Once I went to the Lincoln Memorial. One of the most profound things that President Lincoln wrote is inscribed on the monument. "Both [sides] read the same Bible and pray to the same God, and each invokes His aid against the other. It may seem strange that any men should dare to ask a just God's assistance in wringing their bread from the sweat of other men's faces, but let us judge not, that we be not judged. The prayers of both could not be answered. That of neither has been answered fully. The Almighty has His own purposes."[6]

Basically, this is what we do. We pray what we think God would want, not what He actually does want. What He actually wants for us goes far above and beyond what we want for ourselves. In fact, in greater measure than we know, our prayers are frequently in direct opposition to His desires.

Jesus said, *"The Son can do nothing of Himself, but what He sees the Father do"* (John 5:19 NKJV). So, if Jesus, the Son of God, of His own self could do nothing except that which He saw the Father doing, how do we think we can accomplish anything of eternal value if we cannot see what the Father is doing? Jesus went on to explain how He did not speak of His own self, not His own desires, not His own dreams, not His own wishes. *"I do nothing on my own initiative, but I only speak the truth that the Father has revealed to me"* (John 8:28 TPT).

When you learn how to ascend and descend, from your position in the heavens you can decree, declare, administrate and legislate the desires of God that they would be made manifest in the earth. I have many ascension groups around the earth that are doing this right now. They have set aside their own hopes, thoughts and limitations in order to set their eyes on Him. When they go into heavenly places and they see what the Father is doing, they come back to decree and declare only the things they saw the Father doing. Almost without exception within a short period of time, whatever they declare occurs in their nations as written on the front page of the newspaper and as declared on national news media.

Man is a creature of habit, and we get into our habits. We think we know how to pray and do deliverance. We think we know how to cast out demons and prophesy, but as we move out of the Age of the

---

[6] "Second Inaugural Address." Lincoln Memorial. National Park Service. https://www.nps.gov/featurecontent/ncr/linc/interactive/deploy/html/still_photos/second-inaugural-address.jpg.

Church and into the Age of the Kingdom, much of that functionality is going to pass away.

I am going to give you a perfect example. When we shifted out of the Age of the Church and into the Age of the Kingdom, I had three hundred intercessors, one hundred for each of the three facets of the ministry. I invited them all to come so I could teach them the principles of groaning in regard to a new kind of prayer. I told them much of the way we had been praying was going to pass away. We were going to begin to groan in frequencies that were going to strike the heavens. So, for seven days I taught them about the different sounds in scripture, and for seven days they listened intently. They were in agreement: it was what they really needed and it was what they really wanted.

Now, my intercessors were well prepared. They were sighted and profoundly prophetic. Most of the time they knew where I was and what I was doing. They knew where I was going before I even got there. Once I came back from a trip and they asked, "On Wednesday at 2 o'clock in the afternoon, were you traveling along a big cliff in China when the wheels of your vehicle went off the side of the road?" I asked how they knew that, and they replied that they had seen it! They did see it. They were anointed.

After seven days of teaching them on the new levels of prayer (which, by the way, most of the time goes without words), one of my chief intercessors whom I love very much and who has rescued me from death wanted me to pray for her. She was in the kitchen doing dishes. Everybody else had gone away. She came up to me and asked if she could pull a prayer out of me. I said, "Well honey of course you can! You have rescued me from death many times. Pray whatever you want, but based on what we just learned, I want to lay my hands on your shoulders. You pray, and I will bring my spirit into agreement with what you are praying." However, that wasn't what happened.

This is what she did. She folded her hands and bowed her head, closed her eyes and right away started to cry. "Father, I want my children for the Kingdom of God, for Your righteousness, and I bind every spirit of doubt and unbelief."

Oh, my goodness—something rose up inside of me and the frequency of God struck my spirit. I grabbed her and I shook her. I shook her and shook her, and out of my belly there came a sound: "Noooo!"

She looked at me, stunned, through her thick glasses. Her eyes appeared so big. Her lips started to tremble a little bit, and she asked if she had got off into the old kind of prayer.

I said, "Yes ma'am. You did."

"Okay, give me a minute, just a minute. Give me just one minute." She folded her hands, bowed her head, closed her eyes and started to cry. She said, "Lord, I am so lonely, I want a husband!"

Everything inside of me erupted into a frequency. I grabbed her and shook her again and again. I shook her and shook her, and out of my belly there came this sound: "Noooo! No!"

She looked at me and she asked, "Oh, I did it again, didn't I?"

You see, we are creatures of habit.

She said, "Wait just one minute, just one minute." While I still had my hand on her shoulder, she thought for a few minutes She folded her hands, bowed her head, closed her eyes, and started to cry, "Father, I need money for my business, I want to..."

Out of my belly came an outrageously deep sound: "Noooo! No!" I shook her and shook her and shook her. Then I got right in her face and asked, "Honey, what do you want from God?"

She looked back at me. Her lips started to quiver as tears came down her face. She said, "I don't know what you want me to say."

I grabbed her and held her because I loved her. I loved her dearly. I asked, "Honey, don't you understand? It is not that God does not want your children to be saved. It is not that He does not want you to have a husband or that He wants you to be lonely for your whole life. It is not that He does not want to make every heavenly provision for your business, but He wants to give you HIMSELF! He wants to give you the nations of the earth. He wants to give you the fullness of your inheritance, and you are still praying for your Aunt Bessy's cancer. It is not that those things are not important, but the Word says, "*Seek first the Kingdom of God and His righteousness, and all these things shall be added to you"* (Matthew 6:33 NKJV).

When I tell this story, intercessors will look at one another and remark to one another they hope I never pray for them. God says, *"Yet once more I will shake not only the earth, but also the starry heaven,"* which indicates *"...the removal and final transformation of all those things which can be shaken—that is, of that which has been created—so that those things which cannot be shaken may remain"* (Hebrews 12:26–28 AMP). In other words, everything that can be shaken, will be shaken. Further, *"The kingdom of heaven [that is us] suffers violence, and the violent take it by force"* (Matthew 11:12 NKJV, bracketed addition, mine).

When I was shaking her, everything inside of her was shaken until the only thing not shaken was the Kingdom of God. On that day, she got it! The Word of God says: *"...seek ye first the kingdom of God and his righteousness; and [THEN] all these [other] things shall be added unto you"* (Matthew 6:33 KJV, bracketed additions, mine). When she took her mind off her own self and put it on how to be a co-worker and a co-creator together with God for the establishment of His Kingdom and His righteousness, she got it.

I had known her for thirty-five years. We had been closely attached to one another. She had been praying those same prayers for thirty-five years, with almost no results at all. When she took her eyes off her own needs and set her eyes on Kingdom precepts, within three months all her children gave their lives to Jesus. She met a man and got married. She sold her business for a million dollars and went into mission work in Africa.

I teach on the power of silent prayer and how it contains the groaning and the frequency of our own body. Silent prayer is probably at this moment one of the most powerful prayers because it allows the Holy Spirit to groan inside of us with a groaning that cannot even be uttered.

Silent Prayer and the Kingdom Within

Before we go into the full measure of what this groaning reproduces, I want to talk to you about establishing the Kingdom within through silent prayer. This is the interior way or following the interior path to the path of maturity in the Christian life.

> *Until we all reach oneness in the faith and in the knowledge of the Son of God, [growing spiritually] to become a mature believer, reaching to the measure of the fullness of Christ [manifesting His spiritual completeness and exercising our spiritual gifts in unity].* (Ephesians 4:13 AMP)

Until we learn to pray the way He prayed we will remain in a state of immaturity. This means that we have to come before the Lord without requests for personal matters because we really do not know how to pray as we ought. Ninety percent of the time, we are probably praying in direct opposition to the Lord's desire for us.

If we remain before the Lord without petitioning according to our own will, we will become like soft wax, a perfectly manageable instrument in the hands of God. If we approach God with our own will and motivations, we are focusing on our own needs and are therefore merely being active for activities' sake. We have chosen to do something for God, rather than to be something in God.

As we yield ourselves to silent or internal prayer, we cannot come to God by the strength of our own will. We cannot come out of the fear of missing some big, high "spiritual" experience. We cannot come out of our desire even to be pleasing to Him or out of our own self-induced submission. We cannot come out of pursuit of heavenly experiences. Even when we begin to ascend and descend, we must recognize that it is not our desire for a heavenly experience that matters. What matters is what we do with what we see when we are there. We cannot go because it gives us goose bumps and it makes us feel really good. Too often, we use the Lord's presence for our own self-gratification, instead of being open receivers of what the Lord wants to give us, which is His perfect love.

When you come in silent prayer, you must come with no desire of your own, either earthly or heavenly. You must come only because you love Him, because you are in love with Him and because you are migrating into a state of becoming love.

In the Age of the Church it was okay to do love or give love, but in the Age of the Kingdom we must become love because that is the highest level of His nature. A profound way to do this is through the eternal walk of silent prayer. In it, we come to Him with no petition except to know Him.

I love Peter and Paul. After all the magnificent works they did, they said their one desire was to know Him. Not just to know Him, but to *"know Him and the power of His resurrection, and the fellowship of His sufferings, [by] being conformed to His death"* (Ephesians 3:10 NKJV).

Most people in the church want to know Jesus the overcoming, conquering, victorious hero, but very few of them want to know Him in His suffering. His suffering is vastly different from our suffering. Our suffering is for our personal sanctification, but His suffering is for our perfection.

As people migrating into Kingdom mentalities, one of the things that we have been identified with is the way we identify ourselves with Him in His suffering. We have to be rejected by the people we love the most, by the ones we gave ourselves to and invested ourselves in. Many of us know and understand that level of entering into His suffering.

If we come with no desire except for God alone, whatever comes from within us will be pure and without any kind of selfish motivation. If we are going to become Kingdom establishers—those who are going to establish the Kingdom outside—the first thing we must do is establish the Kingdom within. The best way to do that is through ascension prayer and silent prayer where the groaning of God does all the work.

I find that the times of my greatest level of prayer and communion with the Lord come late at night. I cover up with my quilt, pulling it over my head. It is like the equivalent of wrapping my head within the mantle as Elijah did. I get very quiet. I hold out my hands and I say, "Father, here I am, do with me as You desire."

What happens is amazing. I call it the "bubble up." It feels like I can feel His touch start at the top of my head. It moves down my body like bubbles, then it comes back up from my feet, goes up and down, up and down, and up and down. I do not even say a word, but I believe that what I am receiving is direct anointing from Him.

I am receiving the anointing to be released from human limitations and the anointing to prophesy in the nations of the earth. I receive the anointing to go into the deepest, darkest hell-holes that you can ever imagine and become the measure of light that He created me to be, so that I can drive out the darkness. This is what comes from silent prayer when I allow the groaning or the frequency of the Holy Spirit to shift and change and rearrange me from the inside out.

When we operate from the Kingdom within, we must first depart from self. There are many ways to establish the Kingdom, and there are many diverse realms of the Kingdom. We have the Kingdom of Eternity, the Kingdom of Heaven of Heavens, the Kingdom of Heaven, the Kingdom of our Lord and Savior, Jesus Christ, the Kingdom of the Father, the Kingdom of Earth, and the Kingdom within. If we are going to be used by God to establish His Kingdom in the Earth, we must first establish the Kingdom within.

We establish the Kingdom within not by going upward or outward, but by going inward—inward away from ourselves towards the Holiness of God that lives in our spirit. We have to go to the center of the creature in order to get to the center of the creator, because He lives right in our center. We will truly find Him in a place where there is no longer self. The further away we journey from self, the further we advance towards Him.

There is a preparation that I call "going on to perfection." It is in the dethroning of self that we will find the process that the Lord has laid down for us in moving away from self. Probably one of the hardest things about moving away from self is giving up our right to be right. We must give up our right not to be insulted. If they persecuted Jesus, how much more will they persecute us?

The Lord told me one time as He was preparing me for a third level of anointing that the instant I am in offense, I am in sin because sin is self-defense. He was trying to kill my old self and I was trying to defend myself, which is the exact opposite of what He wanted for me.

When we come to God in this way, our coming will produce a unique sense of rest and peace. It makes no difference what is going on in the world around us, because at that point we have no ungratified wish. We have no unfulfilled desire because our desire has become Him, and Him only. We have no other desire but Him.

During this same time, I went through a very lengthy process to get the third-level anointing. As I was preparing, I felt like that precious anointing was being withheld from me, so I took my chair over to the sea wall and I said to the Lord that I was going to sit on that sea wall until He told me what was standing in the way of me entering into this third level of anointing. I sat there all day long without a word from the Lord. Finally, it was getting to be dusk and I burst into tears and cried. I again said to the Lord that I was not leaving there until He told me what I had to do in order to tap into that third-level anointing.

Although it is inherently personal, I share this with you because it also has to do with the spiritual migration and the process of the church moving out of the Age of the Church and into the Age of the Kingdom.

He spoke to me and said that ninety percent of everything I had done in twenty-five years of ministry had been carnally initiated. Carnally initiated?! I mean, the Lord might as well have taken a sword and driven it straight through my heart!

I began to argue with Him. I reminded Him of how His word says, *"by their fruits you will know them"* (Matthew 7:20 NKJV). What about all the people who have been saved, healed and delivered? What about all the people who have been shifted and changed by the word of the Lord coming out of me? I pointed out all that was fruit.

He responded that it was fruit, and that some of it would last for all eternity. But now He wanted to know what my motivation was. He asked if my motivation was my desire to be recognized in the Age of the Church, and whether my desire was to be indispensable in the lives of the people. He also asked if my desire was to draw the people to myself or to draw them to Him. Was my desire for a name or ministry recognition? What was the internal desire of my heart?

When He asked that, I began to cry because I realized many times we think we are operating according to the Spirit when actually we are trying to produce something for ourselves, in our own lives. So basically, His word to me on that day was that until I was prepared to give up my name and my reputation, my ministry, the anointing, the gifts and fruit of the Spirit in pursuit of nothing more than His presence, I could not have this level of anointing. He exhorted me that on top of that, I could not get it from another man. If I wanted it, I must get it from Him, and Him alone.

I tell you this to show that silent prayer produces an internal yielding so great that you no longer have a desire for anything but Him.

...[T]he Spirit Himself makes intercession for us with groanings which cannot be uttered. (Romans 8:26 NKJV)

The intercession the Holy Spirit makes in and for us is according to the sovereign plan of God to produce what is written on the scrolls in Heaven. They contain the good works that He prepared for you to do before you ever even came to this earth. He intercedes and requests from within us that which is the desire of His heart, not the desire of our own hearts. He does this with a frequency, and that frequency is called groaning.

The request comes from the Holy Spirit, but the desire itself emanates from the Father. This is the will of the Father. Believers will only become one at the request of God which comes through the groaning or the frequency of God from within.

Frequently in the Age of the Church, we taught that we were going to come together in the unity of the Spirit. This unity meant getting together a hundred pastors in the city to come to one place and all pray the same word, at the same time, about the same thing. But that is not unity in the Spirit. Unity in the Spirit is the agreement with Him that is in the invisible realm, with the church that is in the invisible realm and with the church that is on the earth. That is true unity in the Spirit. The more we yield to silent prayer, the more we will learn about that.

When the prayer and the desire for Him only have originated in God, the believer is no longer free to pray for whomever he pleases, whenever he pleases, or even however he pleases. We will effectively have dethroned self.

Often we think we know what the Lord's desire is, especially for those in our own families. But when we start praying our own desires, it is really an attempt to perpetuate our own comfort zones. Rather, we must put ourselves in the unique position to pray exactly as God wants us to pray. When we do, we may be astounded by what comes out of our mouths.

When we are willing to enter into the process to gain the unique quality of radical intimacy with God, it signals a measure of Christian maturity.

Properties of Water

Consider water for a moment. Nothing on earth is more useful than water. Right now, water is the number one topic of discussion at nearly every international symposium. Because the water in the earth is beginning to dry up and much of it is becoming polluted, some of it is dying. In the end time, the Word says that much of the water in the earth is going to be polluted, but for now, let us just talk about pure water.

Water is the most valuable thing in the earth. Man can live without gold, he can live without silver, he can live without money, he can even live without food, but he cannot live without water. Water has no quality of its own, but it can take on a multitude of other forms and different contents. How it is formed and how its content is changed has to do with frequency.

Water is tasteless and can take on an infinite variety of other tastes, depending on what is put in it. If you take a cup of water, boil it (which is done many times by increasing the frequency) and you put a tea bag in it, it becomes tea. If you put water through a coffee pot, it becomes coffee. If you put Kool-Aid in it, it becomes Kool-Aid. If you put lemon and sugar in it, it becomes lemonade.

So, water, even though it has no taste of its own, becomes useful by whatever is put in it. It has no flavor or color, it has no scent of its own, but it can efficiently take on the color or the scent of whatever is mixed with it. Therefore, it has an endless number of uses.

Let us talk about another quality. Water is free-flowing; it has no form of its own. If water comes down freely, it drips all over, everywhere. It takes the form and shape of whatever container the Master puts it in. So, the Master can put the water in a glass, whether in a crystal glass or a pitcher; or the water could be put through a water hose to water a garden. Whatever vessel it is placed in, water will take its form and shape.

One of the ways the Lord spoke to me early on about the baptism of the Holy Spirit was through the analogy of a water hose. I had never had an encounter with a Pentecostal or a charismatic movement, so when I received the baptism of the Holy Spirit, the Lord used a water hose to teach me. I was out in the garden one day. It was springtime in Indiana. Our water hoses had all been balled up and put in the garage for the winter. They were full of spiderwebs and were twisted up in odd shapes. I took one of the hoses and stretched it out.

The Lord spoke to my heart and asked me if the water hose was fulfilling the purpose for which it was created. I did not think it was. I hooked the hose up to the faucet. He told me to turn on the spigot. So, I turned on the spigot and the hose filled up. As it did, the hose straightened out, making all the spiderwebs and everything else come off. He then asked me if I thought the water hose was now fulfilling the purpose for which it was created. I still thought it was not. So, He said to go and turn on the nozzle at the other end of the hose. I lifted up the nozzle and began spraying water over all the plants. He said, "Now! The water hose is fulfilling the purpose for which it was sent."

You see, the water has no form of its own. It can take on the form of ice, vapor, steam, and it can take on the form of liquid. All of which, by the way, are controlled by frequency which treats form the same as it does color. Water is fluid and it yields—it yields to whatever is added to it or to whatever form it is poured into. It takes on the form demanded for its own use. It is pure, it is simple, and that makes it the most useful element in all the earth.

The power of simplicity and purity in prayer comes when we become like water: no shape, no form, no taste, and no smell of our own. We can become whatever the Master desires for us to be. Much of that will happen as we enter into a time of silent prayer during which we allow the Holy Spirit to groan within us. We then become whatever the Spirit wants to put in us.

The human being now has no identity with self. As we yield to the groaning of the Holy Spirit, we abandon ourselves to God. We give up our own hopes and desires. We give up our own form and taste. We give ourselves totally to Him so that we can become the thing that we were created to be, which is the perfect reflection of His glory. God Himself has now become the author of whatever is manifested as a result of our yielding to silent prayer.

The soul no longer has any knowledge of anything of itself. The will no longer sees anything as belonging to itself, including our right to be right. Once we give up our right to be right, we are getting a little bit closer. The mind also enters into this place and has no condition of its own. It does not withhold any part of prayer for its own use. This produces purity and simplicity in prayer.

All Things Work Together

Let us go on with Romans 8: *"We know that all things work together for good to those who love God, to those who are the called according to His purpose"* (v. 28 NKJV). Is that not an interesting statement? How many of us can say that is one of our favorite verses in all the Bible? We know that all things work together for good. All things means all things. That does not mean just beautiful things, hopeful things, graceful things, or righteous things. It can also mean evil things, wicked things, and violent things. Whatever happens in our life will be used to work together for our good. If we yield ourselves as an instrument of God and if we seek Him with all our heart, soul, mind and strength, with everything that is within us, then we can stand before that old rotten devil, our adversary (even as Jesus stood before Pilot), and declare that he has no power over us except that which is given by the Father!

We give the devil so much credit for things which he was not even responsible for initiating. Our paths are led and directed by God Almighty. That means that no matter what happens (and it is true that we can open up our own minds and bodies to attacks from wickedness), the promise of the Lord is Romans 8:28—no matter what happens in your life, it will work together for your good if you are called according to His purpose.

Many people spend their whole life laboring over pains, rejection, betrayal, and many things that were laid on them in their youth, but if they will yield themselves to Him, He will use every one of those things for good. He will raise up the thing that was most painful in all of your life and cause it to be your greatest testimony to His power.

> *For whom He foreknew, He also predestined to be conformed to the image of His Son, that He might be the firstborn among many brethren.* (Romans 8:29 NKJV)

I do not know how to get this way down deep in your heart. The Lord knew you before you were ever born into the earth. You were predestined, you were fore-ordained to be conformed to the image of His Son, that He might be first born amongst many brethren. How many of you know how exciting it is to be called the brethren of Jesus Christ? I mean, really, that is an amazing statement: those that He foreknew. He knew you before you ever came here. He had His finger on your life before you ever came down into the earth. His purpose in foreknowing you and predestining you is so that you can be conformed to the image of Jesus Christ. The Word says we were created to be the perfect reflection of His glory.

> *We can all draw close to him with the veil removed from our faces. And with no veil we all become like mirrors who brightly reflect the glory of the Lord Jesus. We are being transfigured into His very image as we move from one*

brighter level of glory to another. And this glorious transfiguration comes from the Lord, who is the Spirit. (2 Corinthians 2:18 TPT)

Do you really believe that? Do you really believe that you can be the perfect reflection of His glory?

Moreover whom He predestined, these He also called; whom He called, these He also justified; and whom He justified, these He also glorified. (Romans 8:30 NKJV)

We are coming to the age where we are going to be glorified. A lot of people say that God will share His anointing, but He will never share His glory. I am sorry to tell you that is far from the truth. Jesus referred several times in His ministry to us having His glory and us being glorified with Him and in Him.

That they all may be one; just as You, Father, are in Me and I in You, that they also may be one in Us, so that the world may believe [without any doubt] that You sent Me. I have given to them the glory and honour which You have given Me, that they may be one, just as We are one. (John 17:21–22 AMP)

Many of the teachings that we held fast to in the Age of the Church were simply not scriptural, or better said, they were regarded only in part, because we were "seeing through a glass dimly."

What then shall we say to all these things? If God is for us, who can be [successful] against us? He who did not spare [even] His own Son, but gave Him up for us all, how will He not also, along with Him, graciously give us all things? (Romans 8:31–32 AMP)

In the Age of the Church, we were taught that we were poor, miserable sinners and that we were always going to fall short of the glory of God. But Jesus taught that there is going to come a day when we are going to walk in the fullness of our inheritance. What does our inheritance include? Jesus told us: He said that all rule, all reign, all power, and *"All authority has been given to Me in heaven and on earth"* (Matthew 28:18 NKJV). And that which the Father gave Him, He gives to us.

Behold, I give to you authority to tread on serpents and scorpions, and over all the authority of the enemy. And nothing shall by any means hurt you. (Luke 10:19 NKJV)

And I will give the keys of the kingdom of Heaven to you. And whatever you may bind on earth shall occur, having been bound in Heaven, and whatever you may loose on earth shall occur, having been loosed in Heaven. (Matthew 16:19 NKJV)

Of those whom You have given Me, I have not lost even one. (John 18:9 AMP)

When He promises to give us all things, He means He is going to give us all things! Do we earnestly believe that with all our hearts? Then it will come to pass because His word is true—His word is perfect—His Word is *Yes* and *Amen*. Therefore, as Mary said in Luke 1:38, we say, "Let it be unto us Lord, according to Your word!"

CHAPTER 2

Prophetic Sight in the Kingdom Age

PROPHETIC SIGHT in the Kingdom Age requires vision from divine positioning. We have no other pattern to follow but the pattern of Jesus Christ. Jesus came to do a whole lot more than just save us from our sins. He came to be the pattern of how we are to walk in holiness, righteousness and perfection before a perfect God. Therefore, our pattern must be to follow Him.

> *Then Jesus answered and said to them, "Most assuredly, I say to you, the Son can do nothing of Himself, but what He sees the Father do; for whatever He does, the Son also does in like manner."* (John 5:19 NKJV)

If Jesus, the Son of man, could do nothing of Himself, but only that which He saw the Father doing, then we also cannot accomplish anything of eternal purpose unless we know how to see what the Father is doing. Jesus said,

> *I can of Myself do nothing. As I hear, I judge; and My judgment is righteous, because I do not seek My own will but the will of the Father who sent Me.* (John 5:30 NKJV)

I am going to discuss God's demand and purpose for prophetic sight, interpreting prophetic times and seasons, sources and foundations for prophetic sight and what to do with prophetic sight once we receive and interpret it.

A PERSPECTIVE CHANGE

What is prophetic sight? Prophetic sight is the ability to see God's sovereign Kingdom purposes for our lives, the earth, and for all creation, including our universe and all multi-universes. How do we receive prophetic sight? The Word says,

> ... *we do not look at the things which are seen, but at the things which are not seen. For the things which are seen are temporary, but the things which are not seen are eternal.* (2 Corinthians 4:18 NKJV)

In the Age of the Church, the following picture of the visible, above water portion of an iceberg is what our prophetic sight looked like.

Iceberg 1999. (Photograph by M A Felton. © 1999 ButterflyProduction.com, LLC.)

Most everything that we did, and probably ninety percent of all things that were done, was done by what we could see with our earthly eyes, hear with our earthly ears, and feel with our earthly senses. I love the vision of the twentieth-century church as an iceberg. Our sight was limited to the ten percent of the iceberg that could be seen above the water. Everything that we did was dependent on what we realized through our natural senses. We could quantify it all. How many people ran to the altar? How many people fell down on the floor? How many people spoke in tongues? How many goose bumps did we get during worship? Everything was dependent upon our natural senses.

But as we migrate out of the Age of the Church and into the Age of the Kingdom, this next picture, which shows both an above and below water view of an iceberg, represents what the position of our viewpoint will be:

An iceberg in the Arctic Ocean with its underside exposed. (Photograph by Andreas Weith. July 30, 2016.) AWeith [CC BY-SA 4.0 (https://creativecommons.org/licenses/by-sa/4.0)] https://commons.wikimedia.org/wiki/File:Iceberg_in_the_Arctic_with_its_underside_exposed.jpg

I love to illustrate this point with a picture of an iceberg. It helps show that only ten percent of an iceberg may be in the visible realm and ninety percent of it may be in the invisible realm. Paul wrote,

> ...*we look not at the things which are seen, but at the things which are not seen: for the things which are seen are temporal; but the things which are not seen are eternal.* (2 Corinthians 4:18 KJV)

There is more than meets the eye to the purposes behind the establishment of His Kingdom and His righteousness. If we are going to be used as co-workers and co-creators together with Him for the establishment of His Kingdom, we must now learn to set our eyes on the ninety percent in the unseen realm.

Up to the present, we have been serving as infants in the Age of the Church. We have only been functioning at about a ten percent level of functionality, according even to the Word of God. Jesus told his disciples while He was here,

> *I still have many things to say to you, but you cannot bear them now. However, when He, the Spirit of truth, has come, He will guide you into all truth; for He will not speak on His own authority, but whatever He hears He will speak; and He will tell you things to come. He will glorify Me, for He will take of what is Mine and declare it to you.* (John 16:12–14 NKJV)

And Paul explained,

> *That Holy Spirit is the guarantee [down payment; deposit] that we will receive what God promised for his people [of our inheritance] until God gives full freedom to those who are his or we acquire possession of it; the redemption of the possession;—to bring praise to God's glory.* (Ephesians 1:14 EXB)

The word *deposit* is a real estate term, and what that term literally means is a ten percent down payment to secure future ownership. Everybody gets mad when I say we have only been functioning in ten percent. They say, "Are you trying to say that the Holy Spirit is only ten percent?" Absolutely not! The Holy Spirit is the whole ball of wax, but the problem is that the Lord cannot entrust us with more power, knowledge, wisdom or revelation than we can responsibly handle.

If He had shown us in the very beginning how much power He designed us to function in, we would already have destroyed the world many times over, because our hearts had still not been dealt with by the cross. He only releases the measure of revelation that we can handle corporately and universally as the body of Christ. In the Age of the Church, we were functioning in about ten percent of that revelation.

Transfiguration from Old to New

While it's a common myth that the human mind only functions at about three percent of its capacity, what is true is that we have the ability to function at much more capacity than we currently do. A genius, such as Albert Einstein, might give us a glimpse of "the more" that our minds or our brains can accomplish, but even that glimpse falls short of what is possible. I believe our brains still encompass the full revelation abilities and power that the Lord endowed us with when He created us in the garden before the fall. We are in the process of becoming transfigured, purified and resurrected reflections of Him—not for our own edification, but for His glory only.

Transfiguration has already begun to occur. You can hear it in some of the testimonies I share in my teachings. The level of power that we are about to be endued with is greater, higher, deeper, wider and broader than anything ever seen in the earth before. We are about ready to step out of the deposit, which is the operation of the ten-percent function, into the maturing process through which we will grow up into the fullness of the measure of the stature of Christ Jesus.

All rule, reign, power and authority were given to Him in Heaven and in earth by His Father. That which His Father gave Him, He now gives us. The reason the Lord can say He gives us the fullness of all rule, reign, power and authority, is because in the realms of the spirit, there is no such thing as time, space or distance. Everything that can possibly be done has already been done in the realms of the spirit, because the Lamb of God was slain before the foundation of the earth. That means that before the earth was ever even created, the completed work of God was already done. We have simply been working all of it out in the earthly realm. What we are about to step into now is the fullness of His inheritance.

The time is here for corporate ascension. The door of the tabernacle of the congregation has been opened up and we are entering into a whole new realm of functionality which is based on our position in Him and the open door of Revelation 4:1.

After these things I looked, and behold, a door standing open in heaven. And the first voice which I heard was like a trumpet speaking with me, saying, "Come up here, and I will show you things which must take place after this." (Revelation 4:1 NKJV)

This creates a demand for a prophetic shift. We have to draw a line in the sand.

Consider the following image.

Smooth Ripples. (Photograph by Martyn Gorman.) Available on Wired.com in Danielle Venton's "Photographers Capture Mysterious, Beautiful Patterns in Sand." July 25, 2011. https://www.wired.com/2011/07/sand-patterns-gallery/

I love this picture of a line in the sand. Look at the right-hand side. It represents the Kingdom, where everything is completely smooth. The left-hand side is the Age of the Church. It represents us being tossed by every wind and wave of doctrine that comes by. We now have to draw a line in the sand, saying all of the old is over and all of the new has begun. The only way we can step into this new position is to follow in His footsteps, because He is our pattern. We must begin to unlock principles for reformation. That means we have to re-evaluate all of our mindsets and all of our religious traditions by charting new courses in spiritual dimensions.[7]

The Source and Foundation of Prophetic Vision

What are our sources for functioning in accurate prophetic sight? The Word of God is first and foremost. We must learn to live by every word that proceeds out of the mouth of God.

> *But Jesus answered him, saying, "It is written, 'Man shall not live by bread alone, but by every word of God.'"* (Luke 4:4 NKJV)

> *But He answered and said, "It is written, 'Man shall not live by bread alone, but by every word that proceeds from the mouth of God.'"* (Matthew 4:4 NKJV)

According to these scriptures, every word that comes out of the Word of God is our pattern. We truly need to understand that Jesus is the Word.

> *In the beginning was the Word, and the Word was with God, and the Word was God. He was in the beginning with God. All things were made through Him, and without Him nothing was made that was made. In Him was life, and the life was the light of men.*

> *And the Word became flesh and dwelt among us, and we beheld His glory, the glory as of the only begotten of the Father, full of grace and truth.* (John 1:1, 14 NKJV)

If we acknowledge that Jesus Christ is the Word, and Jesus lives in us, then likewise, it means that every word, from Genesis chapter one to the end of Revelation, also lives inside of us. This produces a whole new level of understanding in regard to revelation knowledge. We have to use wisdom to take into account the whole counsel of God. Cults are built on one verse or another verse. Therefore, we must have the wisdom to take into account the whole counsel of God as it regards end time prophetic sight.

---

[7] See my teaching, "Charting New Courses in Spiritual Dimensions," available at globalascensionnetwork.net.

The Word states, *"by the mouth of two or three witnesses every word may be established"* (Matthew 18:16 and 2 Corinthians 13:1, which replaces *may* with *shall*, NKJV). We must take into account the testimonies of and the revelation given to two or three witnesses as we begin to do corporate ascension into the heavenly realms. A thing is established when two or three all begin to speak the same thing prophetically.

Another aspect of functioning in accurate prophetic sight is the ability to recognize the shift from the Age of the Church into the Age of the Kingdom. We have to understand that the Spirit of Prophecy is the revelation of Jesus Christ, which produces redemption. There is a demand on the heart of God for us to have this level of elevated sight.

Our source for functioning in accurate, prophetic sight is the Word of God. There are many different aspects of the Word of God. While every language on the earth communicates, and most are written, the Hebrew language is unique, because the letters with which it is formed and written are living beings. These beings live in the heavenly realms. One of the reasons the Bible says the Word of God is living and active is because the letters themselves are living. Therefore, I encourage you in your study of prophetic sight, to go all the way back to Hebraic interpretation. If you do this on a regular basis, even in your Bible study, you will find that your understanding and revelation will increase.

THE GIFT VS. THE SPIRIT OF PROPHECY

Regarding the Word of God, we have the *logos* word, which is the printed word; the *rhema* word, which refers to Spirit-to-spirit, revelational words. We also have the prophetic word, which is the Spirit of Prophecy—the testimony of Christ Jesus. There is a big difference between the operation of the gift of prophecy and the Spirit of Prophecy. The gift of prophecy is totally conditional. It is based upon a person receiving that gift, embracing it, and doing the things that are required in order for it to be fulfilled. It is temporal, which means it is going to pass away. It operates by permissive will, which means it is totally conditional upon the person who receives that word, volitionally accepting that word. Lastly, it is usually for individuals rather than groups. That means it is for individual edification, building up, strengthening, and preparation for the person to whom that word is given.

The Spirit of Prophecy, on the other hand, is radically different. It is totally unconditional. It will happen, whether a person embraces it or not. Secondly, it is eternal in its nature. That means it will never pass away. It operates by the sovereign will of the Father and is most often given for the redemption of whole geographic territories, rather than for an individual.

A perfect example of this is Jonah. You can read the entire story in the Book of Jonah. Jonah received a word from God telling him to go to Nineveh. Jonah refused, arguing that prophets were stoned in Nineveh. So, he got on a ship going in the opposite direction. The Lord raised up a big fish to come and devour Jonah. When Jonah was in the belly of the fish, being devoured by digestive juices, with seaweed wrapped all around his head, gulping for every last gasp of air he could get, all of a sudden, Nineveh sounded like a really good place to go!

The Lord will never overpower or overtake our individual wills. He has given us our own volition. We have the power of choice and we can choose what path we want to follow. However, He can tweak the circumstances, especially as it involves the Spirit of Prophecy, whose purpose in Jonah's case was for the redemption of an entire geographical territory.

Prophetic sight for the Kingdom age includes five different aspects:

- First, we must have awareness of prophetic times and seasons.
- Second, it requires **greater heights of spiritual vision**. We have to look above and beyond that which we see with our natural eyes. This follows the pattern of Jesus, who went up to high places frequently to see what the Father was doing.
- Third, it requires a **release from traditional, religiously-based thinking habits**. This is called *scotoma*. Scotoma means looking at something over and over, and over and over again, seeing only that which is on the surface, and not that which is

underlying. Much of the Age of the Church labored under spiritual scotomas. That is, they read the Bible to prove what they already knew, rather than read the Word of God to find out what they don't yet know. Greater, by an infinite measure, is the amount that we do not know. If we are going to delve into the mysteries of God, then we must get over the spiritual, religious scotomas, the blindness, to uncover the underlying mysteries in the Word.

- Fourth, it requires **seeing and hearing into the unseen realm**. That is why the Word tells us to not look to the things that are seen. "So we look not at the things which are seen, but at the things which are unseen; for the things which are visible are temporal [just brief and fleeting], but the things which are invisible are everlasting and imperishable" (2 Corinthians 4:18 AMP).
- Fifth, it requires a **rhema understanding** of our spiritual migration and our spiritual identity.

Let's cover a few of these five aspects more specifically below.

TIMES AND SEASONS

Let us talk briefly about the understanding of prophetic times and seasons. The Word says, *"...with the Lord one day is as a thousand years, and a thousand years as one day"* (2 Peter 3:8 NKJV).

In regard to understanding times and seasons, we are standing at the most pivotal point of all human history. We are standing at a place that I call the cross point, between the seventh day of man's communion with the divine nature and the third day of the church (which I discuss in other chapters). If you go to the scripture, understanding that one thousand years is like one day in the calendar of God, you will find that we have two thousand years between Adam and Abraham, two thousand years between Abraham and Jesus, two thousand years from Jesus to the year 2000 (give or take a little because our time is somewhat skewed). 2000, 2000, and 2000 are 6000 years, or in the calendar of God, six days. That means somewhere around the year 2000, we stepped into the seventh day.

If you look up all of the sevens of God, your mind will be totally blown. I will review a few of them here. Each one would require a very detailed teaching. We have seven days of the week, seven days of scripture, seven ages of man's communion with the Divine nature, with the seventh day standing for transfiguration, transformation, glorification, perfection, and rest. That means we are going to be literally transfigured. We are going to be transformed. We are going to come into the glory that we had before the earth was ever even formed. We are coming into the age of perfection and entering the age of rest.

The sevens of God are amazing. We have seven churches, seven stars, seven angels, seven judgments, seven plagues, seven steps to the southern gateways in Ezekiel chapter 40, seven seals, seven scrolls, seven blessings, seven feasts, seven day convocation, seven day healing from the flesh, seven years of labor for Jacob, seven cattle, seven ears of corn, seven days of atonement, seven lampstands, seven lamps, Seven Spirits of God, and all of these each have individual teachings regarding the perfection of the number seven.

When I say we are entering the seventh day, I am referring to the seventh day of man's communion with the Divine nature. The church, on the other hand, is entering the third day. There are two thousand years from the day of Jesus to the year 2000. Two thousand years is two days. Therefore, somewhere around the year 2000, we stepped into the third day of the Church. The third day stands for resurrection and divine intervention. It stands for habitation. We have had in the Age of the Church much visitation—we have believed God visits us and we are anointed from time to time; now, though, we are going to experience habitation—where we are aware of God's presence and leading moment by moment. The third day also stands for divine repositioning. It stands for ascension and resurrection power.

Follow with me now through some of the "third days" of God. In Genesis, on the third day, God created a seed, which is what He created to produce fruit after its own kind. *"And the earth brought forth grass, the herb that yields seed according to its kind, and the tree that yields fruit, whose* seed is in itself according to its kind. And God saw that it was good. So the evening and the morning were the third day" (Genesis 1:12–13 NKJV).

On the third day, Abraham lifted up his eyes and saw the place of sacrifice for his son. *"Then on the third day Abraham lifted his eyes and saw the place afar off"* (Genesis 22:4 NKJV).

In Genesis 42, Joseph released his brothers from prison. *"Then Joseph said to them the third day, 'Do this and live, for I fear God: If you are honest men, let one of your brothers be confined to your prison house; but you, go and carry grain for the famine of your houses'"* (Genesis 42:18,19 NKJV).

In Exodus 19:11, God says, *"...On the third day I will come down in the midst of my people..."* (Exodus 19:11 NKJV).

There are more third days:

> *...the remainder of the flesh of the sacrifice on the third day must be burned with fire.* (Leviticus 7:17 NKJV)

> *He shall purify himself with the water on the third day...* (Numbers 19:12 NKJV)

> *Now it happened on the third day that Esther put on her royal robes and stood in the inner court of the king's palace, across from the king's house, while the king sat on his royal throne in the royal house, facing the entrance of the house. So it was, when the king saw Queen Esther standing in the court, that she found favor in his sight, and the king held out to Esther the golden scepter that was in his hand. Then Esther went near and touched the top of the scepter. And the king said to her, "What do you wish, Queen Esther? What is your request? It shall be given to you—up to half the kingdom!"* (Esther 5:1–2 NKJV)

(Note: Esther represents the church.)

> *After two days He will revive us; On the third day He will raise us up, That we may live in His sight.* (Hosea 6:2 NKJV)

> *Let us know, Let us pursue the knowledge of the Lord. His going forth is established as the morning; He will come to us like the rain, Like the latter and former rain to the earth.* (Hosea 6:2–3 NKJV)

"After two days:" those two days are the time period we entered into in the year 2000.

Do you want to find a pattern for your life for the last few years? I challenge you to go and look up all the references in scripture to the seventh day, and mostly, to the third day. You will find the pattern that your life has taken for the last few years as you are being prepared to walk amongst the overcomers as the end-time establishers of the Kingdom.

Here are a few more third days:

> *For He taught His disciples and said to them, "The Son of Man is being betrayed into the hands of men, and they will kill Him. And after He is killed, He will rise the third day."* (Mark 9:3 NKJV)

> *...And they will mock Him, and scourge Him, and spit on Him, and kill Him. And the third day He will rise again.* (Mark 10:34 NKJV)

Everything written about Jesus in the scripture, everything He did, we are likewise going to do. Our life is going to follow the same pattern as His life. So, get ready, because as we enter into the third day, it will be for resurrection and ascension, and the seventh day is the day for transfiguration, according to the pattern set by Jesus in Matthew 17. His own transfiguration occurred *"after six days,"* which is the time and season we entered into in 2000.

We then go on to discern the times. These Word studies on the seventh and the third day characteristics will show the measure of the spiritual migration that is going to be required of us as we enter into the Age of the Kingdom. I encourage you to be diligent in this. Look the words up in *Strong's Concordance*. Go to a Greek-Hebrew interlinear Bible dictionary, and have discussions with one another in your ascension groups.

A Pattern from Revelation

When I first began to study the Book of Revelation, I noticed a pattern. The pattern is repeated approximately two hundred and eighty-eight times, just in the one book of Revelation: *"I looked," "I saw," "I heard,"* and *"I beheld."*

When I saw that this was a pattern being established for revelation, I decided to check out those four words in the scripture. I looked up the words *looked*, *saw*, *heard*, and *beheld* in the past, present, and future tense in the Word of God. They are in scripture over seven thousand times. You would think if there are words in scripture seven thousand times that we would sit up and take notice of the meaning of those words. So, we will continue to discuss those types of prophetic sight further in this teaching.

When I began to look up the words for prophetic sight (*I looked, I saw, I heard and I beheld*), I found out that there were many different words referring to sight. The first one was *hey* (*Strong's* H1887). That is a present, imperative command. What that word says is, I want you to look—not *if* you want to look, not *if* you think that you might like to look. It is a present, imperative command to "come up here, look and see."

The second word for sight is *nebat* (*Strong's* H5027), which means "to scan." I used to think to scan something meant to just leisurely look it over. But all of a sudden, the Lord radically changed my understanding of what it means to scan.

Recently, my daughter was diagnosed with cancer and she had to have a CAT scan. To have the procedure, she was put in a machine which took multiple pictures from the top of her head all the way to the bottom of her feet. When the scan was complete, they had hundreds of pictures of everything concerning my daughter from within her "unseen realm."

When we ascend to the heavens and see Jesus, He wants us to *nebat* Him—to take multiple pictures. He is multifaceted and multidimensional. Every time we ascend and stand face-to-face with Him, we can take pictures. What He releases to us in that one dimension, when we come back to the earth, bringing the picture with us, we can then function in that dimension. Therefore, it is expedient that whenever we see Him, we are not just content to see Him, but that we take multiple pictures. We need to take pictures of everything we see in the unseen realms so that when we come back, we can accurately manifest those pictures in the earth realm.

Another meaning for the word scan or *nebat* is like a computer scan. On some computers or printers, there is a scan command. What does that scan do? You take a document or picture and put it in the copier. A brilliant blue light passes by that picture, and what comes out on the other end is an exact, duplicate image of the picture you scanned. The ultimate purpose of all revelation is that we should become what we behold. When we ascend into Heaven and scan Jesus, He passes by us with that brilliant, blue-white, blinding light. The whole purpose of His passing by is that we should be reproduced as an exact replica of His glory in all of the earth. That is what we were created to be: the reflection of His glory.

> *...[T]hat he might make known the riches of his glory on the vessels of mercy, which he had afore prepared unto glory....* (Romans 9:23 KJV)

> *The eyes of your understanding being enlightened; that ye may know what is the hope of his calling, and ... the riches of the glory of his inheritance in the saints....* (Ephesians 1:18 KJV)

> *...[W]alk worthy of God, who hath called you unto his kingdom and glory.* (1 Thessalonians 2:12 KJV)

The next word for sight is *tsaphah* (*Strong's* H6822). *Tsaphah* means "to peer into the distance." When we are caught up into the moment of the twinkling of an eye, we can *tsaphah*. We can see the things that were, the things that are, and the things that are yet to come. Actually, you have been doing this all along, ever since you were born into the earth. The only problem is that you do it in your dream life.[8]

The fourth word for *look* is *shuwr* (*Strong's* H7789). *Shuwr* means "to spy out." What does a spy do? A spy goes into unknown territory, gathers information that has been held in secret, and brings it back out to reveal it. That is the whole purpose of a spy. Part of our purpose in our ascension experience with Him is to go and spy out the mysteries that are in the unseen realm so that we can bring back revelatory, mystical information and release it into the earth.

Shuwr also means "to survey." One of the names given for God that is rarely ever talked about is *Architekton*, which means He has been

---

[8] For more information on seeing things that are yet afar off, see "Dreams and Visions" available at globalascensionnetwork.net.

building something since the very beginning. You cannot build a structure accurately unless you have a completed survey. I used to be a real estate agent. I met a person who had built a house on a property that had not been accurately surveyed. They ended up having to tear down half of their house, their garage, and all of their fences because they had unknowingly built on to their neighbor's property. The neighbor did not like that because it encroached on their rights. Since we are called to be co-workers and co-creators together with God for the establishment of His Kingdom, before we can accurately establish and build that Kingdom, we must first *survey*. When we go into the heavens, we must see the things that are there, look at them, and bring back the accurate blueprint of how to build the New Jerusalem in the earth.

The next word for *look* is *atenizo* (*Strong's* G816). This is the same root word from which we get our military command, "Attention!", which means stand up straight, look at me, do not look to the right or to the left, but gaze intently on me. If we are going to see Him properly, then we have to gaze intently: He wants our full attention. I love that, because we look at so many different things, but when we stand face-to-face with Him, His demand for us is to see Him and pay attention. "Pay attention to Me!"

The next word for *see* is *eido* (*Strong's* G1492). This *eido* does not mean just "look at it," it means "to know." It refers to a high level of intimacy, like that which is used for a man to *know* a woman, as in Adam *knew* his wife, Eve. This a level of radical intimacy with God. A lot of people in the Age of the Church read and studied. They knew a lot about God, but they did not *know* Him. Knowing a lot about God is not the same as *knowing* Him or having radical intimacy with Him. I knew a man once who was the third highest rated world expert on the book of Mark. He had read and studied the book of Mark his whole life. He was granted the privilege of handling original manuscripts. But no matter how much he read, he never heard what it was that he was reading, and he never really knew God.

Eidō means we must learn to develop radical intimacy with Him. I can read a whole lot about George Washington. I can read every book written about him and learn a whole lot about him. But unless I actually sit down at a banqueting table and have dinner with him, unless I can watch how he interacts with his business associates, wife and children, I will not really *know* him.

The next word is *katanoeo* (*Strong's* G2657). I love this word. It is the root word from which we get *catatonic*. *Catatonic* is a psychological term used for someone who has their gaze fixed on something so permanently that nothing can distract their attention. You could go to a catatonic patient, give them an injection, and their eyes will not move. You can feed them, and they will not move their eyes. People can come and go, and have conversation, but the eyes of the catatonic are so fixed on something that is out there in a different realm that they are not distracted by anything. The Lord says He wants us to *katanoeo* Him. What He means is, "I want you to fix your eyes on Me, the author and finisher of your faith. I want you to fix your feet on the path that is set before you, not looking to the right or to the left, but to be steadfastly fixed on that path that is set before you." When we ascend to the heavens, we need to *katanoeo* Jesus. We need to keep our eyes fixed on Him, the author and finisher of our faith.

The next word, *nebat*, discussed above, has a few additional meanings. *Nebat* (*Strong's* G5027) means "to regard with favor." So, when we look at Jesus, He wants us to *nebat* Him, to direct our sole attention on Him, to give Him all the favor that He so deserves.

Nebat also means to "take a second look at." There are many things in the Word of God that we need to take a second look at. Jesus is the Word, and in the Word, we have our mind, we have our sight fixed on things being indelibly etched in concrete, when actually He is saying, "I want you to take a second look, at not only Me, but at the Word of God. For there are things in there that I want to show you, that you have not yet seen. Take a second look at Me as the Word. When I begin to release My mysteries into you, it is going to require that you take a second look." Many of our mindsets are still etched by the Age of the Church, and we have to break out of that four-walled mindset. We have to take a second look at the purpose of Jesus, as well as what the sovereign will of God is for the earth, and the meaning of the Word of God.

Horaó (*Strong's* G3708) means "to see clearly, to gaze intently, or to stare at." I have had many face-to-face contacts with Jesus Christ. Every time, I am utterly amazed at the incredible depth of His beauty. Sometimes I can hardly do anything but just stare at Him. I want to encourage you, when you stand before Jesus, to gaze into His eyes, to stare into His eyes. In His eyes, you can see the whole history of humanity, the creation of the galaxies and the universes. Staring into His eyes is one of the most amazing, transforming things you could ever do.

The next word is *katoprismatai* (*Strong's* G2734). I love the word katoprismatai because it is the root word from which we get the word *prism*. And what is a prism? A prism is a piece of crystal that reflects beautiful rainbow, opalescent colors as it refracts light. We are called to be His light reflected. Whenever we are held up against that brilliantly blue, shining white light, we become like a radiant rainbow that can reflect His light to all of the Earth. The whole purpose of our existence is to become that perfect reflection of His image in the earth. The whole purpose for the creation of humanity in the very first place is that we should become His light reflected.

> Once when I was in Israel with a group, we went to the Holocaust Museum. As we went through it, we saw pictures of the unbelievable torture that people endured in concentration camps. When we came out of the exit of the Holocaust Museum, we came to the Children's Holocaust Museum, which is located right behind it. At the Children's Museum, everyone said, "Oh, I cannot go in there. There is no way that I can look at all those awful, hideous pictures of children being tortured and tormented, and brutally, medically abused for 'scientific' purposes."
>
> Many of the group left without going into the Children's Holocaust Museum. I did go in. When I stepped into that

place, it was like an unfolding, magnificent revelation blanketed me on every side. The instant you step through the front door, you leave the light and enter into total, absolute, utter blackness. You have to put your hand on a railing in order to take that first step into the darkness. The floor underneath feels spongy. It is an unsettling feeling, because you are walking on ground that feels unstable.

As your hand follows along the railing, you find that the whole building is in the shape of a nautilus shell (which is, in itself, profoundly prophetic). As you continue along the railing, you turn around one circle, and over your head are three candles called "The Eternal Lights." I thought it was so interesting that in a Jewish museum they would have three candles lit—one at the top and two on each side. You continue along the circular railing until you take that next turn. Oh, my goodness! It is like stepping into Heaven itself.

There are thousands and thousands of shards of mirrors hanging from the ceiling. The mirrors all reflect the light from the three candles that are at the very front. None of them hold their own light: they reflect the three lights that you see when you first enter. It is as if you are literally stepping into the heavens. The mirrors extend from threads on the ceiling, and as you walk through, it is as if you are walking into the midst of the universe. All of the mirrors are singular reflections of the trinity of candles at the very front.

As you follow along with your hand on the rail, you finally come to a little megaphone, an old-fashioned type record player. From it whispers the names of all of the children who died in the camps.

After I walked through the Children's Museum, I came out on the other side in tears, not just for the children, but also for the revelation that encompassed me while I was there. We

> are all created to be reflections of His glory. Those reflections were like walking through the midst of the heavens, through the midst of the stars. The Word says that in the end times, we will be granted the privilege of regathering all of those who have been scattered to the uttermost parts of the heavens, so that all of the reflections of His glory can be reproduced in the earth—the fullness of His glory so that His glory covers the earth as the waters cover the seas.
>
> It was one of the most life-changing experiences I have ever encountered, and I was so sad that everyone was not able to see that we are reflections of His glory.

The next word for see is panah (*Strong's* G6437), meaning "to turn and face." Every time anyone did anything significant in the Word of God, it said they turned. They turned, they turned, they turned. For instance, when Moses was going up the mountain, the Bible says,

> *Then Moses said, "I will now **turn aside** and see this great sight, why the bush does not burn." So when the Lord saw that he **turned aside to look**, God called to him from the midst of the bush and said, "Moses, Moses!"* (Exodus 3:3–4 NKJV, emphasis mine)

If we are going to be those who will stand face-to-face with God, we must turn away from old mindsets that prevent us from entering into the heavenly realms to experience everything of Heaven today. We have to *turn* and go another way. We have to turn and face, therefore when we *panah* Christ Jesus, we have to turn in a totally different direction. That is what happens when we leave the Age of the Church and enter the Age of the Kingdom. We turn and go in a different direction.

Anatheoreo (*Strong's* G333) means "to take another look at." We have to take another look at Jesus. In the Age of the Church, we took the vast, eternal mind of God—so big, so huge, so magnificent, so unlimited—and we tried to bring it down to an earthly environment and take our little, teeny, tiny, finite minds and wrap them around the infinite, unlimited mind of God, to try and make sense of it. We put God in a box, and oftentimes we said, "Well, God can do this, but He cannot do that," and "God can do this, but He will not do that." We limited what God can do through the limitation of our own finite mindsets. But, God is sovereign. He is not *trying* to do anything. He doesn't need our permission when it comes time for Him to activate His sovereign will and plan for mankind in the earth. In order for us to break out of those old mindsets, we have to know, to *anatheoreo* Jesus. We have to take another look at the sovereign purposes of God in the earth.

The next word is *ra'ah* (*Strong's* G7200). Ra'ah means "to see." Sadly enough, it is used in referring to *"..seeing they do not see, and hearing they do not hear, nor do they understand...Lest they should see with their eyes and hear with their ears..."* (Matthew 13:13,15 NKJV). Unfortunately, this *ra'ah* now applies to many people who are living in the age of the sixty-fold who will never enter into the age of the hundred-fold, because they *ra'ah*-ed God and they *ra'ah*-ed Jesus. Seeing, they saw not, and hearing, they heard not. I guarantee there are many of you reading this who have priceless, deeply loved, passionate people that were left behind in their age around sixty in the sixty-fold mindset. I guarantee you, they are not hearing the same thing you are hearing. They are not seeing the same things you are seeing because they chose to *ra'ah* Jesus. The scripture bears repeating: *"I speak to them in parables, because seeing they do not see, and hearing they do not hear, nor do they understand"* (Matthew 13:13 NKJV).

The next word is *chazah* (*Strong's* G2372), meaning "to gaze at or to perceive." The final word is *aramtheoreo* (*Strong's* G2334), which means to discern, or to regard with favor. The Word says,

> *...we do not look at the things which are seen, but at the things which are not seen. For the things which are seen are temporary, but the things which are not seen are eternal.* (2 Corinthians 4:18 NKJV)

These are a few but not all of the words that deal with the issue of the pattern of Revelation, *I look, I saw, I heard, I beheld.* I want to challenge you to go to the Word and investigate those words for yourself. I guarantee you when you go to the Hebrew meaning of what it means *to look at*, and what it means *to see*, that you are going to be radically shifted in your understanding of what we are to receive in our ascending experiences with Him.

There are many different ways to look at Jesus, to perceive Jesus, to behold Jesus, to hear Jesus. The ultimate purpose of all revelation is for us to become the thing that we see. Therefore, I challenge you to get these words that refer to seeing engrafted into your spirit, so that when you are caught up in the moment, in the twinkling of an eye, and carried away to see Him, you will see Him as I AM. You will not just see Him as your savior, healer, deliverer, or your provider. When you see Him as I AM, you will utilize the meanings of all of these words. You will *nebat* Him, *scan* Him, *tsaphah* Him, *atenizo* Him, *eido* Him. You will *know* Him with a radical level of intimacy that will change the way you perceive, and thereby you will activate yourself in positions of elevated sight.

Prayer

Father, we thank You and we praise You that in this day, and in this hour, You are calling us to positions of elevated sight, so that we are enabled by You to see things from the topside downward, rather than from the earth-side upward. Father, I thank You that as this teaching is released, people will find themselves stepping out, stepping up, and stepping into their own unique, divinely designed positions of elevated sight, so they can see what You are doing in the earth and in this hour.

We give You all the praise and all the honor. We release the Spirit of Wisdom, Knowledge and the Revelation of Christ Jesus right now, so the eyes of our understanding may be opened, that we may know our purpose, destiny, and our high calling in Christ Jesus.

I give You thanks, Father, that everyone who reads this will activate these principles for elevated sight in their own lives, that their revelation may logarithmically and exponentially increase as they learn how to ascend, to sit with You in Your throne, to sit with You at Your banqueting table, to go to the halls of intercession, to the halls of Melchizedek, and to the courtrooms of Heaven. Lord, I pray that You will increase the level of their sight in such a way that their whole mind will shift in their understanding of who You are, bearing fruit for all eternity, according to Your divine design. I ask all of these things in the most holy and strong and magnificent name of Yeshua (Jesus Christ), in whose name we pray. Amen.

Chapter 3

OVERCOMING

THE LIFE OF THE OVERCOMER is filled with promises. The concept of the overcomer is taken out of Revelation chapters 1–3. You may be familiar with these scriptures: *"...To him who overcomes I will give to eat from the tree of life, which is in the midst of the Paradise of God"* (Revelation 2:7 NKJV); *"He who overcomes shall not be hurt by the second death"* (2:11); *"To him who overcomes I will give some of the hidden manna to eat. And I will give him a white stone, and on the stone a new name written which no one knows except him who receives it"* (2:17); *"And he who overcomes, and keeps My works until the end, to him I will give power over the nations..."* (2:26). There are more promises to the overcomer in 3:5, 3:12, 3:21, which I encourage you to review.

JACOB AS OVERCOMER

Let's begin by looking at what the Word says about those who overcame in the scriptures. We'll start with Jacob.

> *And He said, "Your name shall no longer be called Jacob, but Israel; for you have struggled with God and with men, and have prevailed."*
>
> *Then Jacob asked, saying, "Tell me Your name, I pray."*
>
> *And He said, "Why is it that you ask about My name?" And He blessed him there.*
>
> *So Jacob called the name of the place Peniel: "For I have seen God face to face, and my life is preserved."* (Genesis 32:28–30 NKJV)

In Hosea 12:2–5, we see Jacob would be justly punished for his ways:

> *But the Lord is bringing a lawsuit against Judah. Jacob will be justly punished for his ways. When he was born, he struggled with his brother; when he became a man, he even fought with God. Yes, he wrestled with the Angel and prevailed. He wept and pleaded for a blessing from him. He met God there at Bethel face-to-face. God spoke to him—the Lord, the God of heaven's armies—Jehovah is his name."* (TLB)

The first point I want to make about Jacob becoming an overcomer is that he struggled with his brother. Whenever we get ready to move out of the Age of the Church and to be qualified as an overcomer, the first thing we are going to do is struggle with our brothers. There are many of you who have precious, wonderful brothers in the old work of God who want to stay in the sixty-fold ministry of the Age of the Church. They are not hearing the same thing you are hearing. They are not seeing the same thing you are seeing and often this causes you conflict. Eventually, their actions will cause defilement, slander, and accusation to be raised against you. The first thing we have to do to qualify as an overcomer is to struggle with our brother.

The second point is that Jacob fought with God. Yes, he wrestled with the angel and overcame. A lot of wrestling is going on as we prepare to move out of the Age of the Church into the Age of the Kingdom. When this happens, we are wrestling with God.

Wrestling with God / Wrestling with Brothers

I myself had to wrestle with God in order to be qualified as an overcomer. When we originally evacuated the Age of the Church and came into the Age of the Kingdom, because my message was so radically different than the message that was given in the Age of the Church, every kind of evil accusation possible came against me.

First, they called me a new ager. I cried to the Father. I went to the Lord. I struggled with God. I said, "Lord, they are saying I'm a new ager! Is it true? Am I really a new ager?"

The Lord just laughed and said, "Well, after all, my darling, it is a new age!" I had to struggle through that with God.

The second accusation they made against me was that I was nothing but a mystic. These struggles came from my brothers, the people that I loved, the people that I travelled with, the people that I spoke with.

From the podium, they said that I was a mystic. I had to come before God and struggle with God and say, "Lord, they are saying that I am a mystic! Is it true, am I really a mystic?"

The Father just laughed and said, "Do you even know what a mystic is? Go look it up."

So, I went to a dictionary and found, as I remember it, eighteen different descriptions of what a mystic is and only two of those were defined as connected with Eastern occult religions. Based on what I learned from the other definitions, the definition I adopted for myself was that a mystic is someone who receives supernaturally derived information from unseen sources through communion with the divine nature. I slapped my knee and said, "Glory to God! I really am a mystic!" But before I could come to that place, I first had to struggle with my brothers and struggle with God. After that, whenever people would come to me and say, "Oh, you are nothing but a mystic," I would say, "Oh, thank you! I am so glad that you can recognize I have communion with the divine nature." We must learn how to agree quickly with our adversary (Matthew 5:25), because doing so dismantles all arguments.

We have to wrestle with our brothers and with God. My brothers were accusing me of being deceived. But having been in deliverance ministry for eighteen years, I knew that the only purpose of the spirit of deception is to deceive a person until they do not even know they are deceived. So again, for six months, I wrestled with God, with God and my brothers.

The people I was struggling with were earth-shaking, nation- shifting apostolic and prophetic names, most of which you would recognize. So, because the Word says there is wisdom in a multitude of counselors (see Proverbs 11:14, 15:22, 24:6), I figured to myself that if no one else was hearing the same thing that I was hearing, then I must be deceived. And so, for six months I wrestled with God. I thought to myself, "Well, if it's the same voice that I heard when I was baptized in the Holy Spirit, maybe I am not even really filled with the Holy Spirit. It's the same voice I heard when I gave my life to Jesus Christ. Oh, maybe I am not even saved!" I wrestled, and I wrestled, and I wrestled. "It's the same voice I heard when… and it's the same voice I heard when… it's the same voice I heard when…. Oh, then perhaps they are right, and I am wrong."

The Peter-Paul Principle

I came to the point where I was drafting a letter of resignation to the ministry because, of all things, I did not want to be accused of deceiving the Body of Christ. I was just about ready to push the send button when my husband came in and said to me, "Wait just a minute. Before we make this decision, we'd better pray and fast."

For the next seven days, I prayed and fasted, wrestling with God and wrestling with the words of men. Finally, on the seventh day I cried out to the Father, "Lord, today I have to know the truth. Are they right? Am I deceived? Am I wrong and are they right?"

Finally, the answer of the Lord came: "It is not that they are wrong and you are right. It is not that you are wrong and they are right. It is simply something called the Peter-Paul Principle."

I asked, "The Peter-Paul Principle? What in Heaven's name is that?"

And He said, "Well, Peter and Paul argued about everything."

Peter would write to Paul and say, "I heard you are making all these new converts. They have to get circumcised according to the Law of Moses." Paul would write back and say, "No, they do not have to because they are not under law, they are under grace." Peter would write to Paul and he would say, "I hear that your new converts are eating unclean foods. You need to straighten up their dietary habits." Paul would write back and say, "No, I don't have to because it's *'Not what goes into the mouth defiles a man; but what comes out of the mouth, this defiles a man'* (Matthew 15:11 NKJV)."

The Lord showed me that they argued about a lot of things, but it was not because Peter was right and Paul was wrong, or Paul was right and Peter was wrong. It was simply that their callings and elections were different. Peter was called to the Jews. Paul was called to the Gentiles. They would never see things from the same perspective again because the Jews operated under the law and the Gentiles operated under grace.

When I saw this, the Lord said: "It is not that they are right, and you are wrong; it's simply that you have different callings. They were called to the Age of the Church. You are called to the Age of the Kingdom, and you are never going to see things from the same perspective again."

In order for me to enter the ranks of the overcomer, the first thing I had to do was wrestle with my brother, then wrestle with God. After that, I had to wrestle with the angel. The Word says, *"...He [Jacob] wept and pleaded for a blessing from him. He met God there at Bethel face-to-face. God spoke to him"* (Hosea 12:4 TLB).

The wounding that came when the separation from the Age of the Church took place was great and devastating. The way that I was healed from all of it and the only way I could escape the pain was by having encounters of being *"caught up in a moment in the twinkling of an eye"* (1 Corinthians 15:52 AMP). I stayed before Jesus, face-to-face and gazed into His eyes. How powerful just to bask in His embrace, feel His breath on my cheek, and hear His whisper in my ears.

JOSHUA AS OVERCOMER

The only thing that kept me from complete devastation at that time in my life was knowing how to stand before God, face-to-face with the Lord, the God of Heaven's Armies, Jehovah is His name.

> *So Joshua did as Moses said to him, and fought with Amalek. And Moses, Aaron, and Hur went up to the top of the hill. And so it was, when Moses held up his hand, that Israel prevailed; and when he let down his hand, Amalek prevailed. But Moses' hands became heavy; so they took a stone and put it under him, and he sat on it. And Aaron and Hur supported his hands, one on one side, and the other on the other side; and his hands were steady until the going down of the sun. So Joshua defeated Amalek and his people with the edge of the sword.* (Exodus 17:10–13 NKJV)

Joshua overcame the Amalekite army with the sword. Why did Joshua overcome? He overcame because he was a champion; he was a warrior. He overcame with the sword. Today, the way we overcome every objection that comes against us is with the sword—the sword of the Word. Because the Word is a sword, our effective weapon in overcoming to the end will always be the sword.

> *For the word of God is living and active and full of power [making it operative, energizing, and effective]. It is sharper than any two-edged sword, penetrating as far as the division of the soul and spirit [the completeness of a person], and of both joints and marrow [the deepest parts of our nature], exposing and judging the very thoughts and intentions of the heart.* (Hebrews 4:12 AMP)

In the midst of this story with Joshua and the sword, though, we don't want to miss what happens with Moses. When Moses was tired, they took a stone. They put it under him, and there he sat. I think it is interesting that he sat on the firm foundation of the stone. The stone was the rock or foundation. One of the hardest things for a Christian to do today is to sit and rest. Moses sat and rested on the stone.

That Moses sat and rested is significant because we are now entering the seventh day of communion with the divine nature.[9] I discussed previously how in God's calendar a thousand years is like one day. As a quick review, remember there were two thousand years between Adam and Abraham, two thousand years between Abraham and Jesus, and two thousand years between Jesus and the year 2000. We are therefore entering the seventh day of communion with the divine nature.

The seventh day is:

1. the day of rest,
2. the day of transfiguration, and
3. the day of perfection.

---

[9] For more, see the teachings on "Prophetic Sight for the End Times" available at globalascenionnetwork.net.

JESUS AS OVERCOMER

Let's look at Jesus as an overcomer in Luke 4. Jesus came to do a whole lot more than to just save us from our sins: He came to be a pattern of how to walk before a perfect, holy, and righteous God in holiness and righteousness. If our life is going to follow the example of Jesus' life, then there are many examples out of His life that we need to take to heart and recognize.

Jesus said, *"Most assuredly, I say to you, he who believes in Me, the works that I do he will do also; and greater works than these he will do, because I go to My Father"* (John 14:12 NKJV). The works that He did, we can do also, is a truth. And not only the works He did, but greater works than He did. Therefore, if we follow the life of Jesus, as He is our pattern for advancement into the Kingdom age, there is no other pattern but His that is laid out. We can really follow, right now.

Even Jesus had to be driven into the wilderness by the Holy Spirit to be tempted of the devil. That is what it says in Matthew 4 and Luke 4. In order to overcome the works of the evil one, He had to be tempted in every way, even as we are tempted, so that He could become the faithful High Priest. He overcame Satan in the wilderness by using the sword of the Word of God against him.

Jesus said,

> *And everything I've taught you is so that the peace which is in me will be in you and will give you great confidence as you rest in me. For in this unbelieving world you will experience trouble and sorrows, but you must be courageous, for I have conquered the world!* (John 16:33 TPT)

And this is what Jesus prayed as he looked up into Heaven:

> *Father, the time has come. Unveil the glorious splendor of your Son so that I will magnify your glory! [...]*
>
> *Father, I have manifested who you really are and I have revealed you to the men and women that you gave to me. They were yours, and you gave them to me, and they have fastened your Word firmly to their hearts.*
>
> *And now at last they know that everything I have is a gift from you.* (John 17:1, 6–7 TPT)

Therefore, the Word of the Lord is that even though we may have trouble, because Jesus overcame the world, we can also overcome to the end.

> *Behold, the hour cometh, yea, is now come, that ye shall be scattered, every man to his own, and shall leave me alone: and yet I am not alone, because the Father is with me. These things I have spoken unto you, that in me ye might have peace. In the world ye shall have tribulation: but be of good cheer; I have overcome the world.* (John 16:32–33 KJV)

> *Jesus spoke these words, lifted up His eyes to heaven and said: "Father, the hour has come. Glorify Your Son, that Your Son also may glorify You, as You have given Him authority over all flesh, that He should give eternal life to as many as You have given Him. And this is eternal life, that they may know You, the only true God, and Jesus Christ whom You have sent. I have glorified You on the earth. I have finished the work which You have given Me to do. And now, O Father, glorify Me together with Yourself, with the glory which I had with You before the world was."* (John 17:1–5 NKJV)

THE TIME HAS COME

Let's review John 17:1 once again—*"Father, the time has come"* (TPT). Say that three times: "The time has come; the time has come; the time has come!" When we understand the significance of the very hour we are living in within the age of the earth, this sentence will make much more sense.

The Third Day of the church is the day for ascension, for resurrection, and for restoration of divine positioning.

> *Beloved, now we are children of God; and it has not yet been revealed what we shall be, but we know that when He is revealed, we shall be like Him, For we shall see Him as He is.* (1 John 3:2 NKJV)

"It has not yet been revealed what we shall be…", but when we see Him as I Am, not just as our savior, healer, deliverer, or provider, but as I Am … then *"we shall be like Him."* The Word goes on to say:

> *It is the same with us. [For] Now we see a dim reflection [obscurely; or indirectly], as if we were looking into a mirror [through a glass darkly], but then we shall see clearly [face to face]. Now I know only a part, but then I will*

know fully, as God has known me [I am fully known]. (1 Corinthians 13:12 EXB)

This means that we can know Jesus as well as He knows us.

That's an amazing statement. What does He know about us? He knows every thought we have, every word we speak, every action we take, how many cells are in our bodies, how many hairs are on our heads. We can know Him just that well as we become the perfect reflection of his glory in all the earth. Isn't that amazing?!

> *Eye has not seen, nor ear heard,*
> *Nor have entered into the heart of man*
> *The things which God has prepared for those who love Him.* (1 Corinthians 2:9–11 NKJV)

We are entering a whole new day—the day I call the Seventh Day transfiguration of the corporate Son of Man. We are approaching the time now when we are going to step into the exact duplication of the pattern of Jesus Christ in the earth.

When we say, "the time has come," it means it is the time for the thing that has not yet been revealed. We have stepped out of the Age of the Church into the Age of the Kingdom. In the Age of the Church, we functioned at a ten percent level of functionality. We know this because Jesus told the disciples, *"I still have many things to say to you, but you cannot bear them now"* (John 16:12 NKJV).

When He got ready to leave, He said, *"And I will pray the Father, and He will give you another Helper, that He may abide with you forever—the Spirit of truth..."* (John 14:16–17 NKJV).

> *In Him you also trusted, after you heard the word of truth, the gospel of your salvation; in whom also, having believed, you were sealed with the Holy Spirit of promise, who is the guarantee (earnest, deposit) of our inheritance until the redemption of the purchased possession, to the praise of His glory.* (Ephesians 1:13–14 NKJV)

The problem is God can never commend to us more responsibility and higher levels of power if we are not able to shoulder the responsibility in a way which benefits the world. If He had shown us in the very beginning how much power we were created to have, we would have destroyed the earth many times over already. We have been living in a very immature state. For the last two thousand years, we have been functioning at ten percent or less of the full capacity He created us to function in. He created us to have dominion over all things.

> *Now I say that the heir, as long as he is a child, does not differ at all from a slave, though he is master of all, but is under guardians and stewards until the time appointed by the father.* (Galatians 4:1 NKJV)

The son (that is us), though we are the heir (that is us, too) of all things, is still subject to teachers, tutors and guides put over him until he reaches the fullness of maturity. At the time appointed by the father, the father will grant to him the fullness of his inheritance. So, what is his inheritance? Jesus tells us what our inheritance is.

> *And Jesus came and spoke to them, saying, "All authority has been given to Me in heaven and on earth."* (Matthew 28:18 NKJV)

Jesus is telling us that all rule, all reign, all power, all authority was given to Him in Heaven and in earth by His Father; and that which He gave to Jesus, Jesus now gives to us.

That is a now-present word. He could speak it in the present tense because in the realms of the spirit, there is no time, space or distance. Therefore, if we are to follow in the pattern of Jesus, we are going to enter into a day of ascension and resurrection power.

When I say that the Age of the Church is over, I do not mean the church itself is ending. The church is eternal and is passionately and forever loved by Jesus Christ. What I am referring to in regard to the transfer of the ages, is that the church is going to move into the day of its greatest glory. In the year 2000, we stepped out of our infantile state and began to grow up into the fullness of the measure of the stature of Christ Jesus (Ephesians 4:13). Therefore, we can say in perfect concert with John,

> *Jesus spoke these words, lifted up His eyes to heaven and said: "Father the hour has come!"* (John 17:1 NKJV)

Because now the time has come for us to step into the fullness of our true inheritance and begin to make our position at the right hand of God the Father Almighty, our manifested condition on the earth.

Glory Restored and Authority Granted

Secondly, Jesus said: *"Glorify Your Son, that Your Son also may glorify You"* (John 17:1 NKJV).

In the Age of the Church, the majority of the world held the church in disrespect. They had no idea who we really were. Because we said one thing and we did another, many people thought we were totally disqualified as being sons of God. The world disregarded us because *"it [had] not yet been revealed what we shall be"* (1 John 3:2 NKJV). But now the glory of God we had in the very beginning is going to be restored to us, the church. Therefore, we are going to be glorified, and the purpose of our glorification is that we may also glorify Him. So, in agreement with the prayer of Jesus we can truthfully say:

> *...[G]lorify your Son, that your Son may glorify you, for you granted him authority over all people, that he might give eternal life to all those you have given him.* (John 17:1–2 NIV)

(Note: those the Father has given Him represent all people.)

> *But we all, with unveiled face, beholding as in a mirror the glory of the Lord, are being transformed into the same image from glory to glory, just as by the Spirit of the Lord.* (2 Corinthians 3:18 NKJV)

Pay close attention to the verse: *"for you granted him authority over all people, that he might give eternal life to all those that you have given Him."* Jesus said, *"While I was with them in the world, I kept them in thy name: those that thou gavest me I have kept, and none of them is lost, but the son of perdition; that the scripture might be fulfilled"* (John 17:12 KJV). Paul advised, *"Let no man deceive you by any means: for that day shall not come, except there come a falling away first, and that man of sin be revealed, the son of perdition"* (2 Thessalonians 2:3 KJV).

When Jesus says that He has authority over all people, that means all people. When John describes every creature, that means all creatures: *"And I heard **every** creature which is in heaven and on the earth, and under the earth and such as are in the sea, and **all** that are in them, saying, 'Blessing and honor and glory and power be unto Him that sitteth upon the throne, and unto the Lamb for ever and ever!'"* (Revelation 5:13–14 KJ21, emphasis mine).

Therefore, when Jesus says we are being granted authority over all people, we can enter into agreement with Him. Why? Because Jesus said *"… the same things I did, you may do also"* (John 14:12)

> *And this is eternal life, that they may know You, the only true God, and Jesus Christ whom You have sent.* (John 17:3 NKJV)

Our only purpose in entering into the fullness of the measure of the stature of Christ is that the world may know the only true God. What is the purpose of Jesus? To point to the Father. Jesus Christ said, *"He who has seen Me has seen the Father"* (John 14:9 NKJV).

And believe it or not, the day is going to come when we can stand with full measure of authority and say, "Those who see us see Jesus, therefore they see the Father because we have been sent."

COMPLETING THE WORK

Being qualified as overcomers is dependent upon us completing the work He gave us to do. Speaking to the Father, Jesus said: *"I have glorified You on the earth. I have finished the work which You have given Me to do"* (John 17:4 NKJV).

I go to many dark, hellish places where there is a lot of death, a lot of destruction, a lot of bloodshed. People say to me: "Aren't you afraid to go to the cannibals? Aren't you afraid to go to the headhunters? Aren't you afraid to go to villages where the heads of 6,000 men have been cut off and their bodies disemboweled?" And I say: "Absolutely not!" Whether I live and whether I die is not the issue. The thing that matters is this: did I complete the work that He gave me to do there?

So, if I go to the cannibals, and I go to the head hunters, and they chop me up into a hundred pieces and they throw me in the stew pot and the end result is that the whole tribe gives their lives to Jesus, then

I have still completed the work that He sent me there for. The way that I bring God glory on earth is by completing the work He gave me to do. *"And now, Father, glorify me in your presence"* (John 17:5 NIV).

When Jesus took Peter, James, and John up to a high place, He actually caught them up.[10] They ascended into a very high place, a place behind the veil, and there, along with Elijah and Moses, Jesus was revealed in all of His glory. So, as the Word says in John 17:5, *"Father, glorify Me in Your presence"*—it is only as we stand in the glory of His presence that we can properly glorify Him.

In Him from Before the World Began

The more we ascend and descend in the Heavenly realms, the more He conforms us to His multifaceted, multi-dimensional image, which culminates in us becoming love, because that is His nature, and the more like Him we will become. It is only then that we can truthfully say: *"And now, O Father, glorify Me together with Yourself, with the glory which I had with You before the world was"* (John 17:5 NJKV).

As overcomers, we all had a glory with God before the world ever even began.[11] In Genesis, you can see how man was created. God created man out of the dust of the earth. That is the creation of our body. Then He breathed on man, and man became a living soul. That is the creation of our soul.

But where is the creation of our spirit? Well, it's not in there because our spirit was not created. We were in Him in the beginning; we'll be in Him in the end. Therefore, we had a glory with Him before the world ever began. *"Before I formed you in the womb I knew you; Before you were born I sanctified you…"* (Jeremiah 1:5 NKJV).

When Job was at his lowest point in all of his trials and in all of the temptations that he went through, when he had lost all of his chil-

---

[10] See the teaching "Seventh Day Transfiguration of the Corporate Son of Man," available at globalascenionnetwork.net.

[11] If you want to find out more, go to "All Creation Groaning." Also, there is a teaching available on the covenants God made with our body, our soul, and our spirit. Find it in the "Order of Melchizedek" PowerPoints at globalascenionnetwork.net.

dren, all of his cattle, and all of his goods, his wife said, "Why don't you just curse God and die?" (see Job 2:9). God visited Him there.

Job's friends came to him saying, "Oh you must have some horrible sin in your life to have these problems."

In devastation and pain, Job sat on a blanket scraping the scabs and puss off his body with a shard of pottery. It was then that God came to him and asked questions like this: "Job, where were you when I hung the stars and the planets in their places? Where were you when I laid down the foundations of the earth? Where were you when I set the boundaries of the sea?"

The answer, I believe, is that Job knows because he was there.[12] "Of course you know all this! For you were born before it was all created..." (see Job 38:21). I don't know how to tell you this: you were there, too. You were there, I was there. We were all there when the earth was created. We were in Him from before the beginning.[13]

Our Purpose: Revealing Him

> *I have manifested Your name to the men whom You have given Me out of the world. They were Yours, You gave them to Me, and they have kept Your word. Now they have known that all things which You have given Me are from You.* (John 17:6–7 NKJV)

Our whole purpose in being separated and set apart is to be those who overcome to the end. Our whole purpose is to reveal Him—not to reveal our own self, not to reveal our own glory, not to show our own power or our own strength. For it is *"not by might, nor by power, but by my spirit"* that all these things will be accomplished (Zechariah 4:6).

Our ultimate goal must be to be able to say, "I have revealed Him." When people can look at us and recognize we are a revelation of the Lord Jesus Christ, when we are actually transfigured in their very presence, we will no longer have to preach the Gospel, because we

---

[12] The words here are not a direct quotation, but are my illustration of God's questions to Job. See Job 38.

[13] For more information, see "All Creation Groaning" on globalascenionnetwork.net.

will have become that which all of creation is groaning for. Jesus says in John 17:6, *"I have revealed You."* Therefore, as Jesus is our pattern, the ultimate purpose for every overcomer must be to reveal Jesus, to reveal the Father—we must reveal the Lord.

We become qualified as overcomers as we recognize it is not us, but He who is in us. We must acknowledge as Jesus did that *"...all things which You have given Me are from You"* (John 17:7 NKJV).

> *You are of God, little children, and have overcome them because He who is in you is greater than he who is in the world.* (1 John 4:4 NKJV)

It's only His authority. It's not by our might, not by our power, not by our gifts, not by our outward manifestation. It is only as we recognize that the thing that is going to be revealed, the mystery of God that has been hidden in Christ since the very beginning (according to Ephesians chapter 1), is in us.

Understanding the Mystery of God

The mystery of God is about to be revealed. How we are going to overcome the world is by understanding the mystery of God. Part of the mystery of God is that the all-knowing, the all-seeing, all powerful, all-mighty, all-present God, who is so big, so huge, so magnificent, could actually fold Himself up small enough to put Himself in us. The mystery of God that is about to be revealed means that that God who folded Himself up so small that He could put Himself in us, is now beginning to unfold. The mystery of God is Christ in us, the hope of glory.

In the Age of the Church we spent all of our time trying to put ourselves in a defensive position against the gates of hell, in order to prevent them from prevailing against us. What resulted was the spiritual warfare network movement, whereby our patterns to defend ourselves against the gates of hell were actually the opposite of those of the Age of the Kingdom.

> *And I also say to you that you are Peter, and on this rock I will build My church, and the gates of Hades shall not prevail against it.* (Matthew 16:18 NKJV)

What that verse means is that the gates of hell will not prevail against the invasion of the Church's offensive action to invade Hell itself. We will charge the gates of hell, and we will take back everything that death, hell and the grave swallowed up.

> *And I will give you the keys of the kingdom of heaven, and whatever you bind on earth will be bound in heaven, and whatever you loose on earth will be loosed in heaven.* (Matthew 16:19 NKJV)

> *Then the seventy returned with joy, saying, "Lord, even the demons are subject to us in Your name." And He said to them, "I saw Satan fall like lightning from heaven. Behold, I give you the authority to trample on serpents and scorpions, and over all the power of the enemy, and nothing shall by any means hurt you. Nevertheless do not rejoice in this, that the spirits are subject to you, but rather rejoice because your names are written in heaven."* (Luke 10:17–20 NKJV)

In verse 19, He specifically says, "Behold, I give you the authority." Authority to do what? *"To trample on serpents and scorpions, and over all the power of the enemy, and nothing shall by any means hurt you."*

Part of entering into the overcomer life, number one, is to recognize and begin to operate in the level of authority that He has already given us. The Word shows us that all rule, all reign, all power, all authority was given to Him in Heaven and earth, and that which His Father gave Him, He gives us. Part of the purpose for which He gave us that authority was to trample on snakes and scorpions, and to overcome all the powers of the enemy.

To overcome means to take dominion over all the power of the enemy that nothing shall by any means hurt you.

I have travelled into deep, dark places. I have eaten monkey brains, yak eyes, rat, cat, bat, buzzard claws, cobra bile, and scorpions (that is an interesting one), but nothing could by any means hurt me. If we believe the Word of God that nothing by any means shall harm us, no matter where we go or what we do, we will not be harmed.

I used to take bottled water with me everywhere I went. On a trip to Africa, I'd planned to go out into the bush. To prepare, I'd packed a case of water in my suitcase, but the suitcase was lost in Amsterdam. I lost another case of water in a suitcase that was misplaced in Bulawayo. By the time I got out into the bush, I had no water.

The people I went to minister to pumped water for me out of a hole in the ground. It looked more like mud than water, and they gave it to me in a filthy, dirty glass. I could barely see through the water. I held the glass up to the sun, and I saw organisms swimming around in the water.

But what does the Word say? It says I can drink any deadly thing and it will not hurt me (Mark 16:18).

So, in spite of what I could see with my eyes, I drank it. In all the places that I have gone, I have never been sick, I have never had a cold, I have never had a flu, any kind of indigestion problem, diarrhea, or any of that, because I believe that as overcomers *nothing* will harm us.

I do not say that to boast, however. Jesus said,

> *Nevertheless do not rejoice in this, that the spirits are subject to you, but rather rejoice because your names are written in heaven.* (Luke 10:20 NKJV)

If we rejoice that the spirits are submitted to us, it's easy to get into spiritual pride. I have done plenty of that in my lifetime. Having cast out demons for eighteen years, I began to think, "Boy, I am really somebody." But rather than rejoicing in the spirits submitting to you, Jesus says to rejoice only that our names are written down in Heaven.

As we leave the Age of the Church and enter into the time of the overcomers, the overcomers are being separated out from the rest of the body. It is good for us to understand what this means. The word *overcome* (from the Old Testament, see *Strong's* H3201) is translated in different verses as *I can, I could, may,* or *might be victorious over*. In the King James Version, *overcome* means "to be able in any and all ways to attain." It means *can, could, endure, might, overcome, have power, prevail,* and *suffer*.[14]

---

[14] Biblesoft's *New Exhaustive Strong's Numbers with Concordance with Expanded Greek and Hebrew Dictionary* shows multiple meanings for the word overcome.

Overcome is defined as follows:

verb (used with object):

1) to get the better of in a struggle or a conflict; conquer, defeat: to overcome the enemy.

2) To prevail over (opposition; a debility, temptations, etc.); to surmount: to overcome one's own weakness.

3) to overpower or overwhelm in body or in mind, as does liquor, a drug, exertion, or emotion: I was overcome with grief.

4) Archaic. to overspread or overrun.

verb (used without object):

5) to gain ultimate victory, win; conquer: a plan to overcome by any means possible.[15]

Clearly, from these definitions of overcome, an overcomer operates from a position of strength.

Casting Down the Accuser of the Brethren

Now, the accuser wants to do everything he can to keep us from attaining the position of an overcomer. But there is good news:

> *Then I heard a loud voice saying in heaven, "Now salvation, and strength, and the kingdom of our God, and the power of His Christ have come, for the accuser of our brethren, who accused them before our God day and night, has been cast down."* (Revelation 12:10–11 **NKJV**)

For the accuser of the brethren to be cast down, we must learn that the real war between good and evil is not out there in the world as much as it is between our own two ears. Every objection that could possibly be made to us coming into the fullness of the promise of God will be thrown at us by the accuser of the brethren that still lurks in the Tree of Knowledge of Good and Evil inside of us (that is our soulish nature).

---

[15] "Overcome." Dictionary.com. Accessed May 28, 2019. https://www.dictionary.com/browse/overcome.

We have a false prophet (who represents the serpent in the Tree of Knowledge of Good and Evil) inside of us who will constantly say: "Oh, I know you would like to be in the ministry, but after all, your first call is to your family. You are not qualified for ministry because you didn't go to seminary and you don't know Greek, Hebrew and Aramaic. I know you would really like to be in the ministry, but you don't have the money, you're not charismatic enough, you're not gifted enough, you're not talented enough, you're not knowledgeable enough. Besides that, remember that atrocious sin you did last week?"

The instant we enter into agreement with any voice that says we cannot be or cannot do all that the scripture says we can, we have taken the mark of the beast. We have agreed with the voice that came out of our soul (the Tree of the Knowledge of Good and Evil) rather than the voice that comes out of the Tree of Life.

The voice that is in the Tree of Life (which is Jesus, through our spirit) says, "We are called, we are appointed, we are anointed, we are elected, we are preferred, we are set aside to be the praise of His glory. We are exalted to be the right hand of God the Father Almighty. We are joint heirs to the Kingdom of Heaven with Jesus Christ. Everything that He has is ours by the adoption of sons. We are the head and not the tail. We are the beginning and not the end. We are a royal priesthood. We are a holy nation. We were known and called by name before we were ever conceived in our mother's womb. We were knit together in our mother's womb by our own Father's hand." Anything that says that we are less than that has to be cast down. How do we do that? We cast down *"arguments and every high thing that exalts itself against the knowledge of God, bringing every thought into captivity to the obedience of Christ"* (2 Corinthians 10:5 NKJV)

It is in our own mind that we have to cast down the accuser of our brethren. While the accuser of the brethren runs rampant in the church, trying to accuse, trying to slander, trying to bring defilement and all kinds of accusations against us, and while we are looking for the anti-Christ manifesting everywhere around the earth, we forget that Jesus said: *"Little children, it is the last hour; and as you have heard that the Antichrist is coming, even now many antichrists have come, by which we know that it is the last hour"* (1 John 2:18 NKJV). He advised us: *"...Do not fear those who kill the body but cannot kill the soul. But rather fear Him who is able to destroy both soul and body..."* (Matthew 10:28 NKJV). Finally, we know *"...they overcame him by the blood of the Lamb and by the word of their testimony, and they did not love their lives to the death"* (Revelation 12:11 NKJV).

Becoming Overcomers

So, how do we become an overcomer?

1. We state our position as being empowered by the blood of the Lamb. If Jesus had not shed His blood, we wouldn't have access to the overcomer life. But because He gave His life, He was wounded for our transgressions, He was bruised for our iniquities; because the chastisement of our sin was upon Him, and by His stripes we are healed from every area of deficiency in our humanity, we can access the realms of the overcomer.

2. We overcome by the word of our testimony. Everybody has a testimony. There is nothing I love better wherever I go in the Body of Christ than to ask the people: "What is your testimony?" I ask not only what your testimony is about how you got saved, but what your testimony is from the operation in the gifting of God that you're walking in right now. The words of our testimony are powerful. Many can fight with us about our interpretation of scripture, but it is hard for them to fight with a testimony that is so personal to us there is no way they can argue against it.

3. They loved not their lives to the death. I love what another minister says about this: "if you're going to be qualified as an overcomer you have to count the cost, you have to pay the price, you have to die the death." That sounds like a simple thing—but it's not. Dying the death is a lifelong process we have to continually go through. We have to count the cost. We have to pay the price. We have to die the death.

So, how do we overcome? We overcome evil with good. By doing good, we can overcome all evil. *"Do not be overcome by evil, but overcome evil with good"* (Romans 12:21 NKJV). In order to die to self, one of the hardest things for us to overcome is our right to be right. Whenever we are slandered, whenever we are accused, and especially when we are falsely accused, our first reaction is to stand and defend ourselves.

When I was preparing to come into a third level of anointing, the Lord told me, "Until you are prepared to give up your name, to give up your reputation, to give up your ministry, to give up the anointing, to give up the fruits of the Spirit, to give up the gifts of the Spirit, in pursuit of nothing more than My presence, you cannot have this third level of anointing."

At that time, I was going through pure hell in preparation for the overcomer life. The most difficult thing to get over was offense. This can be especially true if you're being offended by somebody you love, somebody who really cares about you. As I was preparing to go into that third level of anointing myself, the Lord gave me this word: "The instant you are offended, you are in sin, because offense is self-defense. I'm trying to kill your *self*, and you are trying to defend your *self*."

Sometimes, the most difficult thing for us to give up is our right to be right. It is not easy to follow His example to go like a lamb to the slaughter, not raising a word in our own defense (Acts 8:32).

So, in review, in order to be qualified as an overcomer, we have to:

1. Wrestle against our brother;
2. Wrestle against God (whenever I say that, people say, "What? What are you trying to say?" We have to wrestle against God. We have to see God face-to-face. That is ascension experience.);
3. Overcome to the end.

We overcome to the end by the sword of the Word. In order to overcome the works of the evil one, we have to be tempted of the devil in order to overcome all of those works. Jesus overcame Satan in the wilderness by using the Word of God against him. The Word of God is our sword.

When we can begin to enter the arena of the overcomer, it does not mean that we are not going to have trouble. Jesus says:

> *Remember the word that I said unto you, The servant is not greater than his lord. If they have persecuted me, they will also persecute you; if they have kept my saying, they will keep yours also.* (John 15:20 KJV)
>
> *...[B]ut be of good cheer, I have overcome the world.* (John 16:33 KJV)

As we draw to the end of this chapter, focus on John 17:1. Here is how I lay it out:

1. Father the time has come,
2. to glorify Your son,
3. for the purposes of Your son glorifying You,
4. that we expect and step out and step up, and step into the authority that He gave us, and
5. that we complete the works that He gave us to do, so that
6. we are glorified in His presence with the same glory we had before the world was.

The purpose for us to step into the overcomer life is so that we can reveal Him. As we step into that overcomer place, even the gates of hell shall not prevail against us.

Jesus has given the authority for us to overcome so that nothing by any means will harm us. We have to take authority over the accuser of the brethren in our own mindset to cast down all vain imaginations and every high thing that exalts itself against the honor of the Father.

In conclusion:

1. We overcome by the blood of the Lamb.
2. We overcome by the word of our testimony.
3. We must love not our own lives to death.
4. We must overcome evil by good.

These principles made living and active in us will produce in us the capability to enter the ranks of the overcomers.

Chapter 4

Being an Overcomer

LET'S LOOK FURTHER at the qualifications of those whom the Lord calls *overcomers* in the book of Revelation chapters 2 and 3. In chapter 2, in order to set forth the qualifications for living the overcomer's life, the Lord speaks His judgment in four parts to each of the churches and to the saints within those churches.

The first part of each judgment is His commendation. In nearly every instance, the Lord begins by telling the people of that church what they have been doing right, so that they will be encouraged.

In the second part, He gives them a correction. This correction reveals the thing that they are doing that is not in accurate, proper alignment with His Kingdom design, so that they can know what areas of behavior or what character faults they need to improve upon.

The third part is His commandment. That is His direction for fixing the thing that needs to be corrected, so that they can come into accurate alignment with Kingdom mentalities.

The fourth part is the culmination. The culmination tells them what will result if they are able to overcome to the end. In other words, these will be their blessings.

To summarize, we have the commendation, the correction, the command, and the culmination.

JUDGMENT TO EPHESUS

Now let's look at these seven judgments in more detail. The following verses describe the church in Ephesus. The Lord's commendation to the church at Ephesus is this:

> *I know your works, your labor, your patience, and that you cannot bear those who are evil. And you have tested those who say they are apostles and are not, and have found them liars; and you have persevered and have patience, and have labored for My name's sake and have not become weary.* (Revelation 2:2–3 NKJV)

The correction comes in the next verse: *"Nevertheless I have this against you, that you have left your first love"* (Revelation 2:4 NKJV). That correction is something which all of us have to bear in mind consistently. It is easy (especially if you are in full-time ministry) to get so busy doing the works of the Lord that you forget the Lord of the works. We forget to put Him first and the works second. Verse 5 puts it this way, *"Remember therefore from where you have fallen; repent and do the first works…"* (Revelation 2:5 NKJV). That means turn consistently, daily, hour by hour back to your first love. This verse continues, *"Or else I will come to you quickly and remove your lampstand from its place—unless you repent"* (Revelation 2:5 NKJV). Therefore, we have to repent consistently when we find that we have put the works of the Lord before our first love, the Lord Himself.

The Lord continues, *"But this you have, that you hate the deeds of the Nicolaitans, which I also hate"* (Revelation 2:6 NKJV). Who are the Nicolaitans? Many say they were people who were accused of practicing false religions or of a compromised, syncretized faith, which mixed Christian practice with idol worship. While that may be true, if you take the name Nicolaitans and break it down into two parts, you see that nico- means "victor" or "to lord it over," and -laitans refers to "the laity" or the people. So, what the Lord is saying in verse 4 is this: "You hate the works of the Nicolaitans (or those who lord it over the laity), which I also hate." When God says that He hates something, that is a very strong statement, and it is something to pay attention to.

Here, He hates when church leaders lord it over the laity, perhaps, for example, by trying to control or manipulate the works of the saints or the works of the church through divisive commandments. That was the Lord's correction to the Ephesians.

What then is His commandment? It is essentially this: "Return to your first works."

The culmination is found in the next verse:

> *He who has an ear, let him hear what the Spirit says to the churches. To him who overcomes I will give to eat from the tree of life, which is in the midst of the Paradise of God.* (Revelation 2:7 NKJV)

"*He who has an ear*"—that is an interesting way of putting it. Obviously everyone who is listening has ears. But the Lord is not talking about natural ears. He is talking about spiritual ears. He separates those who have an ear from those who do not because there are those who will not have the spiritual ears to hear what He is saying.

In teaching on the order of Melchizedek, I quote what Jesus said about the fact that after hearing the Word, some receive thirtyfold, some sixtyfold, and some a hundredfold. This is the parable of the sower:

> *Listen! Behold, a sower went out to sow. And it happened, as he sowed, that some seed fell by the wayside; and the birds of the air came and devoured it. Some fell on stony ground, where it did not have much earth; and immediately it sprang up because it had no depth of earth. But when the sun was up it was scorched, and because it had no root it withered away. And some seed fell among thorns; and the thorns grew up and choked it, and it yielded no crop. But other seed fell on good ground and yielded a crop that sprang up, increased and produced: some thirtyfold, some sixty, and some a hundred.* (Mark 4:3–8 NKJV)

God is a logical, mathematical, and a precise God. If you were an elementary school student given a mathematical progression to complete that began "thirty, sixty, _____", and you wrote down "one hundred" in that blank space, your answer would be marked wrong. The logical mathematical progression is thirty, sixty, ninety.

For God to say that His progression is thirty, sixty, one hundred means that ten has been added onto the ninety which would normally follow from that progression. That extra ten represents the order of Melchizedek, the order of the overcomers who are going to be pulled out of the Age of the Church in order to establish the foundations for the advancement of the Kingdom of God and His righteousness in all of the earth. The Melchizedek order represents God's tithe (His "tenth") to the earth, and their responsibility is to co-work and co-labor together with Him for the establishment of His Kingdom and His righteousness in all the earth.

What the Lord is saying, therefore, is that many will not have ears to hear what you are hearing. Some who remain in that sixtyfold will accuse you of being "off," of taking a wrong turn, of adopting wrong or false doctrines because they are not hearing the same thing that you are hearing. But this is by divine design. God Himself sets up a divine dissatisfaction inside those who are being called out of the Age of the Church. Unless we become divinely dissatisfied with the low-level function of the Age of the Church, we will most likely never leave it to search out the "something more" that is coming.

The culmination of the judgment of God to the church at Ephesus is this: *"To him who overcomes I will give to eat from the tree of life, which is in the midst of the Paradise of God"* (Revelation 2:7 NKJV). What is the Paradise of God? Consider this verse from John: *"In the beginning was the Word, the Word was with God, the Word was God"* (John 1:1 NKJV). The Word was made manifest in mortal flesh so that we might behold the glory of the Father. If we understand Jesus is the Word and He lives inside of us, then every single word in the Bible from Genesis chapter 1 all the way to the end of Revelation also lives inside of us. And it is not just the printed words on the page we are talking about. Jesus, as the Word, actually lives inside of us. Therefore every word in scripture lives inside of us.

In saying that, I want also to make the point that you are the Garden of Eden, in the sense that you are the place where God communes with man. The Word teaches there are two trees in the Garden, and we have inside of us those two trees. One is the Tree of the

Knowledge of Good and Evil, and the other is the Tree of Life. Notice that the Tree of the Knowledge of Good and Evil has good in it, but even the good of mankind is out of sync with God's divine design. So, while one tree represents soulish, carnal human nature, the other, the Tree of Life, represents Christ in us, our hope of glory.

When the Lord says He is going to give to us to eat of the Tree of Life, that means we are actually going to sever ourselves from the Tree of the Knowledge of Good and Evil and engraft ourselves into the Tree of Life, which represents Christ. Only in that way, by surrendering every thought to the obedience of Christ Jesus, can we be given the opportunity to eat of the Tree of Life.

Eating from the Tree of Life is extremely important, because in the original garden in Eden, God put both the Tree of the Knowledge of Good and Evil and the Tree of Life, and each reproduced fruit after its own kind. Anytime we partake of the Tree of the Knowledge of Good and Evil, we reproduce things that are temporal and carnal, things that come from our human nature, which reproduces only after its own kind. Therefore the things reproduced after partaking of the Tree of the Knowledge of Good and Evil have no eternal dimension to them.

However, when we partake of the Tree of Life, which is Christ Jesus, we become the express duplicate of His image in the earth, as we are called to reproduce the image of Christ in the earth. We were created to be what? The reflection of His glory. That tree, the Tree of Life, is in the midst of the Paradise of God (Revelation 2:7).

JUDGMENT TO SMYRNA

Let us look at what the Lord says regarding the judgment of the church of Smyrna. The commendation is,

> *I know your works, tribulation, and poverty (but you are rich); and I know the blasphemy of those who say they are Jews and are not, but are a synagogue of Satan.* (Revelation 2:9 **NKJV**)

He commends them like this: "I know your works. I know you have been tried. I know you have endured tribulation. I know that you're poor, but even in the midst of your poverty you are rich." Notice He said, *"I know the blasphemy of those that say they are Jews and are not, but are of the synagogue of Satan."* This is the commendation to the church at Smyrna, the persecuted church.

The correction? There is none. The Lord does not correct them because the people of this church, by experiencing persecution, trials, tribulation, torture, and the shedding of their innocent blood have already brought themselves into perfect, accurate alignment with Christ Jesus.

The Word says you must be identified with Him in the power of His resurrection, and in the fellowship of His suffering:

> *But what things were gain to me, these I have counted loss for Christ. Yet indeed I also count all things loss for the excellence of the knowledge of Christ Jesus my Lord, for whom I have suffered the loss of all things, and count them as rubbish, that I may gain Christ and be found in Him, not having my own righteousness, which is from the law, but that which is through faith in Christ, the righteousness which is from God by faith; that I may know Him and the power of His resurrection, and the fellowship of His sufferings, being conformed to His death, if, by any means, I may attain to the resurrection from the dead.* (Philippians 3:7–11 NKJV)

The church at Smyrna has endured. They understood in a deeper way than we can lay hold of what it means to suffer with Christ Jesus. Our sufferings are much different than His sufferings. Our sufferings are for our sanctification. His sufferings were for our purification or our perfection. Those who did not count their own lives worthy, those who shed their blood for the cause of Christ Jesus, have no correction coming to them.

Here was the command for the believers in Smyrna:

> *Do not fear any of those things which you are about to suffer. Indeed, the devil is about to throw some of you into prison, that you may be tested, and you will have tribulation ten days. Be faithful until death, and I will give you the crown of life.* (Revelation 2:10 NKJV)

The culmination of the Lord's message to the church at Smyrna continues into verse 11:

Being an Overcomer

Be faithful until death, and I will give you the crown of life. He who has an ear, let him hear what the Spirit says to the churches. He who overcomes shall not be hurt by the second death. (Revelation 2:11 NKJV).

This passage is richly packed. *"Do not fear any of those things which you are about to suffer...."*

The first half of my ministry was dedicated to dealing with people in the persecuted church. In my very first encounter with the persecuted church, I went to visit a man called the Living Martyr of China. I sent him a note saying that we were going to come. I planned to bring Bibles and discipleship materials through Donkeys for Jesus, a ministry based in Hong Kong.

We went through intensive training on how to operate in China. Our operation was going to be covert. Because the government had laws against carrying Bibles into China at that time, we had to use code names and code sentences in order to pass any part of the Bible through customs. I have hours and hours of testimony I can give concerning what the Lord did during those trips back and forth into China. But I want to focus on the believers who have been cast into prison, those who have shed their blood, and the many who have died for the cause of Christ Jesus.

The day before I was supposed to meet with the Living Martyr of China, we were caught taking Bibles into the country. I was arrested. But because we had people from twelve different nations with us, the government authorities did not want to cause an international incident. So, they took our passports and assigned armed guards to follow us wherever we went.

I was devastated. My sole purpose was to meet with the Living Martyr of China. When we got to the hotel, a hand-scribbled piece of paper was in my little mailbox. "Dear Mrs. Coen," it read. "Our whole body is longing with anticipation for you to arrive with all of the Bibles and the discipleship material." When I read it, I knew I was not going to be able to go there. If I was caught, I might get a mere slap on the wrist from the Chinese authorities, but he would probably be arrested and thrown in jail.

For the next two weeks we went throughout China, always followed by the armed guards. On the final day before our exit, we had an idea to go into the slums of Shanghai. The slums are dangerous. The day we went in, there was no electricity. People were shouting. Gunshots were going off. People were lying in the streets, drugged out. Even the armed guards did not want to follow us. By the time we came out of the slums, we had lost the guards.

The next day we had to pass through the city where we had been arrested originally. Before we were arrested, a young Chinese man had rescued the book bags full of Bibles. The Lord had later given me the strategy of taking the bags to a hotel in the middle of the night to store them in its luggage room.

So as we came through that city again on our way out of China, I thought to myself, "I wonder if the book bags are still in the hotel luggage room?" When I checked the luggage room at the hotel, sure enough, they were there.

In that city of maybe eighteen to twenty million people, I had a particular address written down on a little piece of rice paper. Everything in the city is built upward, with multiple levels, because if the homes were built side-by-side, they would cover the whole continent due to the vast number of people. All of the houses are small, but they are also very tall. So, address in hand, I hailed a rickshaw, threw the book bags on the back of the rickshaw, and away we went. After driving around for a considerable amount of time, we finally pulled up to a man's home.

When we arrived at the house at the address on the rice paper, the bottom floor had been taken over by a police station. But fortunately for me I got there about noontime, and the police station was empty, as all the police had gone to lunch. I did not even know it was a police station at the time. The assignment they had from the Chinese government was to take down the names of every person who entered that property for the purpose of worshiping Jesus. In fact, on the door that led to the second story of the building, there was a brass plaque printed in eight different languages. It read,

> *It is against the law of the People's Republic of China for anyone to enter these premises for the purposes of worshiping Jesus Christ.*

I opened the door and climbed up the stairs to the second story. My book bags were big, full, and quite heavy. They each weighed about 70 pounds. They hung from the back of my neck almost to the back of my knees. There I was, jerking the book bags up the stairs, banging on all the walls, trying to make my way and drag the bags up to the second story.

When I got to the second story, nobody was there. I sat down and began to pray that somebody would show up to take the bags. Nobody came and nobody came, and I was getting a little antsy about time. I began thinking to myself, "Before long I'm going to have to leave. I have to get back to the airport." If I failed to exit China on that day, they had my passport, which meant I might not be able to get out of the country at all.

All of a sudden I looked over on the left-hand wall. I saw a lashed-together ladder made out of tree limbs leading up to a garret above the second story. I thought, "I wonder if there could be anybody upstairs?" I did not want to leave the book bags without receiving any acknowledgement about where they came from or without putting them into the hands of someone who would be responsible for them. So very gingerly—the ladder was rickety and only lashed together with rope—I climbed up to the third story. When I got there, it was like a garret that would have fit in an episode of *Little House on the Prairie*, the 1970s TV show depicting life on the American prairie in the late 1800's.

The atmosphere of that third-story garret was so holy I fell over on my face. In the hall of the garret area, the trunks from two trees were attached to the floor. Across the sawed-off trunks were 2 x 8 boards laid to make a few rows of seats where the persecuted church could come and meet for their services.

I began to weep. The spiritual climate there was so holy it almost took my breath away. They had no banners, no carpeting, no air conditioning, no sound system and no musical instruments. Even the podium was a mere, bare piece of wood.

I sat there praying and praying in the spirit, weeping and crying, thinking how holy this ground was. But I began to get anxious about arriving at the airport in time, so I got up to leave. When I started to climb down the rickety ladder, I heard a broomstick suddenly fall and hit the floor. I looked around and nobody was there, but I was sure I had heard something hit the floor.

All of a sudden at the far end of that small room, an ancient little Chinese woman stuck her head out from behind a false wall. She had two scarred-over holes where her eyes should have been. For having declared in a public market that she had seen Jesus Christ, her eyes had been burned out of her head with hot pokers. Her ears had been sliced off the sides of her head because she told people they could actually hear from God for themselves. Her lips were mangled, most likely from beatings she had endured for the cause of Christ.

She had stuck her head out, listening to me. Apparently I had gotten very quiet, because just like a little bird, she tilted her head from one side to the other, listening very carefully. I shouted out, "Hello, hello!"

She got so full of joy she began to sing and dance. "Oh American, American!"

With that, all the windows in the third story flew open. Little children flooded in through the windows. The building had little metal windows you push up and hold open with little bamboo sticks. Apparently, a meeting was held the previous night. The children's parents had been arrested and taken off to jail. When I came carrying all the book bags, banging my way up the stairs, they thought I was the police coming back to get them. So, they had scrambled out on the hot tin roof, and pushed down all the windows behind them. They had been sitting out on that hot roof on the adjacent side of the building, just waiting for me to leave.

Being an Overcomer

After they crawled in, they made a big circle around me, dancing and singing. They were excited that I was there at long last. It was one of the most beautiful things I have ever seen. The woman who'd had her eyes put out with hot pokers grabbed my hand and pulled me behind the false wall, where there was a narrow hallway probably only two- or two and a half-feet wide.

At end of that hallway was a tiny bookshelf, maybe only three to four feet high. On the book shelf were eighty-nine copies of the New Testament, one hundred percent handwritten by those little children. Every day they would come in after school and sit down. The Living Martyr would give each of them one page of scripture that they would copy meticulously. Every page was numbered. At the end of their home cell meetings, they would pass the pages back in and would keep them safe to be used again.

The old woman leaned her shoulder into the bookshelf that held the Bibles, and she shoved it out of the way. I do not know how she did it—she could not have weighed eighty pounds soaking wet. Behind the bookcase, a pounded brass-like metal door was hung on the wall with what looked like two giant paper clips. She opened up the small brass door and motioned me to come underneath. I got down on my hands and knees to crawl in. I found myself in a tiny room, maybe three feet wide and five and one half feet long.

Flat on his face, in the middle of the floor, lay the Living Martyr of China. He had been there for ten days praying that God would help me get through with the Bibles I had just delivered. When I saw him, I began to cry. I thought to myself, "Oh my God, if I don't ever do another thing in my life, this is enough!"

When he crawled out, I was honestly amazed that he spoke English. Very few people in China spoke English then, as this happened before China became an internationally schooled nation. He came out and sat down with me. He had spent twenty-seven years in Chinese dungeons, prisons and work camps. Every bone in his body, except four, had been broken for the cause of Christ Jesus.

When I asked him what it was like to live in a place where he was so persecuted for the cause of Christ Jesus, his face lit up and began to shine. He said, "Nancy, I'll tell you the truth. The devil tempts the body of Christ in two ways. One is with extreme persecution and the other is with abject apathy. I can tell you the truth: I wouldn't trade one whiplash on my back, one broken bone in my body, or one year in a Chinese dungeon for all the money in America, because I am a man of sorrow, acquainted with grief, stricken, smitten, afflicted, rejected, who has learned obedience by the things that I have suffered." (See Isaiah 53:3,4 and Hebrews 5:8.)

I looked at him and I thought, "Oh my goodness!" Then in all my pompous American arrogance, in all my American pride—remember this was my first contact with the persecuted church—I said to him, "As a member of the American church, what can I possibly do to help the church in China?"

He threw his head back and laughed the deepest belly laugh I have ever heard. Then he said, "I would prefer to tell you what I wish you would not do."

"What is that?"

He said, "Number one, don't send money, and number two, don't pray for an end to the persecution."

That answer opposes everything about the American gospel. My chin fell down to my chest in disbelief.

He kind of giggled because he knew that would be my response. He continued, "Let me explain. When the people come here from Europe or America and they see the plight of the Chinese church, they go home and immediately collect fifty thousand dollars to send to some poor little home cell pastor who has never ever in his whole life made more than two hundred dollars a year. In two to three months, that home cell pastor will be completely backslidden, and it will cause all kinds of jealousy and competition amongst the other home cell pastors, because money is power, and power corrupts."

I thought to myself, "Whoa, I haven't ever considered that."

He went on. "Number two, don't pray for an end to the persecution. The persecution is our greatest strength! In China there is no such thing as nominal Christianity. Nobody goes to church because it's a good social activity or because their parents built the church, or because they want to see their friends. When somebody comes to Jesus Christ in China, they know they are probably going to lose their job. They might lose their family, their property. They'll probably even lose their home. They might go to jail. They may be tortured for the cause of Christ, and many of them will lose their life for their testimony of Christ Jesus.

"Therefore when somebody comes to Jesus in China, they've already counted the cost, paid the price, and died the death. As a result of that, there is no such thing as nominal Christianity. We send our little eight-year-old children out to raise the dead, and they don't think anything of it. They don't even consider it to be miraculous. They consider it to be part of normal Christian life." He concluded, "That is because of the persecution."

Now do you see why the Lord gave no correction in Revelation 2 to the persecuted church at Smyrna? They already died a death.

The culmination of the Lord's Word to Smyrna is this:

> *Be faithful until death, and I will give you the crown of life. He who has an ear, let him hear what the Spirit says to the churches. He who overcomes shall not be hurt by the second death.* (Revelation 2:11 **NKJV**)

Judgment to Pergamos

The next church addressed is Pergamos. The Lord's commendation is this:

> *I know your works, and where you dwell, where Satan's throne is. And you hold fast to My name, and did not deny My faith even in the days in which Antipas was My faithful martyr, who was killed among you, where Satan dwells.* (Revelation 2:13 **NKJV**)

That is interesting, isn't it: *"among you, where Satan dwells."*

The correction from the Lord to the church at Pergamos is this:

> *But I have a few things against you, because you have there those who hold the doctrine of Balaam, who taught Balak to put a stumbling block before the children of Israel, to eat things sacrificed to idols, and to commit sexual immorality. Thus you also have those who hold the doctrine of the Nicolaitans, which thing I hate.* (Revelation 2:14–15 **NKJV**).

We discussed earlier that the Nicolaitans were those who lord it over the laity, but now let's look at what it means to hold the doctrine of Balaam. All over the earth today there are religious babylons where forms of Christian religious practice have been established, but they are syncretized with local idol worship and tribal customs. By syncretized I mean all kinds of rituals and evil practices from pagan religions have infiltrated Christianity to become part of the local practice in Christian churches.

In Mexico for instance, many of the churches are syncretized, not only with old forms of Catholicism which incorporate forms of witchcraft, but also with Aztec and Mayan based beliefs of the native people. This syncretization means their faith has a form of godliness, but lacks the power thereof (2 Timothy 3:5)

So, the correction the Lord gives to the church of Pergamos is about keeping faith pure. We must not intermarry or intermingle with idol worshipers or those who would cast stumbling blocks before believers. I have found this to be true wherever I go: in churches established in heavily tribal areas, the Christianity there is mixed almost fifty-fifty in some cases with ancient tribal customs.

In this hour, part of our purpose as overcomers is to take that which the enemy has twisted and untwist it, flipping that which is ritualistic and/or satanic into something righteous.

Let me explain. The devil cannot create. All he can do is take something that God created and twist it slightly so that it appears to be the same thing that God created. But actually its source is radically different.

The term wicked does not literally mean diabolical or evil. *Wicked* comes from an old Anglo-Saxon word, wiker, which means "to twist." *Wicked* is related to the word *wick*, as in candlewick. A wick is created by twisting fibers together. Likewise, our English word *wicker* has this idea of materials that are twisted together to form something else. Literally translated then, *wicked* means "the truth slightly twisted."

The devil himself twists words from scripture to tempt people. Remember when he said to Eve, "Did God really say…?" (see Genesis 3:1). Another example of the devil twisting words appears in the gospels. When tempting Jesus, the devil suggested, "Does not the Word of God say…?" (see Matthew 4:6) The devil takes principles laid down in scripture and twists them slightly so that they have a radically different meaning and result than what God intends.

When that happens and the twisted version is accepted as truth, it infiltrates the Church with the appearance of good, but with a purpose to do evil. Everything that the devil does is a slightly twisted counterfeit of a righteous reality. Thus people can look at their faith and say, "We're Christian," at the same time they consistently practice idolatry, some even participating in sacrifices (which is the case, for example, among some people in Mexico).

What the Lord is saying to the church at Pergamos could be paraphrased like this: "This I have against you, that you have mixed your faith with idol worship and that you also keep the doctrine of the Nicolaitans, who lord it over the laity."

His command to the Pergamos church is this: *"Repent, or else I will come to you quickly and will fight against them with the sword of My mouth"* (Revelation 2:16 NKJV). Why does He refer to a sword? We find the answer in Isaiah and Revelation:

> *He has a sword in His mouth. And He has made My mouth like a sharp sword; In the shadow of His hand He has hidden Me, And made Me a polished shaft; In His quiver He has hidden Me.* (Isaiah 49:2 NKJV)

> *He had in His right hand seven stars, out of His mouth went a sharp two-edged sword, and His countenance was like the sun shining in its strength.* (Revelation 1:16 NKJV)

> *Now out of His mouth goes a sharp sword, that with it He should strike the nations. And He Himself will rule them with a rod of iron. He Himself treads the winepress of the fierceness and wrath of Almighty God.* (Revelation 19:15 NKJV)

He is saying, "I'm going to use My word to fight against them, so that which is slightly twisted can be untwisted, and that which is ungodly can be made righteous."

We come now to the culmination, the covenant that God holds with the church of Pergamos. He begins,

> *He who has an ear, Let him hear what the Spirit says to the churches. To him who overcomes I will give some of the hidden manna to eat. And I will give him a white stone, and on the stone a new name written which no one knows except him who receives it.* (Revelation 2:17 **NKJV**)

I love the written Word of God. I love the fact that He is going to give us hidden manna to eat. Everything in the Old Testament is a type and a shadow of something that the Lord is speaking to us personally, even today.

I get really interested when I hear people talk about end-time eschatology. I receive newsletters which proclaim things such as, "We found the Ark of the Covenant. It's under the Temple Mount and we made our way through the stones of the Temple Mount, and we took pictures. But then the officials took the pictures away." The truth of the matter is that the Ark of the Covenant is an infinitely valuable relic.

But the Ark is only a type, a shadow of what we are. We are the Ark of the Covenant. We are the place where God communes with man. Inside of us is hidden manna reserved for another day, just as the Ark in the Old Testament contained a jar of manna from the time of Moses:

> *...the ark of the covenant [was] overlaid on all sides with gold, in which were the golden pot that had the manna, Aaron's rod that budded, and the tablets of the covenant.* (Hebrews 9:4 **NKJV**)

Inside of us is a rod of authority granted only to those who overcome to the end, just as the Ark contained Aaron's rod of authority that miraculously flowered and formed almonds all in one day (see Numbers 17:1–10).

Inside of us are the commandments of God written upon our heart, not just on the tablets of stone contained in the Ark of Moses' time. We are the Ark or the dwelling place of the covenant that God strikes with man. Therefore the Lord says to those who overcome, *"I will give the hidden manna"* and *"I will give him a white stone,"* and *"on the stone, I will give him a new name written which no man knows except them that receive it."*

Notice that if we overcome *to the end*, He is going to give us a new name. In ancient Hebraic culture the nature of a person or a place was described by their name. One's name was aligned with one's nature. Jesus said, *"Most assuredly, I say to you, whatever you ask the Father in My name He will give you"* (John 16:23 NKJV). Therefore, if we are to rely in prayer on this scripture that says we can have whatever we ask for in the name of Jesus, we are really saying that we believe we will receive whatever we ask for in the nature of Jesus. Jesus said, *"Whatever things you ask in prayer, believing, you will receive"* (Matthew 21:22 NKJV). Whatever we ask in the nature of Jesus, believing and not doubting, we receive—we shall have it!

Every time the Lord wants to raise up a man, to bring about change or a shift in the way humanity relates to and communicates with God, He always changes that man's name. Thus Abram became Abraham, Sarai became Sarah, Jacob became Israel, Saul became Paul. God changes their name to indicate a change in their nature, (the shift of the natural man into the spiritual man).

So the new name given to us reflects our spiritual nature. Whenever we call somebody by their name, we prophesy over them everything that is contained in the nature of their name.

For example, my name is Nancy Joy. My parents did not know Jesus until later in life, long after I accepted the Lord, and yet they gave me a name which reflects the nature I grew up with. *Nancy* means "full of grace," and when you combine that with *Joy*, it means "full of grace and full of joy." Whatever name we choose for our children is a prophetic vocalization of what we consider their destiny to be.

I met a young Russian woman in Washington, D.C., whose name was Alona. For her whole life she had been rejected, betrayed, and left out. She always felt like she was a third wheel wherever she went. Fearing intimacy and rejection, she spent her life alone. Her name was Alona, and whenever she came to see me, she poured out to me how she always felt like she was alone.

I told her, "Well, just change your name. If you change your name, you'll change your nature."

She replied, "What should I change my name to?"

"Let's change it to Hannah. *Hannah* means full of grace."

From that day on, her entire life shifted from experiencing betrayal, rejection, and torment to one filled with friends who loved her and sought after her fellowship. Why? She went from a name and nature of being "alone" to being "full of grace."

Once I went to a heavily jihad-oriented city. The jihadist leaders had named the city after Medina, Saudi Arabia, the second-most powerful place in Islam. When I came into that city named after Medina, I asked the pastor of the local church, "What do you want to see accomplished in this city?" He gave me a description of the things he wished to see happen. All those things came from a church-age mentality.

I said, "Two things we have to do. Number one, we have to change the name of the city."

He answered, "How can we change the name of the city? The city is run by jihadist terrorists."

I countered, "Excuse me?! Jesus said all rule, all reign, all authority was given to Him on earth by His Father. That which His Father gave Him, He gave to us." I continued, "The government of this city doesn't lie in that building down there. *You* are the government of this city. The Word says whatever things you sow in Heaven, you also reap in the earth. As long as you sow the word *Medina, Medina, Medina*, you're going to reap jihad, jihad, jihad!"

I concluded, "Just change the name of the city."

"Well, change it to what?" he responded.

I said, "Don't ask me! Go ask your intercessors. The Lord has been speaking to them about it for quite some time."

He went to ask his intercessors, and they freaked out. For eighteen months the Lord had been telling them, "Change the name of the city." The name the Lord gave them was *Goshen*, which means "the place of protection." That night we changed the name of the city by decreeing and declaring to the heavens that the name and thus the nature of the city was changed from *Medina* to *Goshen*, the place of protection.

Not too long after that there was an assault on the whole territory, and every church in the region except one was either burned down or their doors were nailed shut. The only church left untouched was in Goshen, the place of protection.

When God says He is going to give us a new name, that means we are going to receive a new nature. And with our new nature we also are going to receive our spiritual DNA. That means we are going to move out from under the control of our natural DNA into the control of our spiritual DNA.

JUDGMENT OF THYATIRA

Let us go on to the church of Thyatira. Their commendation from the Lord is this: *"I know your works, love, service, faith, and your patience; and as for your works, the last are more than the first"* (Revelation 2:119 NKJV), meaning, "Your works are more than your first love."

Here is the correction:

> *Nevertheless I have a few things against you, because you allow that woman Jezebel, who calls herself a prophetess, to teach and seduce My servants to commit sexual immorality and eat things sacrificed to idols. And I gave her time to repent of her sexual immorality, and she did not repent.* (Revelation 2:20-21 NKJV)

This correction goes back to syncretization, which is rampant in the Age of the Church. There is so much mixture in the church with false religious practices. The purpose of the Jezebel spirit is to shut the mouth of the prophets so that the things she declares will come to pass rather than the things the prophets of God declare. She seduces the servants of God to commit fornication and to eat things sacrificed to idols. This again shows syncretization of the practices connected with idol worship.

We think about idols as being idols of wood and stone, or idols of gold and silver. But what kind of idols do we have in our everyday life? Could the computer be an idol? Could gaming be an idol? Could the television be an idol? Could sports be an idol? What takes our time, our focus, our giftings, our talents, and our creativity away from God?

The Word says we are to give Him a tithe. That is more than just ten percent of our money. It is ten percent of our time, ten percent of our giftings, ten percent of our creativity. Ten percent of everything we have belongs to God. If you consider just the principle of time, for every twenty-four hours, 2.4 of those hours should belong to and are to be dedicated only to the worship and the seeking of God Almighty.

How many people do you know who spend 2.4 hours every day seeking the Lord? Yet some of those same people will watch six or seven hours of TV, most of which is extremely unedifying. TV can become an idol, computers can become an idol—anything that we do that replaces our time of intimacy with the Lord is idolatry.

Let us go on:

> *Indeed I will cast her into a sickbed, and those who commit adultery with her into great tribulation, unless they repent of their deeds.* (Revelation 2:22–23 NKJV)

That means if we have idols in our life concerning food, drink, drugs, or our names, our reputations, even our ministries, we have to repent of making those things more important than the Lord. Our idols can even be spiritual things, such as our gifts, our prophesying, or our manner of worship. If we equate our identification with the Body of

Being an Overcomer

Christ to our gifting, then that becomes an idol. Even worship itself can become an idol if our focus is centered on the action of worship and not on Him whom we worship.

Verse 23 continues the correction:

> *I will kill her children with death, and all the churches shall know that I am He who searches the minds and hearts. And I will give to each one of you according to your works.* (Revelation 2:23 NKJV)

Now here is the command: "*...hold fast what you have...*" (Revelation 2:25 NKJV)—which is what? Good works, patience, longsuffering.

The covenant is this: "*...He who overcomes, and keeps My works until the end, to him I will give power over the nations...*" (Revelation 2:26 NKJV). Until the end of what? It does not mean until the end of time. It does not even mean to the end of your spiritual migration in the earth. It means to the end in terms of death to self. He is saying, "If you overcome and keep My works unto the end of self, to you I will give power over nations."

This is happening already. The Lord is granting to those who qualify as overcomers heavy-duty power to speak to the leaders of nations, in order to reconfigure the spiritual atmosphere in the nations wherever they are co-participating with God. We were created to be co-workers and co-creators together with God for the establishment of His Kingdom and His righteousness in all of the earth (see Ephesians 6).

I believe that in the end times, the leaders of nations will come to us saying, "Show us your ways," and we must be confident in what the Word says: "*...you yourselves are full of goodness, amply filled with all [spiritual] knowledge, and competent to admonish and counsel and instruct one another*" (Romans 15:14 AMP).

Already this is taking place. I have prophesied over more than thirty heads of nations and many of their cabinets. It does not make any difference whether they are Muslim, Buddhist, Confucian, new age, or tribalistic. Once the gift of God is manifest in you, the gift makes way for you, and you are given the authority then to speak to leaders of nations.

He is giving us the power over the nations. Scripture says:

> *"He shall rule them with a rod of iron; They shall be dashed to pieces like the potter's vessel"—as I have also received from My Father; and I will give him the morning star. He who has an ear, let him hear what the Spirit says to the churches.* (Revelation 2:27–28 NKJV)

The morning star is the very last star that can be seen in the heavens as the darkness turns into daylight. *"I will give to him the morning star"* refers to a title referring to Jesus, meaning that we will not only have Jesus, but we will also have the power to drive out all darkness, being the express representation of His light.

JUDGMENT OF SARDIS

Now let us look at the church at Sardis.

> *He who overcomes shall be clothed in white garments, and I will not blot out his name from the Book of Life; but I will confess his name before My Father and before His angels. He who has an ear, let him hear what the Spirit says to the churches.* (Revelation 3:5–6 NKJV)

The sentence *"He who overcomes shall be clothed in white garments"* could be referring to the men in white linen, who have already gone on to become part of the great cloud of witnesses. As overcomers, we are in a state of preparation to become the men in white linen of the future. These are those amongst the great cloud who have gone further than the normal Christian in their pursuit of union with the divine nature, and whose fruit is evident for all eternity to see.

> *Therefore, since we are surrounded by so great a cloud of [a]witnesses [who by faith have testified to the truth of God's absolute faithfulness], stripping off every unnecessary weight and the sin which so easily and cleverly entangles us, let us run with endurance and active persistence the race that is set before us.* (Hebrews 12:1 AMP)

The white garments can represent the restoration of our original, primordial position and condition in Him. The white garments may also be the restoration of the shekinah glory we had with God before mankind ever fell. The white garments may represent our total transfiguration. They are symbolic of many different things, but the truth of the matter is that we already have a garment of light inside of us called our spirit. Our purpose at this time is to take that which was relegated to hiddenness within us and bring it out to make it preeminent once again so we may take over our primordial position in God as sons of light.

Consider these scriptures:

> *For God did not send His Son into the world to condemn the world, but that the world through Him might be saved.* (John 3:17 NKJV)

> *Then Jesus spoke to them again, saying, "I am the light of the world. He who follows Me shall not walk in darkness, but have the light of life."* (John 8:12 NKJV)

Jesus did not come into the world to condemn the world but that through Him the world might be saved. He is saying, "For I am indeed the Light that lights the whole earth, the Light that lights the heart of every man." (See John 1.)

On the outside of us we have a garment of skin, but on the inside we have a garment of light. What we are about in this current age is taking back that garment of light and putting our spirit back into the command position over our soul and our body.[16]

JUDGMENT OF PHILADELPHIA

I love the next church in Revelation 3, the church in Philadelphia. *"These things says He who is holy, He who is true, 'He who has the key of David, He who opens and no one shuts, and shuts and no one opens'"* (Revelation 3:7 NKJV). The commendation comes next: *"I know your works. See, I have set before you an open door, and no one can shut it"* (Revelation 3:8 NKJV). I love that. The Lord continues,

> *For you have a little strength, have kept My word, and have not denied My name. Indeed I will make those of the synagogue of Satan, who say they are*

---

[16] This concept is discussed more in these chapters: Seventh Day Transfiguration and Restoration.

Jews and are not, but lie—indeed I will make them come and worship before your feet, and to know that I have loved you. (Revelation 3:8–9 NKJV)

Verses 10 and 11 go on:

Because you have kept My command to persevere, I also will keep you from the hour of trial which shall come upon the whole world, to test those who dwell on the earth. Behold, I am coming quickly! Hold fast what you have, that no one may take your crown. (Revelation 3:10–11 NKJV)

The next verses contain the promise:

He who overcomes, I will make him a pillar in the temple of My God, and he shall go out no more. I will write on him the name of My God and the name of the city of My God, the New Jerusalem, which comes down out of heaven from My God. And I will write on him My new name. He who has an ear, let him hear what the Spirit says to the churches. (Revelation 3:12–13 NKJV)

The church of Philadelphia is the church of love… brotherly love. Notice that there is no condemnation to the church that *is* love. In the Age of the Church, it is okay to *do* love or to *give* love. In the Age of the Kingdom, we must *become* love because we are growing up into the measure of the fullness of the stature of Christ Jesus, and the nature of Jesus *is* love.

In James 1:17 we see *"[t]here is no shadow of turning with Him"* (NKJV). Therefore, if we are going to be conformed to His image, love can no longer be merely a verb describing an activity. It must move from being an action to becoming a state of being. As we move into the Age of the Kingdom, the same can be said of prayer. It is no longer just an activity. It, too, becomes a state of being. We must *become* love, because the ultimate goal of the overcoming life is to be completely, absolutely and totally conformed to His image.

But we all, with unveiled face, beholding as in a mirror the glory of the Lord, are being transformed into the same image from glory to glory, just as by the Spirit of the Lord. (2 Corinthians 3:18 NKJV)

The end of that is love. Prophecy and all the other gifts are going to pass away. All that is going to remain is faith, hope, and love.

> *Love never fails. But whether there are prophecies, they will fail; whether there are tongues, they will cease; whether there is knowledge, it will vanish away... And now abide faith, hope, love, these three; but the greatest of these is love.* (1 Corinthians 13:8,13 NKJV)

Love will never pass away because when we become love, we become what *all* creation is groaning for:

> *For the earnest expectation of the creation eagerly waits for the revealing of the sons of God. For the creation was subjected to futility, not willingly, but because of Him who subjected it in hope; because the creation itself also will be delivered from the bondage of corruption into the glorious liberty of the children of God. For we know that the whole creation groans and labors with birth pangs together until now.* (Romans 8:19–22 NKJV)

When I go into places of great darkness, people sometimes run at me with spears and machetes to cut my head off. But because I am learning the power of becoming love and because the transfiguration is beginning to make itself visible, people recognize love, and I am not harmed.

My heart reverberates with the frequency of God's love, and though they don't understand it, their Spirit hears that sound and recognizes it. It is a sound they heard in Heaven before they even came to the earth. When they hear the sound of the frequency of God's love, their souls cannot defend it, because it draws them back to the knowledge of who they are and why they were sent here in the first place.

No matter where I go, I find three basic needs all human beings have regardless of background. First, people need to be loved; love is the primary need. Second, people need to give love. And third, people need to know they have a purpose and a destiny here on earth—a destiny that supersedes getting up every day, going to work to earn a paycheck, and coming home to pay bills.

The number one thing every man I have ever met needs is to be loved. When you *become* love (the express reflection of His image), their spirit picks up on that power, and even though their soul may fight and argue against it, their spirit will recognize love.

Even when we go into areas that have been heavily destroyed by militants, or where massive natural destruction is evident everywhere—for example in a tsunami- or earthquake-stricken area—people will chase us down the street just for a touch or a hug. They would much rather have that embrace, that hug, that touch, even more than food, water, medicine or any other thing, because perhaps they are traumatized by having lost forty relatives in twenty minutes. Many come to the medical units asking us to euthanize them because their pain is more than they can bear. The one thing they are looking for above all else is *love*.

The church of Philadelphia was a church that became love. Because they kept His word and worshipped at His feet, because He loved them and they loved Him, there was no condemnation to the church that became love.

> *Because you have kept My command to persevere, I also will keep you from the hour of trial which shall come upon the whole world, to test those who dwell on the earth. Behold, I am coming quickly! Hold fast what you have, that no one may take your crown.* (Revelation 3:10–11 **NKJV**)

Those words imply we have a crown already. If we are qualified as overcomers, we do not have to wait to die and go to Heaven to get a crown. We have crowns already—now! When I talk about being caught up in a moment, in the twinkling of an eye, and carried away to stand with Him face to face, people say to me, "Are you trying to tell me there is no such thing as rapture?"

I say, "Absolutely not. I get caught up in the twinkling of an eye every single day. I get carried away to stand face-to-face with Jesus. I sit down at the banqueting table. I take my crown. I take my rod of authority. I take my robe. Then I come back down here and put every enemy under my feet. Oh, yes—I believe in rapture!"

This is not something that is yet afar off. This is here and now. It is happening in the present. You can learn how to be caught up in a moment, in the twinkling of an eye.

> *For whatever things were written before were written for our learning, that we through the patience and comfort of the Scriptures might have hope.* (Romans 15:4 NKJV)

In other words, everything written of Israel is for teaching and instruction for the Body of Christ today.

Consider this parallel from the history of the Israelites.

The Israelites had the revelation that Messiah was going to come as the overcoming, conquering, victorious hero to overcome all the kingdoms of the world, to sit on the throne of David and rule from the temple in Jerusalem. From scripture they had the revelation He was going to come as a man of sorrow and grief, smitten and stricken, afflicted, rejected—a man who learned obedience by the things He suffered. They had scripture that said He would be wounded for our transgressions, bruised for our iniquities, the chastisement of our sin would be laid upon Him, and that by His stripes we would be healed.

> *He was despised and rejected by men,*
> *A Man of sorrows and pain and acquainted with grief;*
> *And like One from whom men hide their faces*
> *He was despised, and we did not appreciate His worth or esteem Him.*
> *But [in fact] He has borne our griefs,*
> *And He has carried our sorrows and pains;*
> *Yet we [ignorantly] assumed that He was stricken,*
> *Struck down by God and degraded and humiliated [by Him].*
> *But He was wounded for our transgressions,*
> *He was crushed for our wickedness [our sin, our injustice, our wrongdoing];*
> *The punishment [required] for our well-being fell on Him,*
> *And by His stripes (wounds) we are healed.* (Isaiah 53:3–5 AMP)

They had the prophetic word recorded in scripture that said He would be born in Bethlehem: *"But you, Bethlehem Ephrathah, Though you are little among the thousands of Judah, Yet out of you shall come forth to Me The One to be Ruler in Israel, Whose goings forth are from of old, From everlasting"* (Micah 5:2 NKJV).

He would be born of a virgin: *"Therefore the Lord Himself will give you a sign: Behold, the virgin shall conceive and bear a Son, and shall call His name Immanuel"* (Isaiah 7:14 NKJV).

He would be of the line of David: *"When your days are fulfilled and you rest with your fathers, I will set up your seed after you, who will come from your body, and I will establish his kingdom. He shall build a house for My name, and I will establish the throne of his kingdom forever"* (2 Samuel 7:12–13 NKJV).

They had it all right there in scripture. But, for two thousand years they had been taught that when the Messiah comes, He would be an overcoming, conquering king. So when He did come they did not recognize Him because He did not come the way they had been taught.

For two thousand years now the Body of Christ has likewise been taught exactly how Messiah is going to come again, so that when He comes, we fail to recognize Him because He did not come the way we were taught.

Jesus told His disciples things like, *"The kingdom of God has come near to you"* (Luke 10:9 NKJV), *"the kingdom of God is at hand"* (Mark 1:15 NKJV), and *"the kingdom of God is within you"* (Luke 17:21 NKJV). As we can see, the Kingdom has always been here. His own disciples told the people of their day: "Forget about planting your fields, you must get ready because Jesus is coming back." "Forget about getting married, you must get ready because Messiah is coming!" And *why* did they say such things? Because Jesus Himself had told them so: *"Assuredly, I say to you, there are some standing here who shall not taste death till they see the Son of Man coming in His kingdom"* (Matthew 16:28 NKJV).

Unless I am misinformed, the disciples have died. So, either Jesus lied or we misunderstood what He was saying. We are still looking for a day that is afar off, and all the while it is here, and it is now. It has always been here and now! That is why He told His disciples that the Kingdom is at hand: His Kingdom is within you. It is and always has been as close as our heartbeat—as close as our next breath. All we need to do is step into it.

Judgment to Laodicea

Finally, we come to the church of Laodicea, beginning in Revelation 3:15. The first thing to notice is that the Lord makes no commendation. There was nothing good that came out of the church of Laodicea. Therefore, the Lord could not commend them for what they had done well. They had not done anything well. He says to them, *"I know your works, that you are neither cold nor hot. I could wish you were cold or hot. So then, because you are lukewarm, and neither cold nor hot, I will vomit you out of My mouth"* (Revelation 3:15 NKJV).

I had a fabulous, wonderful, dynamic Damascus-road experience when I gave my life to Jesus. Due to a lot of negativity from the church I grew up in, I had become an atheist just as soon as I moved out of my parents' home. I turned away from God, and I had nothing but disdain for the church. I believed God was an excuse for things man could not understand. I believed Jesus was dead, that He was still in the grave and He was not ever coming back again.

But fortunately for me (glory to God!), He had better plans for me than to leave me in that state of denial and unbelief. Because He knew that I was so hard-hearted and so antichrist-spirited that no man could ever convince me that God was real, He just decided to do it Himself.

He showed up in my bedroom in a blinding, brilliant, blue-white light that completely turned my world inside-out and upside-down in the course of one night. I had a divine, epiphanous appearance of Jesus Christ. From that day on, all I could do was grab every homeless, drug-addicted, alcoholic, prostituted person I could find and bring them to my home, telling them, "You have just got to know this wonderful Jesus! He is so magnificent and so beautiful."

Because I was coming out of a time of my life where I was totally cold, totally antichrist-spirited, the Lord spoke to me in a very dynamic way.

After I gave my life to Jesus, the very next weekend I went out and joined the church where all of my country club friends went, thinking they would be totally delighted I'd had a personal appearance of Jesus in my room. It took me about one week in that church to realize no one there had any idea what I was talking about. In fact, even the pastor had no clue what a born-again experience was.

During the course of the seven years I spent in that church because of God's mandate for me, I never met another person who was born-again, saved or filled with the Holy Spirit. I would try passionately to get people to come to my house for Bible study, to read the Word of God and to pray with me, but nobody wanted to read the Word, nobody wanted to pray. They thought that was boring. They only wanted to read *I'm OK – You're OK*, a secular self-help book of that day. In fact in our adult Sunday school class, we spent Easter Sunday one year talking about whether or not Jesus Christ was the Son of God or the son of Joseph—or whether or not the truth of that matter made any difference after all.

That church was not even up to lukewarm in spiritual temperature. But if we had to look at an example of a lukewarm church, let's just say that church had about twenty-eight hundred people, none of whom (other than me) knew Jesus as their personal savior through a born-again experience.

God hates religion. He hates it because it sets up a structure of do's and don'ts. It sets up a pattern for people can follow, thinking they are doing good works, when all the time they are doing dead works, because none of them are hooked into the belief that Jesus Christ is the foundation for everything they do.

That church I was part of had become a social organization where people could come together to spend ninety percent of their time drinking coffee and eating donuts and ten percent of their time talking about whether God really knew our names and whether or not God really interfaced with humanity today. But how many of you know the church is not an organization? It is a living organism. That is one of the reasons why God hates religion.

Let us go on. The Lord said, "...*Because you are lukewarm, and neither cold nor hot, I will vomit you out of My mouth*" (Revelation 3:15 NKJV). That is such a repulsive thought—to think that God Almighty could have so much disdain for the lukewarm church that He would actually spit them out of His mouth.

I hate to say it, but unfortunately this is the state of a great majority of the church in America: *"Because you say, 'I am rich, have become wealthy, and have need of nothing'—and do not know that you are wretched, miserable, poor, blind, and naked..."* (Revelation 3:17 NKJV). They think they are rich because they are increased in goods. They think they have need of nothing but do not understand they are poor, wretched, blind, and naked.

Recently I was in the church in Indonesia where a bunch of well-recognized ministries had come to teach the people of Indonesia how to build their church as a body. I happened to know the people from this particular ministry and had travelled with them many times before. But when they came to Indonesia, they brought along their PowerPoint presentations on how to build a church.

One of the men, whose name you would recognize, stood up and said, "I have a testimony. Twenty-five years ago, I started my church with only four people, and today I have twenty-eight hundred people. And so I'm here today to tell you how to build your church in like fashion."

He showed slides which covered how to develop a youth ministry, how to develop your nursery, how to develop your teaching ministry, etc. "How to raise funds"—that was one of the most interesting of all. When he finished his presentation, he walked up to the man next to me, whom I also knew. I thought, "Oh my goodness. This is going to be very interesting."

The man next to me had borrowed a suit coat to come to this meeting. The sleeves to the suit coat were so far past his fingers he had to constantly pull up the sleeves. He wore a pair of old flip-flops that were nearly worn down to the concrete. He had a little, teeny, tiny spiral notebook with a pencil that was about two inches long because it had been sharpened so many times. He was busily taking notes from the great American preacher who came to teach him how to build his church.

The teacher walked up to him, slapped him on the shoulder, and said, "Now son, let's take you. How many people do you have in your church?"

The man put his head down, and his face turned red. He was quite embarrassed, and in almost a whisper he said, "Well, probably I'm not going to be a very good example because our church is only one year old."

And the preacher said, "Look, son, I'm trying to help you here. Despise not the day of small beginnings. About how many people do you have on your church roll?"

The man said to him, "Well, we don't actually have a membership roll. We don't have what you would call a standard number of people."

The preacher smacked him on the shoulder and said, "Look son, I'm here to help you. I can't help you if you won't help me. So take a wild guess and tell me approximately how many people do you have in your church?"

In almost a whisper, taking a gulp before he even said it, he replied, "Eight hundred and fifty thousand."

I looked at my friend the teacher. His face went totally white. Here, in front of him, was a man who had established a church that was only one year old that had already reached a level of eight hundred and fifty thousand people. And yet, here was this great American preacher who had come from a nation rich and increased in goods, having need of nothing, trying to teach that man how to build a church? I don't think so!

The issue in America is that we think we have everything down pat. We have been the exporter of the Gospel for two hundred years, so we arrogantly think we must have the inside track on how to build a church. I knew this Indonesian man. I had been involved with him for several years. In his meekness and humility he had been able to establish something which does not exist in America. This meek, humble, little man was "richer" than any other person I have known, and I have known many billionaires during my travels.

> *I counsel you to buy from Me gold refined in the fire, that you may be rich.* (Revelation 3:18 NKJV)

All over the world, wherever I have gone, I have seen churches tried by fire. In many of those churches, members have been decapitated. One pastor I visited had his wife's legs blown off in a car bomb, and his son had been beheaded—all for the testimony of their faith in Christ Jesus. This is what is called being tried in the fire. The fire of persecution purifies people. It makes them quite rich, actually.

Let's return to the story I told earlier about the Living Martyr of China. After I left him, I was on my way home, coming from the church in South Korea headed by Paul Yongi Cho. He had given me a book out of his library. I was reading it on the plane on my way back. I put it down in my lap, and thought about the Living Martyr of China. I recalled his statement that his desire was number one, for us not to send money, and number two, not to pray for the end to the persecution.

I lifted up my voice right there to the Lord and I said, "Oh my God, I am so thankful that I live in a country where I'm free to worship You, where I'm free to preach the gospel without fear of imprisonment, where I'm free to have twenty-five Bibles in my own home."

And suddenly the Lord whispered in my ear, "Who is more blessed, really?" Suddenly, I understood that those who had suffered through the fires of persecution had something we really need. Because they had counted the cost, paid the price, and died the death, they had achieved a wealth that goes far beyond money.

The Living Martyr had said that their eight-year-old children went out to raise the dead and did not even think of it as being miraculous.

How much we need that in the United States, so that whatever it takes to bring us to that place where we are tried by fire, we might be truly called rich. Woe unto us who say we are rich and increased in goods and know not that we are poor, blind, and naked. There is a wealth that goes above and beyond monetary substance. That is the wealth and riches that come to people who have been tried by fire.

I knew a man who had been a very poor jihadist terrorist. He gave his life to Jesus Christ, and in three and a half years, he won a million and a half people to Jesus. I would say that he is richer by far than anybody I know in the United States!

The Lord continues speaking to the Laodicean church:

I counsel thee to buy of me gold tried in the fire, that thou mayest be rich; and white raiment, that thou mayest be clothed, and that the shame of thy nakedness do not appear... (Revelation 3:18 KJV)

When we become transfigured beings following in the pattern of Jesus Christ, believers have a garment of light, the *shekinah* that is called our spirit. When we become the light that can drive out all of the darkness, our nakedness and the shame of our nakedness will no longer affect people, but rather wherever we go, people will fall down on their faces crying out, "What must we do to be saved?" Why? Because we have been clothed with the shekinah that we had with God before the world was ever in existence, and have therefore become once again the thing that all creation is longing for, which is the manifestation of the sons of God.

When God came to Adam in the Garden and said, "Adam, where are you?" Adam responded and said: "I heard your voice walking in the Garden and I was afraid because I was naked." He didn't respond that way because he looked down and suddenly saw that he and Eve didn't have any clothes on. Who cares if they were naked? They were the only ones there anyway.

Being an Overcomer

He responded that way because he saw that they had been stripped of something. They were afraid because they recognized they had been stripped of the garment of the shekinah that had allowed them to walk in unfettered union with God prior to the Fall. At that time, they could have direct contact with God, without interference from darkness, *because they were made of the same substance.*

The light of that substance has since migrated into our mortal bodies and now lies hidden within our hearts, while our created part, through the grace of God, has been covered instead by skin.

Continuing, we read: *"... anoint your eyes with eye salve, that you may see"* (Revelation 3:18 NKJV).

I love what Paul said to the Ephesian church in Ephesians 1 (I am paraphrasing): "I pray for you daily that the spirit of wisdom and knowledge in the revelation of Christ Jesus would come to open up the eyes of your understanding, that you would know—that you know, that you know your purpose, your destiny, your high calling in Christ Jesus."

We need to pray consistently for our eyes to be opened so we can see the deeper, wider, broader, richer, higher principles of Christ Jesus, those principles that we can see only when we ascend into the heavens and stand face-to-face with Him. We must cry out to God continually to anoint our eyes. Most of us read the Bible only to prove the things we already know, rather than to see the things we do not yet know or to ask for our eyes to be opened up to the mysteries of God that have been hidden for us. When we pray to the Lord to open up the eyes of our understanding, we begin to read the Word from a totally different viewpoint, from a place of elevated sight, where the words on the page penetrate our spirits and produce instantaneous change. We anoint our eyes to see the higher purposes of God in Christ Jesus.

Jesus says, *"Behold, I stand at the door and knock. If anyone hears My voice and opens the door, I will come in to him and dine with him, and he with Me."* (Revelation 3:20 NKJV). For years and years we have used this verse as a means to evangelize those who are coming out of the ranks of the unbelieving. But this verse is intended for those who have overcome and particularly for those who have overcome to the end.

When I began to come into ascension experiences with the Lord, and I first saw and opened up that door, I was inspired to study the doors and windows mentioned in the scripture. There are many, many different doors and windows in Heaven. The word *door* occurs in 242 verses in the King James Version.[17] One door is mentioned more than any other door. That door is "the door of the tabernacle of the congregation," which is referred to about 133 times, by my count. *Tabernacle* means "dwelling place, the place of habitation." Therefore, the door of the tabernacle of the congregation is the door to the dwelling place of God in the midst of the congregation.

When I teach about corporate ascension experience, this is the door that we go through—the door of the tabernacle of the congregation. In Revelation 3:20, Jesus stands at the door and knocks always, but it is up to us to make the decision to open up that door.

To him who overcomes I will grant to sit with Me on My throne, as I also overcame and sat down with My Father on His throne. (Revelation 3:21 NKJV)

In 1997, I had an experience with the Lord which lasted seven days. During this seven solid days of communion with Him, unfettered by any human contact whatsoever, I experienced things that were nearly unbelievable. At the end of that time, the Lord said, "These are the seven judgments. You have been judged and found ready. Now come and sit down with Me in My throne."

"Come and sit" means come and rest. He was saying, "You have overcome to the end. These are the seven judgments, and now you are prepared to sit down with Me in My throne."

---

[17] See Art and the Bible website, "door" and "doors" entries in the Old Testament and New Testament, available https://www.artbible.info/concordance/d.html.

From that day forward, the focus of my ministry made a gigantic, tectonic-level shift. It put me into a whole new level of ruling and reigning with authority from the throne. To this day many leaders—presidents, kings, tribal chieftains—come to me saying, "Show me your ways in keeping with the Word of God, so that in the end-time we will have power to judge even the nations."

Those things are already present. They are already here, already happening. All we have to do is step out, step up and step into our divine positioning in His throne, secured by Jesus Christ for us at the right hand of God the Father Almighty. *"To him who overcomes I will grant to sit with Me on My throne, as I also overcame and sat down with My Father on His throne"* (Revelation 3:21 NKJV). We are called to be co-laborers and co-creators together with God for the establishment of His Kingdom and His righteousness in all the earth: *"For we are God's fellow workers; you are God's field, you are God's building"* (1 Corinthians 3:9 NKJV), and *"We then, as workers together with Him also plead with you not to receive the grace of God in vain"* (2 Corinthians 6:1 NKJV).

If we are going to be those true co-laborers and co-creators:

1. We have to overcome all the judgments laid down in Revelation 2 and 3;
2. We have to overcome to the end;
3. We have to be seated in our divine position at the right hand of God the Father Almighty in a way that manifests itself in the earth realm.

When this happens, we are going to find that the disdain which the whole earth has had for the Church all these many years is going to suddenly disappear. For the thing that has *not yet* been revealed is going to be revealed.

> *Beloved, now we are children of God; and it has not yet been revealed what you shall be but we know that when He is revealed, we shall be like Him, for we shall see Him as He is.* (1 John 3:2 NKJV)

That means something is coming that is above and beyond—greater than, higher than, deeper than, wider than, broader than anything that has ever happened in the earth before.

When the thing that has not been revealed is revealed, all creation which groans right now for the manifestation of the sons of the living God will hear the frequency. They will see the transfiguration in us, and the whole of humanity will come to see it. Thus the scripture will be fulfilled: *"Arise, shine, for your light has come and the glory of the LORD has risen upon you"* (Isaiah 60:1 **NKJV**).

The Lord is saying, "Though darkness covers the earth and gross, hideous, ugly, despicable darkness the hearts of men, yet My light shall be seen upon you, and the kings of the earth and the unbelievers will be gathered together and converted unto Me."

Why? Because you preach a good message? I don't think so. Why? Because you heal the sick and raise the dead? No! They will come because His light will be seen upon you. This is reserved for those who overcome to the end.

I want to encourage you right now to buy of the Lord fire that you might be rich—gold refined in the furnace of fire that you might be rich. Pray to Yahweh every single day for increasingly elevated sight so you can see things in the Word you have never seen before, that the mysteries of God would be revealed to you, in you, through you, and out of you to a broken, hurting world, so that we might become perfect reflections of His glory in all the earth.

Father, I thank You and I praise You for this message concerning the overcomers. I thank You that the seed of this Word has fallen on good ground, that it will bear fruit, it will be multiplied, and it will last for eternity. According to your Word, let it be done. In the beautiful, magnificent and holy name of Yeshua, let it be done. Amen.

Chapter 5

Revelation

IN THIS CHAPTER we are going to open up the Book of Revelation, and I will begin to teach from perhaps a little different perspective than you have heard before. We begin in Revelation chapter one.

> *The Revelation of Jesus Christ, which God gave Him to show His servants—things which must shortly take place. And He sent and signified it by His angel to His servant John, who bore witness to the word of God, and to the testimony of Jesus Christ, to all things that he saw.* (Revelation 1:1–2 NKJV)

Don't you love God's idea of "shortly"? After all, these words were written two thousand years ago, and we are still waiting for them to come to pass. One important aspect of the first verse, *"... He sent and He signified it by His angel to his servant John...,"* is John's encounter with the angelic being sent as the messenger from heaven with this revelatory download. Through that encounter, John bore record of the Word of God, the testimony of Jesus Christ and of all the things he saw. For the rest of our study in the Book of Revelation, I want you to circle in your own Bible every time you see these words: *he looked, he saw, he heard,* and *he beheld*.

> *Blessed is he that readeth, and they that hear the words of this prophecy, and keep those things which are written therein: for the time is at hand.* (Revelation 1:3 KJV)

Do an exercise with me: put your hand right in front of your face and repeat three times, "The time is at hand, the time is at hand, the time is at hand." Now, look at your hand. Look all the way to where you can see the lines and the pores inside of your hand. Now tell me, how close is your hand? It is as close as your next heartbeat. It is as close as your next breath. The Word of the Lord that begins the whole Book of Revelation is *"the time is at hand."* In other words, what is in Revelation is not for a time that is far off. It is for now.

Every time the disciples questioned Jesus about the signs of His coming, His answer was always the same.

> *And as ye go, preach, saying, The kingdom of heaven is at hand.* (Matthew 10:7 KJV)

> *...The time is fulfilled, and the kingdom of God is at hand: repent ye, and believe the gospel.* (Mark 1:15 KJV)

> *Nor will they say, "See here!" or, "See there!" For indeed, the kingdom of God is within you.* (Luke 17:21 NKJV)

For two thousand years, we've been looking here and looking there, trying to determine when Jesus is coming again. We have been trying to wrap our whole doctrinal eschatology around end-time current events, when all the while, the kingdom we have been looking for is within us. The Kingdom is here. It is now. It has always been here and now.

Notice Revelation 1:3 gives three prerequisites for receiving the blessings of this book:

1. We must first read. (But just because we read does not necessarily mean we hear.)
2. We must hear ("Let those who have ears to hear, hear.").
3. We must keep the things written there.

Some people are content only to read, but even having read, they hear not. Jesus said this: *"Therefore speak I to them in parables: because they seeing see not; and hearing they hear not, neither do they understand"* (Matthew 13:13 KJV). I previously shared about my friend who was an expert on the book of Mark. He had handled and translated the book from original manuscripts. He could read and translate Greek, Hebrew, and Aramaic. But even though he spent half his life learning the book of Mark, he never heard the Word with spiritual ears. He is an example of a person who was *"ever learning, and never able to come to the knowledge of the truth"* (2 Timothy 3:7 KJV). Unfortunately, there are many in the ranks of the church today who read but who do not hear what it is they are reading. These represent the thirty-fold.

On the other hand, there are those who hear the word of the Lord, but don't do it. *"But be ye doers of the word, and not hearers only, deceiving your own selves"* (James 1:22 KJV). In order for us to receive the blessings from Revelation, we must do all three. We must (1) read, (2) hear, and (3) do (or keep) the word. How do we *do* the Word in Revelation? That is a lifelong pursuit that requires ascension experience in Him.

Pursuing End-Time Understanding

When I first gave my life to Jesus Christ, I was so hungry for the Word of God. I was zealous: I would spend twenty hours a day in the Word of God. I had an all-consuming desire to find out about the end-time appearance of Jesus in the earth. I read, reread, and reread again the Book of Revelation. I read over one thousand commentaries concerning the second coming of Jesus Christ. I went to the Library of Congress in Washington, D.C., and I looked up two drawers full of references to the end time appearing of Jesus. (That tells you how long ago it was. We were still using the Dewey Decimal System on file cards then, so to find published allusions to the second coming of Jesus Christ, I had to tediously look up every individual one.)

I was so hungry, so desirous to find out about all the end-time things. I took one of those huge hand-drying rolls that you find in public restrooms and I rolled it down the hallway in my home. Starting at the book of Genesis, I timed, charted, and dated everything from the beginning of the Bible all the way through the book of Revelation. I wanted to figure out the timing for everything for myself. I went back to the kings and wrote down this king ruled these many years, and this king ruled these many years, and his son was born, and his son ruled these many years… I timed the whole Bible from Genesis all the way to the Book of Revelation. I tried to figure out what was going to be the end time, out-working of the appearance of Jesus Christ in all the earth.

I found a very interesting thing: every single generation since the fourth generation of Christianity has earnestly believed with all of their hearts that they were going to be the generation that would be alive when Jesus Christ came back to the earth again. Even the disciples taught their people to forget about planting crops, and forget about getting married, because you have to get ready because Jesus is coming back again soon. Why did they teach that? They taught it because Jesus told them, *"Assuredly, I say to you, there are some standing here who shall not taste death till they see the Son of Man coming in His kingdom"* (Matthew 16:28 NKJV).

Now, unless I miss my guess, the disciples have all passed away. Therefore, either Jesus was lying or He was trying to communicate to them something we still have not laid hold of until this day. That principle is contained in the words *the time is at hand*. The time is at hand. Every time the disciples asked Him what the sign of His coming would be, He told them the same thing: "I tell you the truth, the time is at hand. The kingdom is within you." The time described in the book of Revelation has always been here. It is not anything that is yet afar off. It has always been present, always been attainable and is something that every earnestly desiring, earnestly seeking Christian could lay hold of at any time in human history. That is why Jesus consistently said, *"The time is at hand."*

After three and a half years spending hundreds of hours trying to figure everything out, I finally came before the Lord in tears, crying out to Him: "Lord, I really want to know the truth!"

He laughed at me and said: "If you want to know the truth, you must come to the truth. The truth is not a doctrine. It is a person!"

His directive was clear. If I wanted to know the truth, I would have to *"come up here,"* just as John was directed in Revelation 4:1.

THE RECORD OF THE COMING KING

Second Timothy chapter 3 says everything that was ever written of Israel was for teaching and instruction for the body of Christ today.

For two thousand years, Israel had the full revelation of Jesus Christ. It was written in their scrolls. They read it all the time out of the synagogues.

Israel had the Word that said He was going to come as an overcoming, victorious hero to overthrow all the governments and the kingdoms of this earth, to sit on the throne of David and rule from Jerusalem. They also had the Word that said He was going to come as a man of sorrow, acquainted with grief, stricken, smitten, afflicted, and rejected (Isaiah 53:3), the Word that said he would come as a man who learned obedience by the things that He suffered. They had the prophecy that He would be wounded for our transgressions, bruised for our iniquities, that the chastisement of our sin would be upon His head, and by His stripes we would be healed (Isaiah 53:5). They had the Word of God that said that He would be of the tribe of David, born of a virgin in the city of Bethlehem, and that He would be hung on a tree. But for two thousand years they had only been taught that when the Messiah would come, He would come as an overcoming, conquering king. So, when He came as the suffering servant, they did not recognize Him, because He did not come the way they had been expecting.

If everything written of Israel is for instruction for us today, then we are following exactly in the same pattern. Now, for the last two thousand years we have been taught exactly how Jesus Christ will come again so that when He comes—*when* He comes—we will not recognize Him if He does not come the way that we were taught. As long as we relegate the Book of Revelation to a series of end-time current events immediately surrounding the second coming of Jesus, we follow exactly the same pattern Israel followed.

During World War II, several books were written with so-called conclusive proof that their generation were the ones living in the end times. Their reasons? Hitler was the anti-Christ, Mussolini was the Beast, and Stalin was the false prophet. The case was made that the current events they faced fit the entire scenario of the Book of Revelation. Therefore, they were certain they were in the end time.

We have done the greatest travesty that could be done to this magnificent book by relegating it to a bunch of end-time current events. That is not what it is at all. It is a history of the pilgrimage of the human spirit from the day that we first leave heaven to the day we are completely perfected *in Him*, the day we become one in union with the divine nature.

If Jesus is the Word, and in the beginning was the Word (John 1), if He lives in us and the Word lives in us, then every book of the Bible from Genesis all the way to the end of Revelation also lives in us, because He is the Word and He is in us.

SEEING REVELATION FROM THE KINGDOM WITHIN

I encourage you to set aside your mindset about end-time eschatology and look at the book of Revelation from an entirely different perspective: from the perspective of the Kingdom of God within us being developed.

There are many different levels of Kingdom. There is the Kingdom of Eternity, The Kingdom of the Heaven of Heavens, The Kingdom of Heaven, The Kingdom of our Lord and Savior, Jesus Christ, The Kingdom of the Father, The Kingdom of this earth, The Kingdom Within. If we are going to be used of God to establish His Kingdom outward, we must first deal with the Kingdom Within.

Every word of Revelation has three different applications, for three different times, in three different, distinct applications to us. One is for the past, one is for the present, and one is for the future. Time is an earthly paradigm in the realms of the Spirit. In in realm of the Spirit, everything that can be done has already been done. That is why the Word says the Lamb of God was slain before the foundation of the earth. Therefore, in the realm of the Spirit, the completed work of God was finished before the earth was ever completed.

But, from earth's perspective there is one application for past, one for present, and one for future. There is also one application for your body, one application for your soul, and one application for your spirit. There is one application for the heavenly realm, one for the earthly realm, and one for the demonic realm. You can carry the many different facets of interpretation of the book of Revelation *ad infinitum*[18] to a multitude of layered meanings, meaning that the interpretation is going to depend on the extent of the elevation of your personal sight.

I am not saying that many things in Revelation will not happen in the earth, but I am saying that before they can happen in the earth, they must take place in the Kingdom Within. The Word of God has so many layered applications and it applies to so many different realms and dimensions, that we must lay hold of the one that is most important to us for this time.

As I begin to read through Revelation, I am going to speed through the scriptures quickly. I encourage you to circle every place it says, *I looked, I saw, I heard, I beheld.*

Let's begin in Revelation 1:4.

> *John, to the seven churches which are in Asia: Grace to you and peace from Him who is and who was and who is to come, and from the seven Spirits who are before His throne.* (NKJV)

Notice that He is the same God—the God who is, the God who was, and the God who is yet to come—all at the same time. He is not limited to time, or space, or distance. Jesus does not live in time: rather, time lives in Him. Therefore, if Jesus is not limited to time, space, or distance, then neither are we relegated to time or limited to space, because wherever He is (past, present or future) we may be also. We are in Him and He is in us.

Galatians chapter 4 says though we are heirs to all things, we are still subject to the teachers, tutors and guides put over us until we come into the age of the fullness of maturity when the Father will grant to us the fullness of our inheritance. In the Age of the Church, our teachers, tutors and guides came through the five-fold ministry. At that time, we thought the apostles, prophets, pastors, teachers, and evangelists were the ones called by God to do the work of the ministry. But the Word does not say that. It says the five-fold is called by God to equip and perfect the saints for the work of the ministry.

---

[18] *Ad infinitum*, Latin, "to infinity without end."

In the Age of the Church, we walked in a ten-percent level of functionality. But now—glory to God—we are stepping into the fullness of our inheritance. Being able to step into that fulness is predicated by our interaction with the Seven Spirits before the throne. In the Age of the Church, the five-fold were our teachers, our tutors, and guides, but in the Age of the Kingdom our teachers, our tutors and guides are the Seven Spirits before the throne.

Many Bible commentators might say, "Well, the Seven Spirits represent seven facets of the character of Christ Jesus or seven different dimensions of the Holy Spirit." But that is not true. The Seven Spirits are ancient, sentient beings. If you look up the Spirits of Wisdom, Understanding, Council, Might, Knowledge, Fear of the Lord and Revelation, you will find there are many, many references to them.

The Spirit of Wisdom herself, the Word says, was with God before the earth was created and has written down in the books of Heaven every act that He has ever done. I do not know about you, but I would like to have many encounters with the Spirit of Wisdom. I call upon the Spirit of Wisdom to be present in every meeting that I do because the Spirit of Wisdom and the Spirit of the Revelation of Christ Jesus open up the eyes of our understanding so that we may see, know, understand, and perceive the purpose, the destiny and the high calling of Christ that is ours.

So, it says of the seven Spirits before the throne:

> *That the God of our Lord Jesus Christ, the Father of glory, may give unto you the spirit of wisdom and revelation in the knowledge of him: The eyes of your understanding being enlightened; that ye may know what is the hope of his calling, and what the riches of the glory of his inheritance in the saints, And what is the exceeding greatness of his power to us-ward who believe, according to the working of his mighty power.* (Ephesians 1:17–19 KJV)

> *And has made us kings and priests to His God and Father, to Him be glory and dominion for ever and ever. Amen.* (Revelation 1:5 NKJV)

> *And has made us unto our God kings and priests: and we shall reign on the earth.* (Revelation 5:10 KJV)

Notice when it says he has made us kings and priests, it is stated in past tense. He has already made us kings and priests. He uses past tense, as I said before, because we were kings and priests forever before the earth was even created.

Because He has already made us kings and priests, the status is not something that we can work for, not something we can labor for. It is something Jesus Christ has already done. He has already made a way for us to enter into dominion and rulership as co-workers and co-creators together with Him for the establishment of His Kingdom and His righteousness in all the earth according to 2 Corinthians 6:1.

> *Behold, He is coming with clouds, and every eye will see Him, even they who pierced Him. And all the tribes of the earth will mourn because of Him. Even so, Amen.* (Revelation 1:7 NKJV)

Every eye will see Him, even those who pierced Him. So, this is in reference to the second resurrection.[19]

> *"I am the Alpha and the Omega the Beginning and the End," says the Lord, "who is and who was and who is to come, the Almighty." I, John both your brother and companion in the tribulation and kingdom and patience of Jesus Christ, was on the island that is called Patmos for the word of God and for the testimony of Jesus Christ. I was in the Spirit on the Lord's Day...* (Revelation 1:8–10 NKJV)

Underline this in verse 10: "*I was in the Spirit on the Lord's day.*" We must be *in the Spirit* (which is the mystery of the ascension experience in God) in order to *see* into the realms of Heaven. Our spirit is made perfect already. Our spirit is exalted to the right hand of God the Father Almighty. As soon as we confessed with our mouths and believed in our hearts, we instantaneously became joint heirs to the Kingdom of Heaven with Jesus Christ. Everything that He has is ours by adoption as sons. In the realms of the Spirit, we will never be more perfect than we are the day that we confess with our mouth because the Word says when we make that decision and when we make that confession, He (Jesus) imputes to us his righteousness. So, in the Spirit, we

---

[19] See "Restoration of All Things," a teaching in regard to the second resurrection, available at globalascensionnetwork.org.

are already made perfect. That is the gift and promise made in the Spirit.

But our soul and our body are still full of the flesh. It used to bother me that in one place the Bible says, *"For by grace are ye saved through faith; and that not of yourselves: it is the free gift of God: Not of works, lest any man should boast"* (Ephesians 2:8–9 KJV), but only a few chapters later it says, *"...work out your own salvation with fear and trembling"* (Philippians 2:12). I could never figure out how both of those could be true at the same time. Either salvation is a free gift, or it is not. Either salvation cannot be worked out through works, or we must work out our own salvation with fear and trembling. It took me a bit of time in my spiritual migration to understand that the free gift is for our spirit. It is in our soul and our body that we must work out our own salvation with fear and trembling.

Once I understood the principle of separation of flesh and spirit, it was easy to see that when you confess with your mouth and believe in your heart that Jesus Christ is Lord, your spirit is already exalted to the right hand of God the Father Almighty. You are already made perfect from that day, because on that day, Jesus imputes His righteousness to you. Therefore, in the realms of the spirit, you could never be more righteous than on the day that you confess with your mouth and believe in your heart. That is the position of your spirit. Your body and your soul, however, are still full of the dickens, and it is in those areas that you need to work out your own salvation with fear and trembling.

A Blinding Ascension

In 1997, I was in a prayer meeting with a group of intercessors in a small church in my hometown. The pastor laid hands on my eyes and said: "Lord, give her the eyes of an eagle, that she may see her enemies while they are yet afar off."

As soon as he said that, I fell to the floor crying. My eyelids were sealed shut, and my eyes began to pound in their sockets. My pastor's wife put her hands on my eyes which were pounding so hard that her hands began to bounce on top of them.

Since our prayer meeting was nearly at an end and it was getting late, I asked the pastor to dismiss the intercessors and to leave me alone in church. I knew the Lord was doing something unusual.

As soon as I heard the doors lock, I felt my spirit ascending into the heavens. I went flying upward through a brilliant blue-white tube chute. I came out lying face-down in the Sea of Glass with my arms spread outward. When I lifted up my head, I saw only the feet of the Master. I was so in awe that I put my head back down in the water.

I heard the voice of Jesus saying, "Look at Me."

Trembling, I remembered the power of His presence when I first met Him in my bedroom. I was shaking and almost fearful to look upon His presence.

He said a second time (this time with a little more insistence), "I said, look at Me!"

Still I was apprehensive.

Then, He reached down, grabbed me under my arms, sat me up on my knees, put His hand under my chin and forced my face upwards with the third-time command: "Look at me!"

When I finally opened my eyes, His radiance was overwhelming.

> ...*His countenance was like the sun shining in its strength. And when I saw Him, I fell at His feet as dead. But He laid His right hand on me, saying to me, "Do not be afraid."* (Revelation 1:16 NKJV)

He looked more like lightning and sounded more like thunder.

With eyes flaming like fire, He gazed into my soul and asked: "Are you ready?"

I heard myself saying, "Yes, Lord. I am ready."

With that, a brilliant, vibrating sword came flying out of his mouth —"*out of His mouth went a sharp two-edged sword*" (Revelation 1:15). He took it in his hands and lifted it over my head, again asking: "Are you ready"?

I said, "Yes, Lord. I am ready!"

Then He lifted that giant two-edged sword high over my head and jammed it downward into my body. I could feel the force of it in my natural body and I began to scream in pain. Instantly, my body disappeared and around it was a rainbow-colored aura which was vibrating outward.

Physically, I could feel the force and the incredible frequency coming off the sword. My body curled up in a fetal position, and I began to scream in pain. I endured for a while, but then the pain and vibrations became too intense. I begged the Lord, "It's too much, Lord. Please, take it away!"

Immediately, with tenderness, I saw Him in the realms of the Spirit lift the sword upward. My body came back into view. He waited for a little while, so that my body could endure more. Then, He asked me again for the second time, all the while with the sword lifted up over my head: "Are you ready?"

I heard myself say, "Yes, Lord. I am ready."

With that response, He again slammed the sword with full force downward through my head and into my body—BAM! Again, I felt the force of the sword penetrating and vibrating inside my body with such an intensity that there are no words to accurately explain it. Again, I screamed and cried out in pain. This time, my body began to wrench back and forth, and up and down. My muscles went into spasmatic retaliation. Every muscle, every nerve, every organ, my bones, my ligaments, my tendons all began to respond to this radical frequency ripping through my insides.

After a short time, the pain became more than I could endure. I heard my voice crying out from the earth: "Lord, it is too much! Please, take it away!"

Again, He lifted the sword upward and out of my body, all the while holding it extended over my head. My body, which had completely disappeared while the sword was vibrating in me, slowly came back into view in the spirit.

Patiently, He held the sword over my head while my body reacclimated. Then He asked for the third time: "Are you ready? ... Are you ready? ... Are you ready?"

I was hesitant to respond, but I heard myself saying, "Yes Lord, I am ready!"

Again, with the full force His electric presence could manifest, He slammed the sword down into my body, and again, pain ripped through every cell.

This sequence repeated seven times through the night. Each time ended with me asking Him to please take it away, because I couldn't go on anymore. The whole experience lasted seven hours, with each occurrence lasting a short time longer than the one previous to it.

After the seventh such occurrence, the Lord asked me one final time, "Now are you ready? ... Are you ready? ... Are you ready?"

When I responded affirmatively, He took the sword that had come out of His mouth and put it into my hands. Then, with the lightning heat of His hands coming together around my hands, He fused the sword into my hands, making my hands one with the sword.

With that, He stood me totally upright, lifted my head, and turned me around so that I was looking past the Sea of Glass. As I looked across the Sea of Glass, I saw an army of warriors with their swords all uplifted, standing at perfect attention and all in perfect order. He said: "Now, go and do what I called you to do."

By the end of the night, my body was fully spent. I was lying on the floor, my clothes drenched with sweat. I had no more energy. I had cried and screamed all night long until I had no more tears. My voice had been minimized into a faint whisper because of the hours of intense screaming.

When I came back to myself, my eyes were still sealed. I couldn't open them at all. I had done a Bible teaching that day about the healing of the blind man. I thought to myself, I will crawl on my hands and knees to the back of the sanctuary to get into the bathroom to wash my eyes. Either they will open, or they will not.

As I crawled down the aisle of the church, I heard the voice of my pastor's wife saying: "I saw as it were a woman driven into the wilderness to travail a great travail to bring forth the man-child." Unbeknownst to me, my pastor and his wife had spent the whole night in the church watching what was happening.

She got up to help me to the bathroom. I put my head down to the sink and sprinkled my eyes with water. They opened up right away. I was totally unemotional about the whole event. My only response was, "Well, that was certainly interesting."

It took a long time to digest all that happened that night. But today I know its purpose was to prepare me by filling my mouth with His word to make me an oracle. It prepared me for the intense warfare that I would endure. It gave me the power to overcome all things through the sword of His Word. I also believe it was preparation for yielding to high-level frequencies and the pain associated with them, as I yielded my body to be His instrument to respond to all creation groaning.

Since that day, I have gone through prolonged periods of time when painful groans have come up out of me for the purpose of gaining breakthrough for others. These groanings have produced resurrection from the dead, the restoration of amputated limbs, and temporary dominion in the area of healing. The same groaning has produced the salvations of thousands of people who were hard-hearted and anti-Christ spirited, and it has produced God's redemptive plan for whole geographical territories.[20]

This was just one of many times the Lord has called me by His sovereign will to come up into Heaven to receive the empowerment and equipping I need to bring to completion the good work He has begun in me. The experience had little to do with my volitional participation. It was solely initiated by Him and completed by Him. All I had to do was yield.

Seeing the Things Which Are

> *Write the things which you have seen, and the things which are, and the things which will take place after this.* (Revelation 1:19 NKJV)

Every word written in Revelation is not only about the things that are to come in the hereafter, but the things that are now. Revelation addresses the things that were, the things that are and the things that are

---

[20] See "All Creation Groaning" for further testimonies, available at global-ascensionnetwork.net.

yet to come. Therefore, let's not relegate Revelation to being only about something yet afar off. It says itself: these are *the things which are*.

In chapter 1, verse 12, John writes, *"Then I turned to see the voice that spoke with me. And having turned I saw seven golden lampstands"* (NKJV). In verse 16, John recounts seeing seven stars: *"He had in His right hand seven stars."* The mysteries he saw are then revealed to John: *"The mystery of the seven stars which you saw in My right hand, and the seven golden lampstands: The seven stars are the angels of the seven churches, and the seven lampstands which you saw are the seven churches"* (v. 20). Follow along with me just a minute and every time you see words such as see, look, hear and behold, circle them in the Bible, so you can begin to see the desire of God has always been that we see and hear into the realms of the Spirit.

> *He who has an ear, let him hear what the Spirit says to the churches. To him who overcomes I will give to eat from the tree of life, which is in the midst of the Paradise of God.* (Revelation 2:7 NKJV)
>
> *He who has an ear, let him hear what the Spirit says to the churches. He who overcomes shall not be hurt by the second death.* (v. 11)
>
> *He who has an ear, let him hear what the Spirit says to the churches. To him who overcomes I will give some of the hidden manna to eat. And I will give him a white stone, and on the stone a new name written which no one knows except him who receives it.* (v. 17)
>
> *He who has an ear, let him hear what the Spirit says to the churches...* (v. 29)
>
> *He who has an ear, let him hear what the Spirit says to the churches...* (Revelation 3:6 NKJV)
>
> *He who has an ear, let him hear what the Spirit says to the churches...* (v. 16)
>
> *Behold, I stand at the door and knock. If anyone hears My voice and opens the door, I will come in to him and dine with him, and he with Me.* (v. 20)

Are you getting a pattern here? Chapter 4 starts like this:

> *After this I looked, and, behold, a door was opened in heaven: and the first voice which I heard was as it were of a trumpet talking with me; which said, Come up hither, and I will shew thee things which must be hereafter. And immediately I was in the spirit: and, behold, a throne was set in heaven, and one sat on the throne.* (Revelation 4:1–2 KJV)

"*After this…*" After what? After the churches have all been judged?

> *And He who sat there was like a jasper and a sardius stone in appearance; and there was a rainbow around the throne, in appearance like an emerald. Around the throne were twenty-four thrones, and on the thrones I saw twenty-four elders sitting, clothed in white robes.* (Revelation 4:3–4 NKJV).

> *Then I saw a strong angel proclaiming with a loud voice, "Who is worthy to open the scroll and to loose its seals?" […] And I looked, and behold, in the midst of the throne and of the four living creatures, and in the midst of the elders, stood a Lamb as though it had been slain, having seven horns and seven eyes, which are the seven Spirits of God sent out into all the earth. […] Then I looked, and I heard the voice of many angels around the throne, the living creatures, and the elders; and the number of them was ten thousand times ten thousand, and thousands of thousands… […] And every creature which is in heaven and on the earth and under the earth and such as are in the sea, and all that are in them, I heard saying:*

> *"Blessing and honor and glory and power*
> *Be to Him who sits on the throne,*
> *And to the Lamb, forever and ever!"* (Revelation 5:2,6,11,13 NKJV)

I am setting up the pattern laid down in the Book of Revelation: *I looked, I saw, I heard, I beheld.*

As I began to discern this pattern, I thought to myself, I wonder how important that pattern is to the Lord? I went to my *Strong's Concordance* and I looked up the phrases *I looked, I saw, I heard, I beheld*, in past, present, and future tense in the Word of God. I found that those four phrases are in the Bible over seven thousand times. If God has said something seven thousand times, we might want to sit up and take notice.

In my research about seeing, hearing and beholding, I found there are multitudes of different types of sight.[21] The desire of the Father has always been for us to see Him. That is why He says "look, see, hear, behold, come and see" seven thousand times. The Old Testament prophets and the apostles understood that we could separate flesh and spirit. The Word says in Exodus, *"So the Lord spoke to Moses face to face, as a man speaks to his friend"* (Exodus 33:11 NKJV). Only nine verses later, God says to Moses: *"But He said, 'You cannot see My face; for no man shall see Me, and live'"* (Exodus 33:20 NKJV).

How are both of those possible at the same time? It is because they understood that the whole purpose of the Word of God is to sever and separate flesh from spirit so that our spirit can have face-to-face communion with God Almighty at the same time our soul and our body down here on the earth are doing what they were created to do.

The apostles understood this. That is why Paul said:

> *I know a man in Christ who fourteen years ago—whether in the body I do not know, or whether out of the body I do not know, God knows—such a one was caught up to the third heaven.* (2 Corinthians 12:2 NKJV)

It was common knowledge to early believers, but sometime in the development of the church, it became a negative thing to think that we could sever and separate flesh and spirit and be caught up into the heavens to see the things that are there. Even Jesus' desire for all of his disciples was the same. That is why He told them,

> *Do you not say, "There are still four months and then comes the harvest?" Behold, I say to you, lift up your eyes and look at the fields, for they are already white for harvest!* (John 4:35 NKJV)

In the realms of the Spirit there is no such thing as time, space, or distance. Therefore, we must learn how to lift up our eyes and look into the unseen. The Word says:

---

[21] To find out more about the different types of prophetic sight in the Bible, go to "Prophetic Sight for the Kingdom Age," available www.globalascensionnetwork.net.

> *... we look not at the things which are seen, but at the things which are not seen: for the things which are seen are temporal; but the things which are not seen are eternal.* (2 Corinthians 4:18 KJV)

One of the ways we can peer into the unseen realm is revealed in Revelation chapter 4.

> *After these things I looked, and behold, a door standing open in heaven. And the first voice which I heard was like a trumpet speaking with me, saying, "Come up here, and I will show you things which must take place after this." Immediately I was in the Spirit; and behold, a throne set in heaven, and One sat on the throne.* (Revelation 4:1–2 NKJV)

The Lord tells us to look not at the things that are temporal, and not at the things in the earth, because many people do not believe they can look into the things of eternity. But not only are we to look, we are *to behold* (that is, to consider). I love John. I have often mused about why the Lord would choose John to be the one to bring forth the eternal revelation. All of the other disciples had already been murdered. They had been boiled in oil, hung upside down, crucified, drawn and quartered by the chariots of Rome. Only John was left. John had seen so many things. He had seen his Lord and Savior crucified. I am sure there were times he wondered, "What is this all really about?" Then he saw all his best friends being murdered in terrible ways. He was the only one left.

He was probably around eighty years old when he was exiled to the Isle of Patmos. There he wrote the Book of Revelation. I think many times there, he must have been sitting in a cave all by himself, totally alone, looking back on the things that he had seen during the course of his lifetime. He must have cried out to the Lord, "Lord, what was it all about? What was it all about?" Every day, he would venture into that cave. Day after day, his cry must have been, "Lord, show me: what was it all about?"

One day he lifted up his voice, "Lord, show me what it was all about." All of a sudden, the booming voice of God Almighty responded: "What was it all about? You want to see what it was all about? Okay—here!" And BANG! God opened up the door in Heaven and immediately John was at the throne room.

John was caught up into the heavens to see the things that were, the things that are, the things that are yet to come. He saw great things, huge things, beautiful things, magnificent things, horrible things, ugly things, demonic things. Through the doors of Heaven, he could see everything that was happening in every different dimension and every different realm. I imagine it was like a panoramic-type movie for him. He saw the ultimate revelation of Jesus Christ and he put himself to the project of writing it all down.

I can imagine the people and what they must have been thinking: "Oh John, John tell us. Tell us, were the streets really made of gold?"

And John said, "Not gold, *gold*!"

"John, John, tell us about the throne. Was the throne really surrounded by rainbow colors?"

"Not rainbow—RAINBOW!"

It must have been so difficult for him to put down in human language the vast glory of the things he saw. There was no known verbiage to give accurate description to it. I feel like I understand that difficulty because I have been ascending and descending for over thirty years. Often there are not words to express the magnificence of the things I have been shown. I love the Book of Revelation, and I can tell you, when the Lord caught me up into the heavens for the first time, He showed me things that were, things that are, and things that are yet to come—just like the Word itself says.

On the Island of Patmos

I developed a deep hunger, a thirst in my heart to go to the Island of Patmos and sit in the place where John received the divine download of revelation through the open door. Finally, I was granted permission by the Father to go. On a trip with Chuck Pierce, Cindy Jacobs, Barbara Brierly and others, we had to wait in line to get into the cave where John received his divine revelation of Jesus Christ. We sat out in the hot sun, waiting. I was so excited, so anticipating, so believ-

ing I was going to get into that cave, slip through the open door and see things above and beyond what human imagination is capable of.

When we finally got into the place that contained the cave where John is said to have written Revelation, my heart completely sank. It had been turned into an idol-worshipping temple. There were plastic flowers everywhere. There were incense burners swinging. There was a huge picture of Mary with a tiny baby Jesus flying up to place a crown on her head.

As I walked in and my heart sunk, I said to myself, "Oh Lord, this is a place for divine revelation and they have turned it into idol worship." It made me feel sick.

Then suddenly the Lord tapped me on the shoulder and said, "You teach people 'not to look at what they see with these eyes, rather look to the things that are unseen and eternal.' The open door is still here, all you have to do is close your eyes and go."

That day I was caught up into the heavens and the things that I saw were far above anything ever perceived in the earthy realm. Since that day, I have followed through almost every day, going through the open door, back and forth from Heaven, to see majestic, magnificent, glorious things above and beyond human understanding. Every time I come back, especially after I have stood face-to-face with Jesus, I am totally prepared to meet the day with heavenly resolve.

Becoming What We Behold

Yeshua is multi-colored, multifaceted, and multidimensional. Every time I am caught up into the open door of Heaven to stand in front of Him, I feel His breath on my face. I feel, I can hear and sense His whispers in my ear, and I can reach out and touch His hair. It is so magnificent. Every time I go, it's different. I receive the impartation of one more dimension of His character. And when I come down from that place, I can manifest that dimension of Christ's character here in the earth because I have seen it. Once you see it, you can be it! The ultimate purpose of all revelation is that *we should become what we behold!*

Now the Lord says, "When you behold me as in a mirror reflected, then you shall know me as well as I know you." That is an amazing statement. When we see Him as a mirror reflected, we can actually know Him as well as He knows us. What does He know about us? Every word we speak, every thought we think, every action we take. He knows how many cells are in our body, how many hairs are on our head.

Here, He is saying that when we see Him as in a mirror reflected that we even know Him as well as he knows us (1 Corinthians 13:12). The Word goes on to say, *"Beloved, now we are children of God; and it has not yet been revealed what we shall be, but we know that when He is revealed, we shall be like Him, for we shall see Him as He is"* (1 John 3:2 NKJV).

When we see Him as He is, not just as Savior, protector, healer, deliverer, or provider, but when we see Him as He is, *then* we shall be like Him. *"When you see Me as I am"* means seeing Him as everything from the beginning all the way to the end. If we are caught up every day into the open door of Heaven and carried away to see one more aspect of His character and His nature, then we can manifest that dimension in the earth realm. If we can be conformed to that one dimension of His nature that He reveals to us on a consistent basis, day by day, then we shall be like Him. That is what the Word says.

Entering the Open Door

Heeding His invitation to *"come up here"* through the open door is the most magnificent decision that we can ever make, aside from initially making Him our Savior.

The very first time that I went through the open door, the Lord took me into a huge, vast, unlimited library. On the shelves were ancient scrolls, all rolled up and sealed. The Lord lifted up His hand, took a whole shelf full of the scrolls, collapsed them into one big scroll (as you might collapse an accordion), and He put it on the top of my head. He beat it on the top until it went down into my whole body. Taking in that scroll made me physically dysfunctional. For the next six months, I could hardly function in my human nature at all because I was so full of the Word of God and so full of this magnificent, divine downflow of revelation. I was about ready to explode! I had a difficult time speaking or doing anything in the presence of human beings.[22]

But let's go back to the open door. Who is the open door? Where is the open door? And how do we go through the open door? The Word says,

> *Then Jesus said to them again, "Most assuredly, I say to you, I am the door of the sheep. [...] I am the door. If anyone enters by Me, he will be saved, and will go in and out and find pasture.* (John 10:7,9 NKJV)

The open door to heaven is through Jesus Christ. Jesus is the way. He is the door. No man can come to the Father except through Him. Therefore, we have to recognize that in one aspect the door is Jesus Christ. He is the way that we enter in through the heavenly realms.

The mysteries of Christ Jesus can only be discerned as we are given permission by God to go through the open door called the door of entrance. Paul asked for that door to be opened when he wrote to the Colossians:

> *... Meanwhile [pray] also for us, that God would open to us a door for the word, to speak the mystery of Christ, for which I am also in chains.* (Colossians 4:3 NKJV)

While there are many different doors in the heavens, the door referenced more than any other in the Word of God concerns the corporate ascension experience. It is called the door of the tabernacle of the congregation. That is the dwelling place of the congregation. In the Old Testament, the door of the tabernacle/habitation of the congregation is extremely important. But who has ever heard a teaching on the door of tabernacles of the congregation? Yet it is a door behind which revelation greater than what can be attained by a singular ascension experience is available.

---

[22] There are amazing testimonies available of what the Lord did through that time. Go to www.globalascensionnetwork.net for "Testimonies of an Overcomer."

Behind that door is revelation reserved and set aside for bridal expression through the congregation. Revelation 3:20 says: *"Behold, I stand at the door and knock. If anyone hears My voice and opens the door, I will come in to him and dine with him, and he with Me"* (NKJV). We have often used this as a scripture to refer to evangelizing the heart of a person. You might be familiar with the picture of Jesus standing at the door and knocking on someone's heart. But, Revelation 3:20 has little to do with evangelization. This is a door that is only opened after we come through the qualification as overcomers. To use this scripture for someone who is just starting off with God is a mistake.

When Jesus says, *"I stand at the door and knock, if any man hears My voice and opens the door,"* He means we must, number one, hear His voice, and number two, by our own decision we must decide to open the door. Everything that we do in the realms of the Spirit requires a decision. When we get ready to be caught up into the heavens to see him through that open door, it requires a decision.

People will say to me, "Well, you cannot just decide to go to Heaven." I say, "Oh, yes you can. I do it every single day." Everything you do in the realms of the Spirit requires a decision. You cannot get saved if you do not make a decision. You cannot get filled with the Holy Spirit if you do not make a decision. Ascending and descending from the heavenly realms is the same thing. If Jesus knocks, you make the decision whether or not to open the door.

From Decision to Decree

A pastor once said to me, "That is heresy. You cannot just decide that you are going to go to heaven." He said there had to be a sovereign call or a sovereign election. My response was that right now, the Lord is opening up the doors of heaven for people all over the earth. Once they are caught up in the moment and twinkling of an eye, and carried away to see Him as He really, really is, they come back to the earthly environment and take the thing that they saw and begin to decree and declare it as being so, on the earth.

Historically speaking, I can prove the things that they decree and declare actually manifest in the earthly realm. Once they go and they see the things that are in Heaven, that is when they feel the prayer of Jesus, *"Your kingdom come. Your will be done on earth as it is in heaven"* (Matthew 6:10 NKJV).

> *Even Jesus Himself said: "I speak to you timeless truth. The Son is not able to do anything from himself or through my own initiative. I only do the works that I see the Father doing, for the Son does the same works as his Father."* (John 5:19 TPT)

Jesus ascended and descended frequently. Often He pulled Himself apart from His disciples and went into a high place, alone. That high place isn't a physical mountain: that high place is a heavenly place. And even though there are a multitude of mountains in the heavenly places, He Himself could only do that which He saw His Father doing.

If Jesus, the Son of Man, of His own self, could do nothing except that which He saw the Father doing, how do we think that we can accomplish anything if we cannot see what the Father is doing? And how do we see what the Father is doing? We have to be qualified, we have to go through the door, and we have to look.

Revelation 4:1 says, *"After this"* or *"After these things."* After what? After the judgment of the churches, after the overcomers have been qualified and are ready. So after this, John says,

> *After these things I looked, and behold, a door standing open in heaven. And the first voice which I heard was like a trumpet speaking with me, saying, "Come up here, and I will show you things which must take place after this."* (Revelation 4:1 NKJV)

THE PROPHETS SAW

The open door has always been available. The Old Testament prophets knew this reality. That's how Isaiah could say, "I saw the Lord."

> *In the year that king Uzziah died **I saw** also the Lord sitting upon a throne, high and lifted up, and his train filled the temple.* (Isaiah 6:1 NKJV)

That's how Ezekiel could say, "I saw."

> *Now it came to pass in the thirtieth year, in the fourth month, in the fifth day of the month, as I was among the captives by the river of Chebar, that the heavens were opened, and **I saw** visions of God.* (Ezekiel 1:1 KJV)

> *And **I saw** as the colour of amber, as the appearance of fire round about within it, from the appearance of his loins even upward, and from the appearance of his loins even downward, **I saw** as it were the appearance of fire, and it had brightness round about. As the appearance of the bow that is in the cloud in the day of rain, so was the appearance of the brightness round about. This was the appearance of the likeness of the glory of the LORD. And when **I saw** it, I fell upon my face, and I heard a voice of one that spake.* (Ezekiel 1:27–28 KJV)

> *And the cherubims were lifted up. This is the living creature that **I saw** by the river of Chebar.* (Ezekiel 10:15 KJV)

> *This is the living creature that **I saw** under the God of Israel by the river of Chebar; and I knew that they were the cherubims.* (Ezekiel 10:20 KJV)

> *And the likeness of their faces was the same faces which **I saw** by the river of Chebar, their appearances and themselves: they went every one straight forward.* (Ezekiel 10:22 KJV)

> *Moreover the spirit lifted me up, and brought me unto the east gate of the LORD'S house, which looketh eastward: and behold at the door of the gate five and twenty men; among whom **I saw** Jaazaniah the son of Azur, and Pelatiah the son of Benaiah, princes of the people.* (Ezekiel 11:1 KJV)

That's how Daniel could say "I saw."

> *Thus were the visions of mine head in my bed; **I saw**, and behold a tree in the midst of the earth, and the height thereof was great.* (Daniel 4:10 KJV)

> ***I saw** in the visions of my head upon my bed, and, behold, a watcher and an holy one came down from heaven...* (Daniel 4:13 KJV)

> *Daniel spake and said, **I saw** in my vision by night, and, behold, the four winds of the heaven strove upon the great sea.* (Daniel 7:2 KJV)

*After this **I saw** in the night visions, and behold a fourth beast, dreadful and terrible, and strong exceedingly; and it had great iron teeth: it devoured and brake in pieces, and stamped the residue with the feet of it: and it was diverse from all the beasts that were before it; and it had ten horns.* (Daniel 7:7 KJV)

***I saw** in the night visions, and, behold, one like the Son of man came with the clouds of heaven, and came to the Ancient of days, and they brought him near before him.* (Daniel 7:13 KJV) (Emphasis mine on "I saw" in the above verses.)

They could say they *saw* because they understood and believed they had access to the heavens. And these are just a few of the references to the Old Testament prophets who had regular ascension experiences in which the secrets and mysteries of God were revealed to them. Run a *Strong's* reference check on the words *I looked, I see, I saw, I have seen*, etc. You'll be amazed at how many times the Lord refers to these words.

The Simplicity of Seeing

When the Lord says, *"Come up here,"* it is a present imperative command. It does not mean, "Hey, if you think you may be interested in coming…," or "Hey, if you think you might like to see…," or "Hey, if you think you might want to, come on up here." It is a present imperative command. "Come up here!"

A lot of people say, "Well, I do not know how to go up there." I tell people it is so, so simple. Why do we make it hard? What makes it hard is what lies right between our own two ears—our carnal nature which tells us it is impossible. Our soul will try to talk us out of doing the things of God all the time.

I have been doing this for over thirty years and still on occasion my soul asks, "Are you sure that this is really what God said?" "Hey, are you sure that this is what you really saw in the heavenly realms?" But all you have to do is close your eyes, listen for the voice of the Lord, which says, "Come, come, come up here. I have many things I want to show you." The Word says that when John heard the voice of the Lord, instantly, immediately, right now, his spirit was severed and separated from his soul and his body and it was thrust into the heavenly realms to see the things that were, the things that are, and the things that are yet to come.

I tell people all the time it's so, so simple. You have actually been ascending and seeing all along. You have just not been aware of what it is that you have been doing.

Let's take a look at how this works in terms of the way that we are created. We know from Genesis that God created man in His own image. God is a trinity. He is the Father, the Son and the Holy Spirit. They are all three in one. But, even though they are all one, each one of them has a radically different administration and radically different purpose within the Godhead.

We know God's presence is everywhere. He is omnipresent. But the manifestation of His presence is not. Therefore, just for picture's sake, I want you to picture Him up in the heavenly realms as His manifested place of residence. The Father looks down on the earth and says, "You know, Son, I created man to love me, to worship me, to have intimacy with me. But now we have this sin problem down there. So, I am going to send You down to the earth to deal with the sin problem."

Jesus leaves Heaven and all the unending worship of the angels. He comes down into the earth to be wounded, bruised, beaten, falsely accused and hung on a cross to deal with the sin of mankind. So, when Jesus is in the earth, what do you have then? You have the Father and the Holy Spirit in the heavens, and Jesus here on the earth.

When Jesus got ready to go away, He told His disciples, "I am going back to the Father, but don't worry. I am going to send you the Holy Spirit." So, after Jesus accomplished His purpose here on the earth, He went back to the Father and He sent the Holy Spirit down to the earth. So, now what do you have? You have God the Father and God the Son in the heavenly realms, and you have the Holy Spirit here on the earth. They are manifesting in two different realms at the same time.

We were created in the image of God. Therefore, we are also a three-part being. We have a body, we have a soul, we have a spirit.

They are three in one. But even though they are only one being, all of the three have a totally different administration and function.

Following the pattern of the trinity, at night when you lay down in your bed, your body, your mind, your will, your emotions and your memory which lives inside of your soul go sound asleep, but your spirit never sleeps. Your spirit has no need for sleep.

Your spirit is caught into the heavens to see the things that were, the things that are, and the things that are yet to come. The problem is in the morning when you wake up, you don't remember the exploits that you were doing in the heavenly realms while your body and your soul were sound asleep. Why? Because your memory lies in your soul.

Here is how precognition would manifest in the human or in the earth realm: you might be carrying on your normal everyday activities, when, say, you get into a conversation with somebody. All of a sudden, the hair on the back of your neck stands straight up. You look around the room and you have this overwhelming feeling. You think inside your spirit: "Oh my goodness, I feel as if I have been in this conversation before."

You sit there, quietly watching. You know everything that every person involved in the conversation is going to say. She is going to say this, the baby's going to cry, the doorbell is going to ring, the phone is going to ring and the dog is going to bark. Then he is going to say this… and it all happens exactly the way that you know that it is going to happen.

But your soul, that part that exalts itself against all that is God or godly, sits upright in your body and says, "You stupid woman, you could not have been in this conversation before. You only met these people today." And yet, there you are, watching the whole thing unravel with an amazing sense you know exactly what everybody is going to say.

Because you do not understand what just happened, you take that experience, you set it on a back shelf somewhere, and you call it a *déjà vu* and you try very quickly to forget about it. When, in essence, what really happened was one night your body, your soul, your mind, will, emotions and memory went fast asleep. Your spirit was caught up into the heavens to see the things that were, the things that are, and the things that are yet to come. On that particular day, the things that you saw in the heavens which were yet to come were downloaded into the present into the earth realm and your spirit picked up on it. But your soul rejected it because it was impossible to believe that you were accessing the throne of God while you were asleep. These activities frequently occur when we are caught up to go through that open door.

Let's take another example. Have you ever been driving around in your car and maybe you are in a place that you have never been before? Suddenly, you have an overwhelming feeling deep down inside: "I feel like I have been here before." You drive down the road and you think: "There is going to be a church up ahead. After that there is going to be a city building. Then I will turn right and there is going to be a city park, and across from that there is going to be a lake, and then I am going to go over a railroad track…" Then it happens exactly the way that you know that it's going to happen.

Your soul, that part that exalts itself against all that is God or godly all the time, sits straight up in your body and says: "You stupid man. You have not have been in this place before. This is the first time you have even been in this state." And so, you take the experience, set it on a back shelf somewhere, and you call it *déjà vu*. In truth, you have been there before. In truth and in reality, you have been in that conversation before. In truth and in the reality of heaven, you have been in that location driving your car before. The issue is that in the realms of the spirit, there is no such thing as past, present, or future. The thing you saw that was yet afar off was downloaded into the earth's time and your spirit picked up on it. In truth, you have been ascending and descending ever since you came to the earth. You most frequently do it while your body and your soul are sound asleep.

Because your memory lies in your soul, you don't remember where your spirit was during your hours of sleep. Many people claim they don't dream at all. Yet it has been scientifically proven that we dream at least 80% of our sleeping hours. The problem is we only remember what occurred in our dreams just as we are falling asleep or immediately before we wake. What happens while we are in REM sleep, we have no conscious memory of.

In the Age of the Church, we were taught that we are poor, miserable beings who are always going to sin. Some said it this way: "We are just human beings having a spiritual experience." But in truth, exactly the opposite is true: we are spirit beings having a human experience. We are just passing through here. This, here on earth, is a momentary part of the eternity of our spirit. Our spirit has no beginning; our spirit has no end. Our spirit was in Him in the beginning, our spirit is in Him in the end.

My grandchildren used to come to me and say, "Hey Mimi, how old are you?"

I would look at them and say, "Well, honey, I am ancient."

They would say, "No, really—how old are you?"

I would insist, "Well, really—I am ancient."

"What do you mean?"

So I would explain, "Well, I was in Him in the beginning. I am going to be in Him in the end. That means my spirit—which is the real me—had no beginning and had no end. It was in Him the whole time. That means I'm ANCIENT!"

As we begin to pursue being caught up in the twinkling of an eye and carried away into heavenly places, through that open door, we are going to begin to realize that the book of Revelation is infinitely more than a bunch of end-time current events surrounding the second coming of Jesus Christ.

Everything in this book represents the things that we can set our eyes upon. This has been the Lord's desire since the very beginning. He has a name that very few people ever talk about. That name is *Architecton*. Since the very beginning, He has been building something. He has been building the creative, co-working counterpart for Himself called the Bride of Christ. The only way we can manifest the Bride of Christ in the earth is to be caught up in the moment, in the twinkling of an eye and be carried away through the open door of revelation.

When I mention being caught up in the moment of the twinkling of an eye, I mean it is an instantaneous thing. It is not something you have to labor over or make happen. I have a little granddaughter. (She is not so little anymore.) When she was two-and-a-half years old she came to me one day and said, "Mimi, Jesus came into my room last night."

I said, "He did?" (I was trying to sound incredulous.)

She said, "Yes. He took me up that thing that goes like this." Though she had no previous reference to a spiral staircase into the heavens, she made a spiraling motion with her hands. She continued, "He took me to Heaven."

"He did? What did you see?"

And she began to tell me all of the things that she saw in her heavenly experience at the invitation of Jesus Christ Almighty. I have been to all the places that she described and I knew that everything that she was saying was one hundred percent accurate.

Today, she is a beautiful young woman. All she has to do is shut her eyes and she is there. She does not have to figure it all out. She does not have to make it make sense. The Word says the wisdom of man is foolishness to God (1 Corinthians 3:19), and the wisdom of God is foolishness to man. If you try to make sense out of ascension experience you are never going to ascend, because in the understanding of God, all of our wisdom applied to trying to figure out how it all works is total foolishness.

Believe in the Kingdom; Believe in Rapture Now

When I respond to critics who say you cannot access Heaven, I tell them that like them, I believe in rapture. But why wait for something as if it is yet afar off, when we can access it *now*?! When I ascend, I sit down with Him at the banqueting table. I take my rod of authority. I take and receive the crown He gives me. I put on my cloak. I take the rod of authority and I come back to earth and put every enemy under my feet.

The disciples would pursue Jesus and ask, "What is going to be the sign of Your coming?" His answer was always the same: "I tell you the truth: the Kingdom is within you. The Kingdom is at hand." It is as close as your next breath. It's as close as your next heartbeat. It's here, it's now, it has always been here and always been now. When we relegate it to some kind of future magnificent event, we put it off to another time in the same way those in the age of Israel did. They put off the coming of Jesus Christ for a day yet afar off when all the while He was walking right in front of them.

> *Lift up your heads, O you gates!*
> *And be lifted up, you everlasting doors!* (Psalm 24:7 NKJV)

I love that scripture. When you look at the Book of Revelation from the viewpoint of the Kingdom within us, it means that *we* are gates and *we* are the everlasting doors. Jesus told us He went in advance. He opened the door. He prepared the way for us so that wherever He is, we also may be.

In the same way, we are being called in this hour to go in advance of others to open the doors for them. ("If you would be my disciple... then do as I do!") We are going to begin to open up the doors of Heaven and invite people from all over the nations of the earth to come and join us in ascension experience, to be caught up in the moment and the twinkling of an eye, carried away to stand face-to-face with Him.[23] Jesus is a door, and so are we! I cannot imagine how anybody could live a more exciting life than I live. I believe ascension experiences which are currently rare will become the normal Kingdom advancement process.

"*Eye has not seen, nor ear heard, Nor have entered into the heart of man The things which God has prepared for those who love Him*" (1 Corinthians 2:9 NKJV). The things yet ahead are so big, so huge, so magnificent, that we can hardly conceive of them with our current-day mindsets. If we imagine the biggest, most glorious events ever, we will still (at this time) fall short of the glory He has planned for us.

When people say to me, "Oh, you are such a mystical revelator. I wish I could have the level of revelation you walk in." I say to them,

---

[23] This is the purpose behind the development of Global Ascension Network.

"Honey, I do not know how to tell you this, but we are barely scratching the surface. Ten years from now, the thing that we think of today as being so big and so huge will seem like a small thing compared to the revelations of the future! The day will come when we will laugh at the fact that we once thought ascension was a big revelation."

The Lord has called us to be revealers of mysteries, mysteries that have been hidden. He desires *"... to make all see what is the fellowship of the mystery, which from the beginning of the ages has been hidden in God who created all things through Jesus Christ"* (Ephesians 3:9 NKJV). Part of the mystery is about ready to be revealed. The all-knowing, all-seeing, all-powerful God, is so big, so huge, and so magnificent. He created with just four words all of the universe, as well as all alternative universes. Yet in all His grandness and magnificence, He also folded Himself up so small and put Himself inside of us. He is ready to unfold the mystery. There are things coming that are so mystical, so high, so above and beyond anything that we could ever conceive of at this present moment.

But the Lord has prepared all this for us, because His whole purpose in His sovereign unfolding of His divine design for human kind is to create for Himself a perfect co-creative, co-working counterpart to stand with Him and work with Him in the heavens for the creation of a whole new Heaven and a whole new earth.

We are going to be involved in that creation. Can you imagine anything greater than that?! We have power deep down inside of us that we are not even aware of yet. The Lord could not previously make us aware of the level of power He created us to walk in because up until the present time we have been functioning at a very low level of maturity, because our heart, corporately speaking, has not yet been dealt with by the cross. He can only reveal the measure of power to which we can respond responsibly.

Accessing Our Inheritance Through Love

As we grow up into the fullness of the measure of the stature of Christ Jesus, the Word says He will impart to us the fullness of our inheritance. What is the fullness of our inheritance? Jesus was *"ap-*

pointed heir of all things" (Hebrews 1:2), and we know we are made joint heirs (Romans 8:17). Jesus told us, *"All authority has been given to Me in heaven and on earth"* (Matthew 28:18 NKJV), and that which the Father gave to Him, He now gives to us.

Notice that is a present word and part of the reason that is a present word is because in the realms of the spirit everything that can be done has already been done. There is no past, no present, no future: it has already been done because the Lamb of God was slain before the earth was even created. What else is a part of our inheritance? Jesus said all things—all things! *"And He put all things under His feet"* (Ephesians 1:22 NKJV).

We are the heirs to all things created. Everything that has ever been created, those things that are on the earth, under the earth, over the earth in the sky, in the sea (Revelation 5:11–15), in the galaxy, in the universe—they are all our inheritance because we are joint heirs to the Kingdom of Heaven with Jesus Christ. Everything that He has created is ours by the adoption of sons (Romans 8).

The only way that we can lay hold of this principle and make it a living reality in our mindsets, in our daily life, in our daily conversations, is that we must *become* the message. We must become the love of God. In the Age of the Church, it was good enough for us to *do* love or to *give* love. That is a verb type of love. But in the Age of the Kingdom we must *become* love because that is His nature and we are called to be conformed to His image and nature. We are called to be co-workers (1 Corinthians 3:9) and co-creators together with Him.

If we are going to be conformed to His image, our image must be love. Love is not an activity: it is a state of being. It is the state of manifesting His nature, which is love. When our hearts are moved by the same thing that moves His, and when our hearts beat with that frequency of love, the whole world will respond, because we will, at long last, have *become* what all creation is groaning for.

The more that we are caught up through the open door of Heaven, the more we stand before His throne, the more that we recognize the twenty-four elders and the seven Spirits before the throne, the more like Him we become. The more that we interface with all the angelic beings and with the great cloud of witnesses, the more we see Him as He is, and the more aware we are that we are called to be seated with Him in His throne, the more power He can entrust us with. That is what the Word says in Revelation: *"To him who overcomes I will grant to sit with Me on My throne, as I also overcame and sat down with My Father on His throne"* (Revelation 3:21 NKJV). Therefore, our whole purpose is to rule and reign with Him. Then, we will be co-rulers, co-makers, co-creators, and co-heirs together with Him to all things that have ever been created. This can only be made manifest in our life as we make our decision to be caught up into the open doors of Heaven, to be those who are given magnificent mysteries that have not yet unfolded in the earth. For to us it is given to know mysteries of God:

> *... Unto you it is given to know the mysteries of the kingdom of God...* (Luke 8:10a KJV)

Father, I thank You and I praise You that the seed of this Word has not gone forth to return void, that just as the dew and the rain do not come down from Heaven without watering and refreshing the earth and bringing forth seed for the sower and bread for the eater, so your Word will fulfill the purpose for which it is sent.

I thank You that every heart and every person reading will be changed from one image to another, from one glory to another by Your Word. For Your Word is sufficient for all things! Your nature is sufficient for all things! Your name is sufficient for all things! Your grace is sufficient for all things!

Lord, I thank, You that Your Word is living and active and that it has gone forth today to sever and separate flesh from spirit. I thank You that this is going to be a point of no return for people who have established in their heart their desire to be caught up into the open doors of Heaven to see You, to see the magnificence of the things You have created.

And we promise when it happens, we will give all the honor, all the power, all the blessings, all the glory to You, the Lamb of God who sits on the throne forever and ever. In Jesus' most holy, magnificent and strong name we pray. Amen.

....

There are many ways that the Lord desires for us to see Him. There are many invitations that He makes to us to come up into the doors of Heaven. These doors can lead you into the most amazing places above and beyond anything you can fashion inside of your own intelligence. It goes above and beyond our capacity to even believe or hope for those glorious things to become manifest in the earthly realm. But that is God's plan and purpose. He wants it even more than we do!

Chapter 6

Seventh Day Transfiguration

It is an important hour in earth's history. I believe we are living in the greatest day ever. It is a place I call the cross point between the third day and the seventh day. It is a place I call the beginning of the transfiguration of the corporate son of man. In this place, the sons of God are about ready to be revealed for who they are.

For most of us, *who we are* has not yet been revealed. We do know we are children of God:

> *Beloved, we are God's children right now; however, it is not yet apparent what we will become. But we do know that when it is finally made visible, we will be just like Him, for we will see Him as He truly is.* (1 John 3:2 TPT)

Who we are going to become, as John says, is "just like Him." What is it going to take for us to come into the fullness of the measure of the stature of Christ in His transfigured state? I believe when we see Him as the I Am—not just as our savior, healer, deliverer and provider, but as our I Am—then we shall become like Him.

> *Jesus said to them, "I give you this eternal truth: I have existed long before Abraham was born, for I Am!"* (John 8:58 TPT)

And not only will we become like Him, but the Lord says when we are caught up in a moment in the twinkling of an eye to stand and see

Him face to face as in a mirror, we shall know Him as well as He knows us. The Message translation puts it very well:

> *We don't yet see things clearly. We're squinting in a fog, peering through a mist. But it won't be long before the weather clears and the sun shines bright! We'll see it all then, see it all as clearly as God sees us, knowing Him directly just as He knows us!* (1 Corinthians 13:12 MSG)

That is an amazing statement. What does Jesus know about us? Everything. He knows how many hairs are on our heads, how many cells are in our bodies, every thought we have, and every word we speak. He knows everything. A lot of people say we cannot know the thoughts of God and we cannot know the mind of God. I tell them we can because I have seen Him as the I AM. I have seen Him as more than just savior.

KINGDOM GOSPEL REVEALED THROUGH JESUS' PATTERN

There is a big difference between the gospel of salvation and the gospel of the Kingdom. The gospel of salvation gives you access to see the Kingdom, but seeing the Kingdom and entering the Kingdom are two different things. The gospel of the Kingdom allows you the governmental authority to become co-workers and co-creators together with Him for the establishment of His Kingdom and His righteousness. Jesus came to do so much more than save us from our sins. He came to be the pattern and the example of how we are to walk in holiness, righteousness and perfection with a perfect God.

We have been taught in the Age of the Church that we are poor, miserable sinners who will always sin and who cannot ever be perfect. I am here to tell you that this is the worst lie that Satan has ever perpetrated against the church. Jesus himself said, *"Go. From now on sin no more"* (John 8:11 AMP), and *"Therefore you shall be perfect, just as your Father in heaven is perfect"* (Matthew 5:48 NKJV). That's pretty darned perfect! Would He command us to do something and then not make a way for us to be able to do it? We are entering into a whole new day. Ascension prayer is the way that the Lord is making.

Jesus set the standard: if we are going to be His disciples, we must follow Him. *"Then said Jesus unto his disciples, 'If any man will come after me, let him deny himself, and take up his cross, and follow me'"* (Matthew 16:24 KJV). So, let's follow the pattern Jesus set up. He came to be the pattern of how we are to walk in holiness and truth before a Holy God—in purity, righteousness and truth. Therefore, if we are going to seek Jesus with all of our heart, soul, mind, strength and everything that is in us, our lives must follow the same pattern that His did.

The Day of Glorious Revealing

That pattern Jesus set includes one thing very few people ever talk about. Consider the pattern set up by Jesus in Matthew 17.

> ***After six days*** *Jesus took with him Peter, James and John the brother of James, and led them up a high mountain by themselves. There he was transfigured before them. His face shone like the sun, and his clothes became as white as the light.* (Matthew 17:1–2 TPT, emphasis mine).

We are entering into a place called "after six days," which is the seventh day. The seventh day is man's communion with the divine nature, all the way back to Adam in this present creation. The church, however, is only entering the third day, two thousand years between Jesus' death and the year two thousand, at which time it stepped out of the second day into the third day. The third day stands for ascension and resurrection power. The seventh day stands for transfiguration and perfection.

Historically speaking, every thousand years the Lord comes to do a new thing. For His people to come into the fullness of what He designed us to be, He lays down a whole new way of communicating in the realms of the Spirit. Every thousand years, He raises up a man to change the way humanity communes with Him.

The current move of God is bringing about the revealing of the sons of God. Let me repeat: it has not yet been revealed what we shall be, but when we see Him as I Am, not just as our savior, or our healer, or our deliverer, or our provider, but when we see Him as I Am, as everything from beginning to end, then we shall be like Him.

It has not yet been revealed, but the message for us is that we have stepped into the day of the glorious revealing. In the year two thousand, we stepped out of the Age of the Church into the Age of the Kingdom. That does not mean that the church is ending; it means that the church is coming into a day of a higher level of function than we have ever produced before, because we are entering the day called *"the revealing of the sons of God"* (Romans 8:19 NKJV).

> *Beloved, now we are children of God; and it has not yet been revealed what we shall be, but we know that when He is revealed, we shall be like Him, for we shall see Him as He is.* (1 John 3:2 NKJV)

There is something that has not yet been revealed that is going to be revealed in us.

> *But as it is written, Eye hath not seen, nor ear heard, neither have entered into the heart of man, the things which God hath prepared for them that love him.* (1 Corinthians 2:9 KJV)

> *For I consider that the sufferings of this present time are not worthy to be compared with the glory which shall be revealed in us.* (Romans 8:18 NKJV)

> *For the earnest expectation of the creation eagerly waits for the revealing of the sons of God.* (Romans 8:19 NKJV)

When Matthew says Jesus *"led them up,"* it means He took them up into a high place. *"Now after six days Jesus took Peter, James, and John his brother, and led them up on a high mountain by themselves"* (Matthew 17:1 NKJV). Jesus took them up behind the veil and revealed Himself in the fullness of His glory. What did they see? They saw Jesus transfigured into the glory He had with the Lord before the earth ever was. (Note: we also had a glory with God before the earth ever was.)

From the Thousands to the One

Why was it that of all his disciples, He only took Peter, James and John? It is curious to me that Jesus had many disciples. At one time, people pressed in for everything He could do for them, for everything

He could give them. At one time, Jesus had thousands of disciples, but inside those thousands who followed and thronged Him wherever He went, were the 500 who received the Holy Spirit with tongues of fire (1 Corinthians 15:6). They had a different level of relationship with Him than the thousands.

Inside of the 500, however, there were 120 who had an even different level of relationship with Him. Out of the thousands, they were the ones who obeyed the command of the Lord to go to Jerusalem and not to leave until they had received the power of the Holy Spirit (Acts 1:15).

In the midst of the 120 who stood and waited for the coming of the Holy Spirit to descend in that room on that morning, there were seventy who had a different level of relationship with Him. Those seventy were those upon whom He laid His hands. He breathed on them and commissioned them: *"And as you go, preach, saying, 'The kingdom of heaven is at hand.' Heal the sick, cleanse the lepers, raise the dead, cast out devils. Freely you have received, freely give"* (Matthew 10:7–8 NKJV). The seventy had a different level of relationship with Him.

This was so even among His own twelve disciples. I questioned the Lord: since He had twelve, why did He only call Peter, James and John? It is because they had a different level of relationship with Him. The thousands followed Jesus only followed for what He could give, do, or provide for them. These three wanted more than the thousands, more than the 300, more than the 120, more than even the twelve.

Even amongst the three, there was one. John was the only one who would stand with Him, who would be identified with Him in the hour of His suffering. That one, John, was the only one who lived to see the full revelation of Jesus Christ.

You are reading this today because you have a different level of relationship. You are called by the Lord to become His personal expression and the manifestation of His glory in all of the earth. *"Jesus led them up... apart"* (Mark 9:2 NKJV). Many of you have been pulled apart. You left the existing work that you were in.

Some of you are still in the old structure, yet all of a sudden you have found what used to thrill you in that structure now makes you want to vomit. Why? The Lord has infused His people with holy dissatisfaction. Inside of you, you know, that you know, that you know *there is more*, and you want *the more* of God and you want to get it today. I am here to tell you that before you finish this chapter, you are going to have an ascension experience with God in which you stand at His throne and see Him face-to-face. You will never be the same again. In the pattern of Jesus, your face is about ready to shine like the sun. Let us give God the glory.

Moses and Elijah at the Transfiguration

When Peter, James, and John went up to the high place with Jesus, they witnessed an amazing change in Jesus.

> *He was transfigured before them. His face shone like the sun, and His clothes became as white as the light. And behold, Moses and Elijah appeared to them, talking with Him.* (Matthew 17:2–3 NKJV)

I wondered to myself, Lord, why did Moses and Elijah appear there with Jesus? Why not Abraham? He was the father of faith. Why not David? He was the precursor of Christ. Why not Isaiah or Jeremiah? Get this down in your heart, because you are going to begin to manifest the spirit of Moses and the spirit of Elijah. Why? Because there is always an appearance of a Moses and an Elijah before a transfiguration.

Moses was the sovereignly-called, ordained vessel of God to overthrow governmental Babylon. He took the most powerful government ever manifested in the ancient world and brought Pharaoh to his knees until Pharaoh declared the God of Moses was God. Moses was granted power to do signs, wonders and miracles. He was granted power to bring the people out of years of slavery when they were cast down, pushed down, forced down, and kicked down.

Secondly, when his response to God regarding the destruction of the people was that he would rather God write his name out of the

Book of Life than destroy the children of God's name (Exodus 32:32), Moses identified himself with Christ.

Like those Moses led, we are about ready to come out of the state of being pushed and forced down. It is going to happen and when it does, it is going to be glorious. Through signs, wonders and miracles, God is going to empower us to bring billions out of their slavery to the governmental systems of this world.

Not only was Moses a deliverer, but he uttered powerful words. Can you imagine telling God to repent? Moses did! After the people of Israel built a big gold idol to worship, God was so upset with them that He was going to wipe them off the face of the earth. God said, *"I have seen this people, and behold, they are a stiff-necked (stubborn, rebellious) people"* (Exodus 32:9 AMP).

Moses boldly replied to God: *"...repent of this evil against thy people"* (Exodus 32:12 KJV), and he told God to

> *...remember Abraham, Isaac, and Israel (Jacob), Your servants to whom You swore [an oath] by Yourself, and said to them, "I will multiply your descendants as the stars of the heavens, and all this land of which I have spoken I will give to your descendants, and they shall inherit it forever."* (Exodus 32:13 AMP)

Elijah was the sovereignly called vessel of God designed by God specifically to overcome religious Babylon. There are Elijahs sitting around here who are going to overthrow, pluck up, uproot, and destroy religious Babylon because God hates religion. He hates it because it sets up a pattern of "if you do this" and "if you do that." If you go to mass seven times a week, if you bake a thousand cookies for the youth fellowship, if you teach Sunday school, if you are an elder or a deacon, then you can earn God's love. He hates that! He hates it because it prevents people from entering into intimacy with Him. What He really wants is for us to have radical intimacy with Him. What He really wants is to embrace us, to hold, empower, equip and to prepare us to accurately rule and reign with Him. God is good!

So, there they were. Moses and Elijah both appeared, talking with Jesus. Many of you are beginning to manifest either the power of Moses (the intercessor, deliverer) or the power of Elijah (the spirit of reformation). Elijah called down fire from heaven and overthrew the prophets of Baal. The most important thing he ever did is very rarely talked about.

> *And he (Elijah) said to her (the widow woman), "Give me your son." So he took him out of her arms and carried him to the upper room where he was staying, and laid him on his own bed. Then he cried out to the Lord and said, "O Lord my God, have You also brought tragedy on the widow with whom I lodge, by killing her son?" And he stretched himself out on the child three times, and cried out to the Lord and said, "O Lord my God, I pray, let this child's soul come back to him." Then the Lord heard the voice of Elijah; and the soul of the child came back to him, and he revived.* (1 Kings 17:19–22 NKJV)

When Elijah was in the house of the widow, he spread himself over her dead son and called forth life out of death. The boy was raised from the dead. Right now, there are five-and-a-half billion dead sons in the earth. Our purpose is to spread ourselves over them and call forth life out of death. When we are transfigured, we will be empowered to do that.

How many of you know that you have a calling as an intercessor? Moses was not the only great deliverer of people from the bondage of slavery. Many of you are going to be deliverers from the poverty and lack that has struck your people.

There are 5.5 billion people in the world who are still asleep, and they are the ones being called. The ancient call is to raise them from their sleep. This is going to come as Moses and Elijah begin to empower you and equip you with a level of empowerment that the church has never witnessed before.

The first time I visited a certain church, a gentleman there was sitting, minding his own business. All of a sudden, I put my head down and I ran full force into his belly. I head-butted him until he was totally whacked out. Why? Because he was called to operate in the power of Elijah. There are those of us who are going to be aligned with this movement. God is preparing our spirit because we are going to become the most massive and greatest reformation force in the entire annals of human history because His purpose is to restore all things.

Peter and the Age of the Church

Needless to say, Peter, James, and John were amazed at the sight of the transfigured Jesus speaking with Moses and Elijah. Peter spoke out. *"Then Peter answered and said unto Jesus, 'Lord it is good for us to be here'..."* (Matthew 17:4 NKJV). Isn't Peter's statement typical of human arrogance? He continues, *"...if you wish, let us make three tabernacles: one for you, one for Moses, and one for Elijah"* (Matthew 17:4 NKJV).

Notice the details in how the Lord responds to Peter. "While he was still speaking, behold, a bright cloud overshadowed them; and suddenly a voice came out of the cloud, saying, *"This is My beloved Son, in whom I am well pleased. Hear Him!"* (Matthew 17:5 NKJV). The words were not even out of Peter's mouth yet when the Lord told Peter, "Be quiet!" He wanted Peter to stop speaking so he would hear His beloved Son.

Peter represents the Age of the Church. The Age of the Church was destined by God to establish some things in the earth realm. Now the Age of the Church is over, and the Age of the Kingdom is here. Yet we do the very same thing Peter did. We want to build a tabernacle wherever we last saw the glory of God. So, we have a Catholic tabernacle, a Lutheran tabernacle, a Methodist tabernacle, a Baptist tabernacle, a Presbyterian tabernacle, an Assembly of God tabernacle, a Charismatic tabernacle, a Church of Christ tabernacle. But God is not coming for a Catholic, a Methodist, a Lutheran or a Baptist church. He is coming for one body of Christ, united with a singular mind, with a concentration of thought and agreement with the unseen Kingdom realm.

Falling in the Fear of Lord

When the disciples heard the voice, *"This is My beloved Son,"* they fell down on their faces, greatly afraid (Matthew 17:6). The first time I ever saw Jesus, I fell down on my face and I was greatly, greatly afraid, too. I was an atheist. I had been raised in a legalistic Lutheran church. In order to become a member of our church or even to take communion, we had to go to catechism classes three hours a day, three days a week for three years. Before we were allowed to take communion, we had to take an oral examination in front of the entire congregation.

The Word says, *"For the gifts and the calling of God are irrevocable [for He does not withdraw what He has given, nor does He change His mind about those to whom He gives His grace or to whom He sends His call]"* (Romans 11:29 AMP). From my very earliest age, I was a seer. I did not know what that was. I did not know there was such a thing as a modern-day prophet, and I certainly did not know I was one. I did not know anything about the Lord at that time. I would walk into a congregation of legalistic people who were ritualistically bound up by religious spirits, and I would see them as holy, pious and perfect. But the Lord would say to me, "Yeah, well, he is having an affair with his wife's best friend. And he is going out with his secretary. She just had an abortion, and that one is stealing from her employer. He's cheating on his taxes." The Lord just went right down the line. I didn't know how I knew all of those things; I just knew them because I was a seer.

One of the primary gifts of believers in some nations is that they are raised by God to be seers. The prophetic mantle on the nation is going to be completely enfolded and wrapped up around them until they are released to prophesy the future according to the plans of God.

I was a heathen. I was rebellious. I led people away from the Lord. I told people, "God is only a figment of man's imagination. Man just made up God to give them an excuse for anything they cannot understand. Jesus is dead like any other man. He is in the grave and He is not ever coming back." I had a photographic memory, so as a child I knew the Bible better than most any Christian I ever met. Because I could quote it better than they could, I would use the Word of God to pull people away from their faith.

My little daughter struck up a relationship with a young friend who lived down the way. My husband was an up-and-coming executive— the fair-haired child of the corporate world at the time. We lived in a nice house. Right around the corner from us was a little shack. When I say a shack, I mean there were linoleum pieces pounded on the outside of the house to keep the rain from coming in.

Seventh Day Transfiguration

The couple who lived there were what I called *backhills*, Kentucky hillbillies. They'd both dropped out of school when they were in the second and third grades. They'd eventually run away from their homes. He'd turned to drug addiction and she'd turned to prostitution. I had nothing but disdain for them. They had all of these children, but they were so poor and full of lack they could only eat meat once a week. Anyway, that is a long story.

One day, my daughter went down to their house and because it started to rain, she ended up going in. I thought, "Oh God, now I am going to have to go down and get her out of the house of those poor, stupid, ignorant, greased-back Kentucky hillbillies." I thought they were the furthest thing down the ladder from where I was. I was into power, prestige, position, money and all those kinds of things. I thought country club life was just *it*.

I walked to the house and beat on the door trying to get my daughter out of there. When the man of the house opened up the door, Jesus music came flying out. I thought, "Oh God, they are not only poor, dumb, ignorant Kentucky hillbillies, on top of everything else, they are Christians"—like that was the lowest rung on the ladder. (God has a sense of humor!)

I grabbed my daughter out of there and paddled her on the way home. I told her, "Do not ever go into that house again. Those are not our kind of people!" I walked her away from there and I never went back to his house.

I learned much later that on that day when the man of the house opened the door, he received a word of knowledge from God. It was about me. God had told him: "I am going to use this woman in the nations of the earth to win millions of people to Jesus Christ. Your assignment from Me is to pray for her every day, every single day, until she gives her life to the Lord."

About three months later, my family moved twenty-five hundred miles away from Indiana to Texas. When I got to Texas, I had completely forgotten about the man, but every day the man and his wife and the whole church prayed for me to meet Jesus. After several years, I was still preaching that God was dead, that He is just a figment of man's imagination and all that kind of garbage. (Thank you, Lord, that you did not leave me there, still just as hard-hearted and anti-Christ spirited as ever!)

One day, the man and his wife went to a Kenneth Hagin seminar on how to win the lost through spiritual warfare. They came back and put into action all the warfare principles they learned. As close as we can figure, within one week of that time, I woke up hearing voices, audible voices coming out just like they were all around me. It was like those cartoon characters where you have a man with an angel on one side and the devil on the other side, with both talking in his ears.

I heard one voice say, "Behold, I stand at the door and knock. If you open the door, I will come in and sup with you and you with me."[24] Immediately this other voice would pop up and say, "You know that God is only a figment of man's imagination. You know man only made up God to give himself an answer for all the things he could not understand." Then the first voice would pop up on my left shoulder and say, "But I loved you so much that I gave My Son just for you." Then immediately I would hear the other voice pop up and say, "Jesus is dead and in the grave. He is not ever coming back again." The voices were roaring and roaring. They went on for a solid seven days, 24 hours a day, without end.

At the time, I had three successful businesses and three very small children which demanded a lot of time and work. I did not have time for these voices, but I was so pig-headed and stubborn, I was not going to yield to them. One day I was walking down the hall of my real estate company's offices and a voice was following me down the hall, saying: "Go somewhere and pray. Go somewhere."

I got so mad I shook my fist at the ceiling there in the middle of my real estate company, and I shouted, "I do not believe in God and I don't believe in Jesus Christ and you cannot make me pray! You cannot make me!" I was shouting. All of my agents started poking their heads out of their doors, looking at me and thinking I had really gone off the deep end.

---

[24] Cf. Revelation 3:20.

Seventh Day Transfiguration

During the course of that week, I lost about twenty pounds. I did not sleep for five minutes in seven days. At the end of the seven days, I was so sleep-deprived that I thought to myself if I did not get some sleep that night, they were going to have to put me in the hospital. They were going to have to shoot me up with something because I could not even think anymore.

I would lay down in my bed and the voice would say, "Go somewhere and pray. Go somewhere and pray."

I would get so mad. I finally sat up in my bed and shook my fist at the ceiling. I said, "Okay, you want me to pray? I will get up and pray, then you can go away and leave me alone!" So, there I was, talking to a God whom I did not believe in but who appeared to be living in the ceiling of my house.

I got out of bed to pray. I got down by the side of my bed. Because I had been raised in a liturgical church, I knew a lot of legalistic, ritualistic prayers. I remembered them all. I recited, "I believe in God Almighty, the maker of Heaven and Earth, and in Jesus Christ the Son." "Our Father, that art in Heaven, hallowed be Thy name. Thy Kingdom come. Thy will be done… and blah, blah, blah." The more I prayed, the madder I got. I just could not get any peace.

So finally, after about an hour of repeating old, rote-memorized prayers which did me absolutely no good, I said, "Okay, Lord." I was still being snotty, not at all yielded. I do not think I even wanted Jesus. I just wanted some sleep. I said, "Okay, I confess in all of the years that I went to church I never really learned how to pray. So if You want me to pray, by God, You are just going to have to tell me what to pray."

All of a sudden, as soon as I said, "You are just going to have to tell me what to pray," there was a dynamic explosion of light in my room. It was so blinding that I fell over on the floor, grabbed my head and I yelled, "Please don't kill me, please don't kill me!" I knew that was exactly what I deserved.

In the overwhelming light of His presence, I started confessing. I had a lot to confess. I had a lot to repent of and I started repenting from the bottom of my heart. I said, "And God, I am so rebellious, when I was only months in my mother's womb, I used to kick her on purpose just to make her hurt." I actually said that, which probably was the truth. But I also made up things that I did not even do, just to make sure I had covered every single base.

Once in the middle of that night, I picked up my head. My face and eyes were all swollen shut. I had snot all over my face, all stuck in my hair. I went to wipe my eyes. When I did, I could see every bone in my body as if an x-ray was going straight through me. I turned around and looked at the wall. His light was so brilliant, so magnificent and so powerful that I could see the 2 x 4s behind three inches of plaster.

Bob and I have been married nearly 50 years. Throughout all those years, I can count on one hand the number of times he awoke after 5:30 in the morning. But on this morning, my husband didn't get up until 7:30. I was still on the floor. He looked down and said, "What the heck are you doing on the floor?" By then, I had experienced a real, divine revelation of who Jesus Christ was.

I jumped up on the bed and I said, "Oh, honey you're just never going to believe it! Jesus Christ was sitting right here on our bed."

He looked at me like I was whacked out. He called a friend of ours who was a psychiatrist. He said, "You'd better come over here. My wife has taken a long walk off a short pier."

The Word says, *"They fell down on their faces and they were greatly afraid."* I was greatly afraid after my encounter. I knew that day the fear of the Lord is really a real thing. Now, of course, the Lord does not want us to be afraid of Him: He wants us to be in awe of Him. I was most definitely in awe during that night.

ARISE AND SEE JESUS ONLY

Let's return to Matthew 17. After Peter, James and John fell down in fear at the sight of Jesus transfigured, with Moses and Elijah, *"...Jesus went to them and touched them and said, 'Stand up. Don't be afraid'"* (Matthew 17:7 EXB). Another translation of His command here is: *"Arise, and do not be afraid"* (NKJV). When we arise in ascension, our sight becomes elevated. We see similar direction from Jesus in

John 4:35. *"Do not say, 'It is still four months until the harvest comes?' Look, I say to you, raise your eyes and look at the fields and see, they are white for harvest"* (AMP). Jesus told the disciples to lift up their eyes. Even now, if we will look, the harvest is here. When the disciples do look up, the result is this: *"When they had lifted up their eyes, they saw no one but Jesus only"* (Matthew 17:8 NKJV).

In the Age of the Church, there were anointed, powerful, magnificent speakers. Many of us put all of our devotion, money, and tithes into blessing them. In that age, doing so was purposeful. However, in the Age of the Kingdom, I say, thus saith the Lord, "You are going to see no man but Christ, and Him only!"

Seeing Christ and Him only is a future thing. The three disciples Jesus took up with Him at His transfiguration asked questions we still must ask. Why is He coming? And How is he coming?

> *The disciples asked Him, "Then why do the scribes say that Elijah must come first?" He answered and said, "Elijah is coming and will restore all things."* (Matthew 17:10–11 AMP)

THE SPIRIT OF ELIJAH PRECEDES RESTORATION

Many of the paradigms we held during the Age of the Church will change. In end-time eschatology we were taught that Jesus is going to split the sky and ride down from the heavens on his white horse. He is going to catch us up in a moment, in the twinkling of an eye and carry us away to Heaven. We will sit down at a banqueting table where we will have a huge, wonderful, magnificent party, while the rest of the earth burns and goes to hell.

I do not think so!

If we are to follow in the pattern of Christ, we need to look at and understand what He did and what He told us. He left the heavenly realms and the unending, glorious worship and praise of all of the angels. He came down into tribulation to be wounded and bruised, cursed and hung on a cross. He was pierced and nailed down, and then He died so that we could be one with the Father.

But, what do we want to do when we face trials? We want to get out of tribulation, go to Heaven and have a party in the sky while the whole earth burns and goes to hell.

Again: I do not think so!

I have news for you: Jesus tells us He is not coming back again until Elijah first rises up to restore all things (Luke 1:17; Malachi 4:5–6; Matthew 17:11). We assumed in the church age that Jesus was coming to restore the Kingdom. It is not Jesus who is the restorer of all things. It is us! *We* are called by God. *We* are anointed by God. *We* are prepared by God to become the restorers of all things in God. We are to become the spirit of Elijah.

Our purpose is to follow the example of Jesus. He said, *"…I say to you that Elijah has come already, and they did not recognize him, but did to him as they wished"* (Matthew 17:12a AMP). Do you have anyone in the body of Christ doing whatever they wish against you? Perhaps this is because you are following in the pattern of Jesus. Jesus said, *"'The Son of Man is also going to suffer at their hands.' Then the disciples understood that He had spoken to them about John the Baptist"* (Matthew 17:12b–13 AMP).

What did He say? We can put it this way: Jesus will not come back until the spirit of Elijah first comes to restore all things (Luke 1:16–17). The thing that has been birthed by the Age of the Church is now born. The Word says, *"Now these things happened to them as an example and warning [to us]; they were written for our instruction [to admonish and equip us], upon whom the ends of the ages have come"* (1 Corinthians 10:11 AMP). Therefore, we can look at the pattern that was set by Israel and by Jesus, and we can learn from their examples.

Israel had the full revelation of Jesus Christ written down in their scrolls. They had the Word—the prophetic word—that said,

> *…Behold, your King (Messianic King) is coming to you;*
> *He is righteous and endowed with salvation…*
> *…His dominion shall be from sea to sea [absolutely endless]*
> *And from the River [Euphrates] to the ends of the earth.* (Zechariah 9:9, 10 AMP)

In the New Testament, we see it said like this:

Seventh Day Transfiguration

He [Jesus] will be great and eminent and will be called the Son of the Most High; and the Lord God will give Him the throne of His father David; and He will reign over the house of Jacob (Israel) forever, and of His kingdom there shall be no end. (Luke 1:32–33 AMP)

Jesus was coming as an overcoming, conquering, victorious hero to overthrow all the governments and kingdoms of the world, to sit on the throne, and rule from the throne of David and from Jerusalem. But scripture also says,

He was despised and rejected by men,
A Man of sorrows and pain and acquainted with grief;
And like One from whom men hide their faces
He was despised, and we did not appreciate His worth or esteem Him.

But [in fact] He has borne our griefs,
And He has carried our sorrows and pains;
Yet we [ignorantly] assumed that He was stricken,
Struck down by God and degraded and humiliated [by Him].

But He was wounded for our transgressions,
He was crushed for our wickedness [our sin, our injustice, our wrongdoing];
The punishment [required] for our well-being fell on Him,
And by His stripes (wounds) we are healed. (Isaiah 53:3–5 AMP)

For two thousand years, they had been taught that when the Messiah comes, He will come as the overcoming, conquering, victorious hero. When He came as the suffering servant, they did not recognize Him because He did not come the way they were taught.

Now we must ask: are we following in the pattern of Israel? Yes: because for the last two thousand years we have been taught exactly how Jesus is going to come again. So, the question stands before us: will we recognize Him if He does not come the way we have been taught? That is a sobering question.

He is coming to restore all things. Elijah—the spirit of Elijah—represents reformation. We are moving out of one age into another age, and that requires a transition in the way we operate. The Age of the Church had the purpose of teaching, tutoring and guiding us, bringing us up and encouraging us. Unfortunately, when we move out of one age into another age, we become agitated because we think they did not tell us the whole truth. But they did tell us the truth, at least for the day and the time they were living in.

> *For we know in part, and we prophesy in part [for our knowledge is fragmentary and incomplete]. But when that which is complete and perfect comes, that which is incomplete and partial will pass away... For now [in this time of imperfection] we see in a mirror dimly [a blurred reflection, a riddle, an enigma], but then [when the time of perfection comes, we will see reality] face to face. Now I know in part [just in fragments], but then I will know fully, just as I have been fully known [by God].* (1 Corinthians 13:9–12 AMP)

The Lord can only give us as much as we can be held responsible and accountable for. If the Lord had openly revealed to us before the time who we really are as the sons of God, we would have destroyed the earth many times over already, because the knowledge would have been out of time and out of season and our hearts had not yet been dealt with by the cross.

Revelation Increases as Transfiguration Approaches

A ministry friend of mine once said: "One day, we are going to look back and say, 'Can you imagine we thought that we were walking in revelation?'" As the Lord opens up the heavens, revelation is going to increase day by day, hour by hour, minute by minute, second by second, until we are explosive with the power of God. What we are tapping into in this hour is barely scratching the surface. That is good news! The spirit of reformation has come.

For about two thousand years there was something that was conceived in Israel, something that was travailed for in Israel, but when that thing was born, it was a differently functioning entity from what they knew or expected, called *the church*. Israel operated under law; the church operated under grace.

Now, for the most recent two thousand years, there has been something that has been conceived in the Age of the Church, and travailed for in the Age of the Church, but now it is born. It is a completely differently functioning entity from what we've known. In the days ahead, as we arise as sons of God, the differences you are going to see are going to be greater than the differences between the age of Israel and the Age of the Church. Israel functioned under the law, the church functioned under grace, and the Kingdom functions under perfection.

We are moving into what we are doing. We are moving back into our primordial estate. As we become translated into the sons of light, the day is going to come when we will no longer need to preach the gospel because wherever we go, people will fall down at our feet. In the grocery store and at the gas station, they will fall down at our feet and cry out, "What do we have to do to be saved?" It is not even going to take signs and wonders and miracles, because we are the signs, we are the wonders, and we are the miracles of God.

There is coming a day which is just now beginning to unfold when those of us who are called to manifest the sonship of God Almighty in the earth will be revealed. It is the transfiguration. When the transfiguration occurs, we will no longer have to preach the gospel. We will no longer have to do signs and miracles. We will no longer have to raise the dead. Wherever we go and whatever we do, we will become a recognizable, visible light. When that happens, every rank of darkness will be instantaneously evacuated. The Buddhist ranks, the witchcraft ranks, all of the new age ranks are going to be totally, completely vacated, because we will be revealed for who we are— the sons of God. *"For the creation was subjected to futility, not willingly, but because of Him who subjected it in hope"* (Romans 8:20 NKJV).

In church age traditional thinking, this is what we used to believe: "We believe in an all-knowing, all-seeing, all-powerful, almighty God. He is so big, so huge, so magnificent, that He is going to give away ninety percent of what He made to the devil!" I do not think so! For scripture tells us, *"...the creation itself also will be delivered from the bondage of corruption into the glorious liberty of the children of God"* (Romans 8:21 NKJV).

What this refers to is the ultimate restoration of all things.²⁵ It says that the creation will be delivered. That means that we are still in a level of bondage, and the level of that bondage that is brought upon us, is our subjection to the gravitational pull of the earth. This is why ascension is so important. Because when we learn to get caught up in a moment, in the twinkling of an eye, carried away to stand before Jesus Christ face-to-face, trust me, the things of earth will grow strangely dim. We will find that we are delivered from the bondage of the corruption that we have been held down to, and we will be led by His Spirit into a day of perfection.

In the Age of the Church we were taught, "You can never be perfect. You are always going to sin. You are always going to fall short of the glory of God." But Jesus said: "Go and be perfect." And not just perfect, but *"perfect as my Father in Heaven is perfect"*: *"Therefore you shall be perfect, just as your Father in heaven is perfect"* (Matthew 5:48 NKJV). To me, that is pretty darn perfect. Would Jesus command or demand of us something that He does not make a way for us to fulfill?

I have waited for this moment to come to the nations and release the sons of God to arise and become all that God has desired for them to be since before the foundations of the earth. Some of you reading today are going to be totally, utterly, completely changed, shifted and rearranged. I think there is nobody who has a heart as full as mine. God is so good and awesome! I am excited about what He is going to do.

We welcome all the angels, the great cloud of witnesses and the whole of the heavens to join together in unity of spirit, for singleness of mind and unity of purpose. Praise the Lord! Thank you, Father.

---

²⁵ To find out more about what this verse means in its greatest depth, "the creation was not subject to vanity willingly, but because of him who subjected it to the same, in hope," see the recording on the "Restoration of all Things."

Chapter 7

Restoration

This chapter is about global transformation or what I call *the restoration of all things*. If we are going to be called by God to restore all things, first, we have to believe that all things can be restored. Second, we have to see how that is going to happen. Because this has proven to be a controversial message, I would like to share how this revelation came down from Heaven. I intend to use only scriptures the Lord laid down for me. Before we begin, I will share my own personal experience.

My Journey Towards Believing God Restores All

Early in my spiritual journey, I did not have any teachers. I joined a liturgical church. No one there was born again. Nobody knew about the baptism of the Holy Spirit. Nobody wanted to read the Bible. No one wanted to pray. So, I spent the first seven years of my spiritual life mostly by myself. Because I'd experienced an epiphany of Jesus in my bedroom, I instantly developed an intense zeal for Him and I experienced a tremendous, insatiable hunger for the Word of God. I did not know then there was such a thing as a modern-day prophet. I especially did not know I was going to be one. But I had a craving to find out all I could about the end-time appearing of Jesus Christ.

I had three businesses at the time. I handed the work over to management so I could immerse myself in the Word of God, often for as many as twenty hours a day. I could not get enough of the Word. I would wake at three or four o'clock in the morning with questions. To find answers, I would search through my *Thompson Chain Reference Bible*. My desire to find out about the end-time appearing of Jesus

Christ in the earth was deep. I read more than a thousand books on the second coming of the Lord Jesus Christ. Through my research, I found that since Jesus walked the earth, every generation has earnestly believed with all their heart that they would be the generation that would be alive when He came back again. Even His is own disciples thought so. Why? Because He told them: *"Assuredly, I say to you, there are some of you standing here who shall not taste death till they see the Son of Man coming in His kingdom"* (Matthew 16:28 NKJV).

The Book of Revelation is a story of the spiritual migration of the human spirit from the day it first leaves God until the day it is perfected in Him. Knowing that Jesus is the Word, we need to understand what it means to be *in* Christ and to have Christ *in* us. *"In the beginning was the Word, and the Word was with God, and the Word was God"* (John 1:1 NKJV): the Word was made manifest in mortal flesh so that we could behold the glory of the Father. Therefore, if Jesus is the Word and Jesus lives in us, then every word in the Bible, from Genesis to Revelation, lives inside of us because Jesus is in us and Jesus is the Word.

Each book I read concerning the end times presented its own scenarios and backed them up with scripture. One reference book read something like this: "There will be a heavenly collision and the sun and the moon will collide." I thought, "Oh yes, that must be right because it's backed up by scripture." When the New Testament was written, John did not have the language to talk about planes and bombs. He referred to locusts with stings in their tails, but the commentaries I read interpreted that imagery as airplanes carrying bombs. "Oh, yes," I thought. "This must be right because it is what scripture says."

Every book I read was backed up one hundred percent by scripture. Yet, I began to notice every commentator gave a different interpretation. I became confused. The more I read, the more confused I became. Which scenario was right after all?

I've told this before, but I think it bears repeating. One day I was in my prayer closet, crying out to the Lord. "Father, I really want to know the truth."

The Lord laughed and said, "If you want to know the truth, you must come to the truth. The truth is not a doctrine: it is a person."

I thought to myself, "Well, that is right, but I have already come to Jesus. I have already received the baptism of the Holy Spirit."

The Lord said, "No! You must *come* to the truth (Jesus)."

Since my children were going away on a retreat and my husband was on a seven-day business trip, I took my Bible, a little piece of carpet to sit on, and a pup tent out into the wilderness all by myself. For seven days I sat there, waiting to find out the truth.

On the first day, my mind was still inundated with end-time eschatology. I would consider Isaiah and say, "Oh, Isaiah is looking forward and Revelation is looking back. When Daniel says something, he is looking forward, but Revelation is looking backward." I could not break my established mindset concerning end-time eschatology.

On the second day, I started the same way. I started with the Word, from the Old Testament to the New Testament, back and forth again. Then, on the third day, as I was sitting with my eyes closed, the doors of Heaven opened up. I heard the call of the Lord: "Come up here. I want to show you the things that were, the things that are, and the things that are yet to come."

This was in 1997. Since that day, I have been consistently and daily caught up in a moment, in the twinkling of an eye and carried away to the throne of God to receive downloads of wisdom which do not come from books. I discovered the true Wisdom that can come only from intimate union with Him.

About the fifth day into my journey, I came across Revelation 5, which says:

> *Then I looked, and I heard the voice of many angels around the throne, the living creatures, and the elders; and the number of them was ten thousand times ten thousand, and thousands of thousands, saying with a loud voice: "Worthy is the Lamb who was slain to receive power and riches and wisdom and strength and honor and glory and blessing!" And every creature which is in heaven and on the earth and under the earth and such as are in the sea, and all that are in them, I heard saying: "Blessing and honor and glory and power be to Him who sits on the throne, and to the Lamb, forever and ever!"* (Revelation 5:11–13 NKJV)

When I read those verses, I rejected them. I thought, "That is not right. It does not mesh with my church tradition at all." *Every* creature? I shoved it away. "I am misreading, or I got an interpretation of that verse that is not in line with church doctrine." So, I rejected it. All the fifth day, I struggled, pushing those verses away.

On the sixth day, the verses kept coming back to me. Finally, I cried out to God, "Alright, Lord: if you want me to investigate these verses I will, but cults have risen up from misinterpretation of one scripture or verse. Therefore, if this is really a truth that You are trying to reveal to me, I want You to show me where else this is in scripture. You said to 'Take into to account the *whole* counsel of God.'"

So, as God is my witness, for the next two days I randomly moved from Old Testament to New Testament, and everywhere I put my finger down, the message that God's intention was to see all things restored and made one in Him was right there in front me.

The intention of God and His unfolding sovereign purpose is that all creatures everywhere, including those under the earth, would know Him and the power of who He is. For years we have been taught the all-knowing, all-seeing, all-powerful and all-loving God, who is so big, so huge, so magnificent, is ultimately going to give away ninety percent of everything He made to the devil. Suddenly, I began to question that doctrine.

I came out of the desert with five hundred scriptures, all of them confirming His plan to restore all things. The primary one was Matthew 17:11, which I discussed previously in Chapter 7: *"Jesus answered and said to them, 'Indeed, Elijah is coming first and will restore all things'"* (NKJV). Essentially, Jesus said, "I am not coming back to the earth again until first the spirit of Elijah comes to restore all things."

The elders which are among you I exhort, who am also an elder, and a witness of the sufferings of Christ, and also a partaker of the glory that shall be revealed. (1 Peter 5:1 **NKJV**)

I have been ascending and descending in the spirit for more than forty years now. When you learn to be caught up in a moment in the twinkling of an eye, you can see the things that were, the things that are and the things that are yet to come. I have been invited by Yahweh to manifest as a joint heir, a co-creator and co-participant with Him in the restoration of all things. I have been a participant in the second resurrection, and I have seen the result of all things being restored in God. It is so magnificent, so majestic, so overwhelming to have been given the privilege to see the dynamic unfolding of Yahweh's sovereign plan for mankind.

This may be a divisive message, but I hope by the time we get done with this chapter, you will see the truth in it.

Reconciling Eternal Judgment and Every Knee Bowed

Israel was focused on the image of the Messiah appearing as an overcoming king, but that focus did not keep Jesus from coming as a suffering servant. The apparently conflicting prophecies about how He would come were both true at the same time. Similarly, our understandings concerning hell and everlasting fire have are apparently conflicting. But, one does not negate the other from being accurate. The restoration of all things is the day when the Lord comes to revive and revitalize all men everywhere, that God may be the all-in-all.

Let's consider how to reconcile the doctrine of eternal judgment with the restoration of all things. In Hebrews, Paul advises moving beyond a basic understanding:

> *Therefore, leaving the discussion of the elementary principles of Christ, let us go on to perfection, not laying again the foundation of repentance from dead works and of faith toward God, of the doctrine of baptisms, of laying on of hands, of resurrection of the dead, and of eternal judgment.* (Hebrews 6:1–2 NKJV)

Those first elementary principles include good works, the doctrine of baptisms, the laying on of hands, faith towards God and the doctrine of eternal judgment. Set these things aside now, Paul says, and come up to perfection.

To be called by God to reconcile all things, we need to be able to understand and defend this position from the Word of God: Hell had a beginning and hell will also have an end.

> *And the sea gave up the dead which were in it; and death and hell delivered up the dead which were in them: and they were judged every man according to their works. And death and hell were cast into the lake of fire. This is the second death.* (Revelation 20:13–14 KJV)

What is the purpose of fire? It purifies. If we believe that God is the all-consuming fire, this verse would lead to the fulfillment of God's sovereign word and He would be the all-in-all (1 Corinthians 15:28), where *all* means *all things*. There are mysteries here which have not yet been revealed, including the manifestations of the second death and the second resurrection. We sing variations of the words "every knee shall bow and every tongue confess" from Romans 14:11 and Philippians 2:10–11 in multiple songs and preach about them all the time. But have we ever fully listened to what the Word says?

It is written:

> *As I live, says the* Lord, *every knee shall bow to Me, and every tongue shall confess to God.* (Romans 14:11 NKJV)

> *[T]hat at the name of Jesus every knee should bow, of those in heaven, and of those on earth, and of those under the earth, and that every tongue should confess that Jesus Christ is Lord…* (Philippians 2:10–11 NKJV)

Do you believe *every* knee will bow and *every* tongue confess that Jesus Christ is Lord? Or do you only believe that those who have already confessed with their mouth and believed in their heart that Jesus Christ is Lord? We must verify that with the scriptures above. Additionally, Hebrews 6:13 shows no name is greater than God's name.[26] Do we believe that? If we do, that is the answer to the restoration of all things.

---

[26] *"For when God made a promise to Abraham, because He could swear by no one greater, He swore by Himself"* (NKJV).

Restoration

Many misunderstand the message I share of the restoration of all things as a universalist message. It is not a universalistic message. There is only one name under Heaven by which man can be saved—the name of Jesus Christ. He is the door. He is the way to the Father. No man can come to the Father except by Him. No man can see the Kingdom of God unless he confesses with his mouth and believes in his heart that Jesus Christ is Lord. If we do not confess with our mouth and believe in our heart that Jesus Christ is Lord, we will go to hell.

But hell is not the end. The Lord has a totally different ending in the unfolding of His sovereign plan for us. He says:

> *Look to Me, and be saved,*
> *All you ends of the earth!*
> *For I am God, and there is no other.*
> *I have sworn by Myself;*
> *The word has gone out of My mouth in righteousness,*
> *And shall not return,*
> *That to Me every knee shall bow,*
> *Every tongue shall take an oath.* (Isaiah 45:22–23 NKJV)

When God swears something by His own name and out of His own mouth, are we so ignorant as to believe that He cannot do the thing He swears to? He is a sovereign, covenant keeping God, and He will do what He says He will do. *"If we are faithless, He remains faithful; He cannot deny Himself"* (2 Timothy 2:13 NKJV).

Notice next that the creatures are singing and rejoicing. They are not wailing and screaming in torment. This is evidence Hell will be done away with.

> *And every creature which is in heaven, and on the earth, and under the earth, and such as are in the sea, and all that are in them, heard I saying, Blessing, and honour, and glory, and power, be unto him that sitteth upon the throne, and unto the Lamb for ever and ever.* (Revelation 5:13 KJV)

Does this verse mean *every* creature will honor God? Can we really believe that? If it really means every creature, we must believe that all of creation, including the sea creatures, will ultimately be found worshipping the Lamb forever and ever.

ALL MEANS ALL, SO IS DEATH THE END?

God's sovereign intent and purpose is found throughout Ephesians chapter 1, but I am going to highlight verse ten. I encourage you to read the entire book of Ephesians because it is full of the unfolding of God's sovereign plan for mankind. It says: *"in the dispensation of the fullness of the times..."* (note: we are living now in the dispensation of the fullness of time) *"...He might gather together in one all things in Christ, both which are in heaven and which are on earth—in Him"* (Ephesians 1:10 NKJV).

The question is: Do we believe He will gather together *"in one all things in Christ"*?

Consider next Acts 2:17. *"And it shall come to pass in the last days, says God, That I will pour out of My spirit on all flesh..."* (NKJV). Do we believe when He says *all flesh* that He really means *all flesh?* What does that mean for satan worshippers, New Agers, Buddhists, followers of Confucianism, Shamans and tribal people? Are they included in *all flesh?*

Wherever I go in the world, I find people having personal epiphanies of Jesus in their dreams. I have hundreds of testimonies from people in the Muslim world who have been bowing down in mosques when suddenly Jesus Christ appears in their midst. They have given their lives to the Lord and have left Islam. Because of dreams and visions they have, even seventh-generation hajj leaders are leaving Islam to follow Jesus. Jesus, Himself, appears in their dreams and calls them to come to Him... *and they do.*

Do we really believe the whole earth is going to be filled with all the knowledge of God? *"For the earth will be filled with the knowledge of the glory of the Lord as the waters cover the sea"* (Habakkuk 2:14 NKJV). Scriptures like this are not just beautiful poetry. They reveal God's intention for all things. The glory of the Lord is going to cover the earth even as the waters cover the sea.

First Corinthians 15 deals with the issue of separation of flesh and spirit and the restoration of the soul of every living being. When I refer to *every living being*, I even count those who have died. Because of church age teaching, we think that when people die and go to hell, that it is all over for them. I do not know how to tell you this, but they go on with God for long time after they leave the earth realm. A multitude of scriptures deal with this issue.

The Word says: *"...by man came death, by Man also came the resurrection of the dead"* (1 Corinthians 15:21 NKJV). This verse is a precursor to the second resurrection. And there is a second resurrection coming.

> *For as in Adam all die, even so in Christ all shall be made alive. But each one in his own order: Christ the first fruits, afterward those who are Christ's at His coming. Then comes the end, when He delivers the kingdom to God the Father, when He puts an end to all rule and all authority and power.* (1 Corinthians 15:22–24 NKJV)

If we believe that *all* mankind will not be saved in Christ, then we must say that in Adam *all* did not die. But the word *all* means *all*. It means *completely encompassing*: so in First Corinthians, I believe it refers to every single solitary creature that has ever lived or been created. If we say that all mankind will be made alive in Christ is not the truth, then we must also say that in Adam *all* did not die.

The first fruits represent the church. If and when "He puts an end to all rule and all authority and power" (v. 22), that means satan no longer has any power. "For He must reign till He has put all enemies under His feet. The last enemy that will be destroyed is death" (1 Cor 15:25–26 NKJV).

Let's look at the next verses:

> *For "He has put all things under His feet." But when He says "all things are put under Him," it is evident that He who put all things under Him is excepted. Now when all things are made subject to Him, then the Son Himself will also be subject to Him who put all things under Him, that God may be all in all.* (1 Cor 15:27–28 NKJV)

But God gives it a body as He pleases, and to each seed its own body. All flesh is not the same flesh. There is one kind of flesh, of man. There is another flesh of beasts, another flesh of fish and another of birds. There are also celestial bodies and terrestrial bodies; but the glory of the celestial is one, and the glory of the terrestrial is another. (1 Corinthians 15:38–41 NKJV)

The scripture above refers to separation of flesh and spirit. We have a spiritual body and we have an earthly body. But the glory of one is vastly different than the glory of the other. We have a terrestrial body—that is this body, our flesh—and we also have a spiritual body that is full of light. In the realms of the spirit, we have one glory. That glory is pure, undefiled, perfected light. I refer to that glory as the revealing of the thing that has been hidden in Christ since the beginning.

We need to keep in mind *"it hath not yet been revealed what you shall be."* The following scriptures help lay it out. Paul was preaching *"to make all see what is the fellowship of the mystery, which from the beginning of the ages has been hidden in God who created all things through Jesus Christ…"* (Ephesians 3:9 NKJV). John wrote, *"Beloved, now are we the sons of God, and it doth not yet appear what we shall be: but we know that, when he shall appear, we shall be like him; for we shall see him as he is"* (1 John 3:2 KJV). And we learn: *"Eye hath not seen, nor ear heard, neither have entered into the heart of man, the things which God hath prepared for them that love him"* (1 Corinthians 2:9 KJV). These verses all infer that our eyes have not yet seen the greatness of the things He has prepared for us. If we imagine in our hearts the greatest, grandest scenario ever, what is coming will still be so much greater than anything we can imagine at this time.

There is something that has not yet been revealed which shall be revealed when we see Him. *"For I reckon that the sufferings of this present time are not worthy to be compared with the glory which shall be revealed in us"* (Romans 8:18 KJV). The purpose of ascension experience is for us to see Him as He is. The seventh day transfiguration of the corporate son of man is coming, when the glory that we had with God from before the beginning will finally be revealed, as we follow Him in the pattern that was set before us in Matthew 17. (See Chapter 7 on the Transfiguration.)

Jesus said: "If you want to be my disciple, follow me." He came to be the pattern of how we are to live in holiness, righteousness, and perfection before a perfect Father. Therefore, if we truly seek Him with all our heart, mind, will, and strength, our lives will follow the same pattern that His did, including the transfiguration.

Creation of Body, Soul and Spirit

Let's look more closely at 1 Corinthians 15, beginning in verse 39.

> *All flesh is not the same flesh: but there is one kind of flesh of men, another flesh of beasts, another of fishes, and another of birds. There are also celestial bodies, and bodies terrestrial: but the glory of the celestial is one, and the glory of the terrestrial is another. There is one glory of the sun, and another glory of the moon, and another glory of the stars: for one star differeth from another star in glory.*
>
> *So also is the resurrection of the dead. It is sown in corruption; it is raised in incorruption: It is sown in dishonour; it is raised in glory: it is sown in weakness; it is raised in power: It is sown a natural body; it is raised a spiritual body. There is a natural body, and there is a spiritual body.*
>
> *And so it is written, The first man Adam was made a living soul; the last Adam was made a quickening spirit. Howbeit that was not first which is spiritual, but that which is natural; and afterward that which is spiritual.* (1 Corinthians 15:39–46 KJV)

It's clearly laid out: there is a natural body and there is a spiritual body. The body goes down as a natural body and then it is raised a spiritual body.

I want to take a minute on that verse to explain how man was created. We have very little understanding of the separation of flesh and spirit. If you go to the creation of man in Genesis, you will find the Word says: *"And the Lord God formed man of the dust of the ground, and breathed into his nostrils the breath of life; and man became a living being"* (Genesis 2:7 NKJV). Man was created out of the dust of the earth. That is the creation of our body. Then God breathed in him and he became a living soul. When He breathed into man and man became a living soul, that was the creation of our soul.

We must consider: Where is the creation of the spirit addressed? It is not stated in Genesis 2:7. It is not there because the spirit of man was not "created," as such. Our spirit is eternal. It was in God in the very beginning. It will be in God in the very end.

If it is true that our spirits are not created but eternal, how did our spirit unite with our body and our soul to become the trinity of man that the Lord created us to be? I can tell you because I was there. You were there also. You simply do not remember it. At the very moment of conception, in the very moment the male sperm strikes the female egg, there is an instantaneous flash of light that joins them. Even atheistic scientists call it the "God particle." I call it our spirit, coming from Heaven in order to join with our body and our soul, which are temporary.

Job was devastated after all his children and all his cattle had been killed. He was sitting on a carpet scraping off bloody scabs from his body with a shard, when three of his friends came to him and said, "There must be great sin in your life because otherwise you would not be having this trial." (See Job 4:7, 8:5–6; and 11:4–6.) Even Job's wife came to him and said, *"...Curse God and die!"* (Job 2:9 NKJV). He was in the most devastating part of his trial when the Lord came to him and asked (paraphrased), "Job, where were you when I laid down the foundations of the earth? Where were you when I hung all the stars and the planets in the sky? Where were you when I set out all the boundaries of the sea? You know, because you were there" (see Job 38 NKJV). God makes the statement: *"you were born then"* (Job 38:21). Job was in Him in the very beginning and so were we.

Severing Flesh from Spirit, Frequency

The whole purpose of the Word of God is to sever and separate flesh from spirit. Our spirit has a greater glory than our flesh.

Let's go back to the question: How did the spirit of man unite with the soul and the body of man? I can tell you. It was the very first utterance out of the Word of the Lord as He was brooding over the earth. He did not speak in English; He spoke in frequency. The brooding frequency is the sound that a mother hen makes over her eggs to produce the hatching of her chicks. In the Bible it says, *"Let there be light."* But, of course, Yahweh wasn't speaking English. In the realms of the Spirit, there is no language "but a cry." His "brooding frequency" caused all things to be created.

Adam could walk in pure, undefiled communion with Him without any separation at all because he was made of the same substance, which is light. There are four nouns used to describe Yahweh: *"God is love"* (1 John 4:8,16); *"God is Spirit"* (John 4:24); *"God is fire"* (Heb 12:29); and *"God is light"* (1 John 1:5).

> *And they heard the sound of the Lord God walking in the garden in the cool of the day, and Adam and his wife hid themselves from the presence of the Lord God among the trees of the garden. Then the Lord God called to Adam and said to him, "Where are you?" So, he said, "I heard Your voice in the garden, and I was afraid because I was naked; and I hid myself."* (Genesis 3:8–10 NKJV)

Interestingly, Christian art frequently pictures Adam and Eve in the garden looking down as if saying, "Oops! We don't have any clothes on." So, they are shown picking leaves off the trees to cover up all their nakedness (Genesis 3:7). Who cares if they are naked? They are the only ones there anyway. Who is going to see them?

When Adam said, *"...I was naked..."* (Genesis 3:10 NKJV), he recognized he had been stripped of something called *shekinah*. The word *naked* according to *Strong's* H2834 means "to be stripped of" or "uncovered." *Shekinah* (note: the word itself is not in scripture, but is used in rabbinic teaching), interpreted from Hebrew means at its root the dwelling place or the settling place of divine nature (see *Strong's* H4908). The shekinah gave him permission to have pure, undefiled communion with the Lord Jesus Christ, because with it he was "the dwelling place of God's nature."

Paul saw it this way:

> *For we know that if our earthly house, this tabernacle [our natural body], were dissolved, we have a building of God, a house not made with hands*

[our spiritual body], eternal in the heavens. For in this we groan, earnestly desiring to be clothed upon with our house which is from Heaven [redemption of the body], that, being so clothed, we shall not be found naked. For we that are in this tabernacle do groan, being burdened: not because we would be unclothed, but clothed about, that mortality might be swallowed up by life. (2 Corinthians 5:1-4 KJ21, bracketed additions mine)

We are coming to a place where we are going to take back what was stripped off. We are going to take back that shekinah. That place is called the seventh day transfiguration of the corporate Son of Man. The level of glory we will walk in will be powerful and magnificent because it comes with the restoration of dominion, the dominion over all things. Therefore, every creature on the earth, under the earth, over the earth, in the sky, and in the sea will see and be drawn to us because we have finally become what all creation is groaning for.

There is a natural body and there is a spiritual body. We need to understand that even though we have three parts—a body, soul and spirit—we are created in the image of our Father who has three parts: Father, Son and Holy Spirit. Even though they are three in one, with one mind, they have three totally different manifestations, administrations and functions of operation. Our spirit is the same.

"And so it is written, 'the first man Adam became a living being.' The last Adam became a life-giving spirit. However, the spiritual is not first, but the natural, and afterward the spiritual" (1 Corinthians 15:45–46 NKJV). The first man is the man of the earth—he is earthy. The second man is the Lord of Heaven. So they are also in the earth and in the heavenlies. Such are they also that are in the heavenlies.

One of the reasons I teach ascension experience is because the more we ascend, the more we are caught up in the heavens to see Him. He is multifaceted, multi-dimensional, and multi-colored. Each time I ascend, He releases an understanding of a different facet of His character. When I come back down, I can manifest the facet of His character I have seen and touched. The purpose of all revelation is that we should become what we behold: *"And as we have borne the image of the man of dust, we shall also bear the image of the heavenly Man"* (1 Corinthians 15:49 NJKV).

In the Age of the Church, we were taught that the only way we could attain a heavenly image was to die and go to Heaven. There we would get a harp, sprout wings and float around all day on a cloud. That is not true. We have so limited God with our thinking. The sovereign design of God is for us to be restored to and brought into total alignment with original creation, so that the shekinah-glory of the Lord will again be seen upon us. Thus shall be fulfilled the prophetic word of Isaiah 60:

> *Arise, shine; for thy light is come, and the glory of the LORD is risen upon thee. For, behold, the darkness shall cover the earth, and gross darkness the people: but the LORD shall arise upon thee, and his glory shall be seen upon thee. And the Gentiles shall come to thy light, and kings to the brightness of thy rising. Lift up thine eyes round about, and see: all they gather themselves together, they come to thee: thy sons shall come from far, and thy daughters shall be nursed at thy side. Then thou shalt see, and flow together, and thine heart shall fear, and be enlarged; because the abundance of the sea shall be converted unto thee, the forces of the Gentiles shall come unto thee.* (Isaiah 60:1–5 KJV)

The kings of the earth, *all* the Gentiles (the unbelievers), all the sons and daughters, and all the abundance of the sea shall come. Why? Do they come because we can preach a good message, because we have communicated the gospel to them, because we can heal the sick or raise the dead? No! They come because *"His light shall be seen upon us."* That *light* is the seeable, tangible, touchable light of God: His glory shall be seen upon us.

> *Now this I say, brethren, that flesh and blood cannot inherit the kingdom of God; nor does corruption inherit incorruption. Behold, I tell you a mystery: We shall not all sleep, but we shall all be changed—in a moment, in the twinkling of an eye, at the last trumpet. For the trumpet will sound, and the dead will be raised incorruptible, and we shall be changed. For this corruptible [our terrestrial body] must put on incorruption [our celestial body], and this mortal [terrestrial body] must put on immortality [our celestial body].* (1 Corinthians 15:50–53 NKJV; bracketed additions, mine)

> *Who shall change our vile body [terrestrial], that it may be fashioned like unto his glorious body [celestial], according to the working whereby he is able*

even to subdue all things unto himself. (Philippians 3:21 KJV; bracketed additions, mine)

All this has to do with the ultimate purposes behind communion. The Bible says: *"For this reason, many are weak and sick among you, and many sleep, because they have not rightly discerned this principle"* (1 Corinthians 11:30 NKJV). The principle of the restoration of all things and the restoration of eternal life is in the mystery of communion.

> *So, when this corruptible has put on incorruption, and this mortal shall put on immortality, then shall be brought to pass the saying that was written. "Death is swallowed up in victory." "O Death, where is your sting? O Hades, where is your victory?" The sting of death is sin, and the strength of sin is the law. But thanks be to God, who gives us the victory through our Lord Jesus Christ.* (1 Corinthians 15:54–57 NKJV)

There are more verses which talk specifically about the restoration of all things.

> *But I say to you, love your enemies, bless those who curse you, do good to those who hate you, and pray for those who spitefully use you and persecute you that you may be the sons of your Father in heaven; for He makes His sun to rise on both the evil and on the good (He) and sends rain on the just and the unjust... For if ye love them which love you, what reward have ye? do not even the publicans the same? And if ye salute your brethren only, what do ye more than others? do not even the publicans so? Be ye therefore perfect, even as your Father which is in heaven is perfect.* (Matthew 5:44–48 NKJV)

If our desire is to be conformed to His image and His nature (which is love), that means we must likewise love both the good and the evil, the just and the unjust. We must *become* love like His love—eternal, uncompromising, unconditional, and without "shadow of turning."

In addition to the above, Jesus goes on to say to his servants,

> *"The wedding is ready, but those who were invited were not worthy. Therefore, go into the highways, and as many as you find, invite to the wedding." So those servants went out into the highways and gathered together all whom they found, both bad and good. And the wedding hall was filled with guests.* (Matthew 22:8–10 NKJV)

The father was preparing a wedding for his son. He sent invitations to the friends of the bridegroom, but they were too busy. They said, "We just bought a new field. We have to plant our field." They were too busy because they had just gotten married and had to pay attention to their wives.

In my personal Nancy Coen lingo, the friends of the bridegroom were too busy with their programs. They were so busy with what they saw as the works of the Lord that they had forgotten the Lord of the works (Revelation 2:4). Therefore, the father directed his servants to send invitations to those in the highways and the byways. This should serve as a warning to us in the church. We can be the friends of the Bridegroom, yet still find ourselves standing outside the wedding feast.

> *And when the king came in to see the guests, he saw there a man which had not on a wedding garment: And he saith unto him, Friend, how camest thou in hither not having a wedding garment? And he was speechless.*
>
> *Then said the king to the servants, Bind him hand and foot, and take him away, and cast him into outer darkness; there shall be weeping and gnashing of teeth. For many are called, but few are chosen.* (Matthew 22:12–14 KJV)

The Word says:

> *Every valley shall be filled, and every mountain and hill brought low;*
>
> *The crooked places shall be made straight and the rough ways smooth;*
>
> *And **all** flesh shall see the salvation of God.* (Luke 3:5–6 NKJV, emphasis mine)

There are hundreds of verses that deal with this issue. We say them. We sing them. We preach them, but we really do not hear what we are saying.

> *And when His disciples James and John saw this, they said, "Lord, do You want us to command fire to come down from heaven and consume them, just as Elijah did?" But He turned and rebuked them, and said, "You do not know what manner of spirit you are of. For the Son of Man did not come to destroy men's lives but to save them."* (Luke 9:54–56 NKJV)

God's Permissive vs. Sovereign Will

> *Therefore, I exhort first of all that supplications, prayers, intercessions, and giving of thanks be made for all men, for kings and all who are in authority, that we may lead a quiet and peaceable life in all godliness and reverence.* (1 Timothy 2:1–2 NKJV)

Today, multitudes of prayers go up concerning the leaders in this nation. Unfortunately, in the Age of the Church we used about ninety percent of our prayer time to pray in direct opposition of God's will. We think we know the will of God, but most of the time we are trying to maintain our own comfort zone.

When somebody in leadership does not seem to be from God, we automatically assume that they are not. But the Lord raises up and takes down those in power. *"For by him were all things created, that are in heaven, and that are in earth, visible and invisible, whether they be thrones, or dominions, or principalities, or powers: all things were created by him, and for him"* (Colossians 1:16). Therefore, whoever is in power is there by divine design to perform and perfect something that is above and beyond our level or our ability to understand. *"For this is good and acceptable in the sight of our God our Savior, who desires all men to be saved and to come to the knowledge of the truth"* (1 Timothy 2:3–4 NKJV).

This is scripture. We say it is not the will of God that any should perish. Is God's will be going to be overcome by the will of man? No. He has a sovereignly ordained plan to bring all things into Christ, that He shall be all in all (1 Corinthians 15:28). God is God, after all. He is not *trying* to do anything. He will bring to completion the desire of His heart, whether it agrees with our doctrines or not.

Many people believe the greatest thing God has given man is independent will, but God will not allow man to override His own will. What will happen to mankind is ultimately similar to what happened to Jonah.

Jonah heard a word from the Lord: "I want you to go to Nineveh." Jonah says, "No way. I am not going to Nineveh. They burn or stone prophets there." Jonah defies the will of God, gets on a ship, and goes in the exact opposite direction. The Lord yields to the will of Jonah, and virtually says, "OK. Have it your own way."

But then God raises up a big fish. When Jonah was in the belly of the whale being devoured by its digestive juices, wrapped up and smothered by seaweed, gasping for his last breath of oxygen, suddenly, Nineveh looked like a really good place (Jonah 1:1–3:3). The Lord does not overpower our will, but sometimes He will tweak our will or our circumstances so that we end up fulfilling His desire. The word of the Lord to Jonah was not meant for Jonah's own personal gain. It was for the redemption of a whole geographical territory. It went above and beyond Jonah's personal benefit.

There are multitudes of people who will say, "Absolutely not!" to God, but the day is coming when the Lord will tweak their circumstances. Even though they are in the belly of the earth, burning up with fire, they will have their souls tweaked. They are going to make decisions to follow Jesus Christ. That is the word of the Lord.

> *[E]very eye will see Him, even they who pierced him.* (Revelation 1:7 NKJV)

> *The Lord is not slack concerning his promise, as some count slackness; but is longsuffering toward us, not willing that any should perish, but that all should come to repentance.* (2 Peter 3:9 NKJV)

> *For it is written:*
> *"As I live, says the Lord,*
> *Every knee shall bow to Me,*
> *And every tongue shall confess to God."* (Romans 14:11 NKJV)

He wants all to be saved. If we say He cannot possibly save all men, we are saying that God cannot perform His own will. But God's will is sovereign. For two thousand years, we have been living according to the permissive will of God, but now we are coming into the activation of the sovereign will of God.

Jesus was going to be crucified even if the disciples did not want it, because it was God's sovereign will for His Son to give His life so that we could once again be one with Him.

From that time Jesus began to show His disciples that He must go to Jerusalem, and suffer many things from the elders, chief priests, and scribes, to be killed and raised the third day.

Then Peter took Him aside and began to rebuke Him, saying, "Far be it from You, Lord; this shall not happen to You!"

But He turned and said to Peter, "Get behind Me, Satan! You are an offense to Me, for you are not mindful of the things of God, but the things of men." (Matthew 16:21–23 NKJV)

Jesus knew that in his love for the Lord, Peter was actually tempting Him not to fulfill the very purpose for which He was sent. Many today do not understand the sovereign will of God. Jesus was going to the cross one way or another because it was part of the Father's sovereign will, not part of His permissive will. Ask yourself this: is the Lord able to perfect and perform His sovereign will? I think so!

People tend to give credit to the devil—"Oh, the devil did this, the devil did that, the devil brought this into my life!"—when ninety percent of the time, it is God. While by our own volition and faulty decisions we can open the door and give the devil a governmental right to attack us, God's promise is that He will cause *"all things to work together for good to those who love God, to those who are the called according to His purpose"* (Romans 8:28 NKJV).

When we seek the Lord with all our heart, mind, and strength, with everything that is in us, we can stand before any accuser and follow Jesus' example. Jesus stood before Pontius Pilate, who said: *"Are You not speaking to me? Do You not know that I have power to crucify You, and power to release You?"* (John 19:10 NKJV). Jesus' response was: *"You could have no power at all against me, except it were given thee from above"* (John 19:11 KJV).

God is sovereign, and His will shall be done in due season. *"For there is one God and one Mediator between God and man, the man Christ Jesus who gave Himself a ransom for all, to be testified in due time"* (1 Timothy 2:5–6 NKJV). In other words, we have been looking from the traditions of the Age of the Church. The restoration of all things does not oppose the existence of hell. Hell is a real place. However, it does add to our understanding. Those burning in hell are not there for all eternity. The restoration of all things in no way minimizes the cross. In fact, it maximizes what Jesus did, which was to become *"a ransom for all."*

I do not believe that *everlasting fire,* as found in the Word, means *eternal fire*. Based on the Greek for *everlasting (Strong's* G166), which is based on its root *aiōn (Strong's* G165), I believe *everlasting* in the context of *fire* means "until the end of the age" (*Strong's* G106) or "until the end of an eon." *Strong's* definition of *aiōn* is "properly, an age; by extension perpetuity (also past); by implication the world; speciallly (Jewish) a Messianic period (present or future): - age, course, eternal, (for) ever (-more), [n-]ever, (beginning of the, while the) world (began, without end). Compare G5550."

The end of another age is coming. At the end of that age there will be a move of God to cause His sovereign will to be manifested in the earth.

The Word says God is the Savior of all men: *"For to this end we both labor and suffer reproach, because we trust in the living God, who is the Savior of all men, especially of those who believe"* (1 Timothy 4:10 NKJV). Do we really believe He means *all* men? He is the Savior of all men but especially of those who believe. Those of us who have salvation right now carry it in earthly vessels. Yet still, Jesus is the Savior of *all* men.

> *In Him was life, and the life was the light of men.* (John 1:4 NKJV)

> *For I say, through the grace given unto me, to every man that is among you, not to think of himself more highly than he ought to think; but to think soberly, according as God hath dealt to each one a measure of faith.* (Romans 12:3 NKJV)

The measure of light given to every man may be covered over by gross, ugly, hideous, despicable darkness, but in the heart of every man there is a light. It may be dim, but there is a light. Not because I said so, but because Jesus said so. This light is their spirit. When their spirit hears the truth through the frequency of Heaven, which is love, they yield and surrender every time because there is a memory in their spirit of where they came from in the beginning.

> *This man came for a witness, to bear witness of the Light, that ALL through him might believe. He was not that Light, but was sent to bear witness of that Light. That was the true Light which gives light to every man coming into the world.* (John 1:7–9 NKJV, emphasis mine)

In every man there is a light. It does not matter what kind of evil, wicked, depraved things they have been subject to, there is still a light inside them. When we allow the measure of light in us to speak to the measure of light in them, we can say, "Lazarus come forth," and they will come. When we learn how to speak spirit to spirit through the frequency of love, they will come.

I have hours and hours of testimonies of when I have spoken into the hearts of the most despicable, ugly, wickedly satanic, Jihadist, and shamanistic high priests that you can imagine. When I allow the level of light in me to speak to the level of light that is in them, every defense inside them totally melts. What happens is the separation of flesh and spirit.

When the Lord brooded over the earth *["Then God said, 'Let there be light'"* (Genesis 1:3 NKJV)], the first thing that happened was separation in the firmaments. When we become the express representation of that light (which is a frequency), His light goes forth and severs and separates soul and spirit. His light (which is the frequency of love) speaks to them spirit to spirit without any interruption or interference from their soul.

I have seen hundreds won to Jesus Christ by allowing the measure of light that is in me (Jesus) to speak to the measure of light that is in them. When I look at them with earthly eyes, I see what is despicable, ugly, and evil. But God said, *"That was the true Light which gives light to every man coming into the world"* (John 1:9 NKJV), and *"For God did not send His Son into the world to condemn the world, but that the world through Him might be saved"* (John 3:17 NKJV).

You know these verses. All scripture is ripe with these types of verses. The problem comes when we read the Word of God to prove what we think we already know, rather than read it to find out what we do not yet know. Trust me: there is a whole lot we do not know yet.

Restoration

In this hour, the Lord is beginning to release mysteries that have been hidden since the very beginning. All over the world, mystical people are being caught up into the heavens to see the final outworking of God's plan for mankind. They are beginning to receive divine downloads concerning the capacity of God Almighty to save all that He created.

Let's review what the Bible says about the restoration of all things:

- *All things were made through Him; and without Him nothing was made that was made.* (John 1:3 NKJV)
- *The Father loves the Son, and hats given all things into His hand.* (John 3:35 NKJV)
- *Jesus [knew] that the Father had given all things into His hands, and that He had come from God, and was going to God.* (John 13:3 NKJV)
- *For by him were all things created, that are in heaven, and that are in earth, visible and invisible, whether they be thrones, or dominions, or principalities, or powers: all things were created by him, and for him.* (Colossians 1:16 KJV)
- *And he is before all things, and by him all things consist.* (Colossians 1:17 KJV)
- *And, having made peace through the blood of his cross, by him to reconcile all things unto himself; by him, I say, whether they be things in earth, or things in heaven.* (Colossians 1:20 KJV)
- *Thou art worthy, O Lord, to receive glory and honour and power: for thou hast created all things, and for thy pleasure they are and were created.* (Revelation 4:11 KJV)
- *Thou hast put all things in subjection under his feet. For in that he put all in subjection under him, he left nothing that is not put under him. But now we see not yet all things put under him.* (Hebrews 2:8 KJV)
- *While I was with them in the world, I kept them in thy name: those that thou gavest me I have kept, and none of them is lost, but the son of perdition; that the scripture might be fulfilled.* (John 17:12 KJV)
- *... Jesus beheld them, and said unto them, With men this is impossible; but with God all things are possible.* (Mathew 19:26 KJV)

- *For I have come down from heaven, not to do My own will, but the will of Him who sent Me. This is the will of the Father who sent Me, that of all He has given Me I should lose nothing but should raise it up at the last day. And this is the will of Him who sent Me, that everyone who sees the Son...* (John 6:38–40 NKJV).

And who is it that sees the Son? *"[E]very eye shall see Him, even they who pierced Him"* (Revelation 1:7 NKJV). And what happens when they see Him? *"...[E]veryone who sees the Son and believes in Him may have everlasting life; and I will raise him up at the last day"* (John 6:40 NKJV).

Let's consider:

> If all things were created by Him (including all things both in Heaven and in earth), for Him, in Him and for His pleasure;
>
> If all things ever created were commended into His hands by His Father;
>
> And if, of all the things given to Him by His Father, He has lost nothing, except the son of perdition;
>
> If He has put all things under His feet, and there is nothing left that was created that was not put under Him;
>
> If every eye will see Him, and all who see Him will be raised up on the last day;
>
> If we, at this time, have not yet seen everything put under Him,
>
> And if, in our mindsets the restoration of all things is not possible, but *"in Him all things are possible,"*

then what does all this say about our current inability to see the eternal sovereignty of the unfolding of a plan that has been already been accomplished in the realms of the spirit, but has not yet manifested in the earth realm?

Time is an earth-based paradigm. In the realms of the spirit, there is no such thing as time, space, or distance. Everything that can ever be done, has already been done. That's why the Lamb of God was slain before the earth was ever created. If the Lamb was already slain and the sovereign plan of God was already completed before creation, then what was the purpose of the cross?

God took something that was done thousands of years before in the invisible realm of the spirit and brought it down into the visible realm, because He knew the demand of the heart of man to see something! Jesus came and was manifest in mortal flesh so that we could see the glory of the God in the form of Jesus Christ. *"And the Word was made flesh, and dwelt among us and we beheld his glory, the glory as of the only begotten of the Father, full of grace and truth"* (John 1:14 NKJV).

Jesus came to destroy the works of the devil. He came to destroy death, hell and the grave. But the devil is still lurking about, and people are still dying and going into the grave. So did Jesus complete the purpose for which he came? The answer, of course, is *yes*! But now, as we enter the fullness of the dispensation of time, He is going to take the thing that was totally finished and accomplished in the invisible realm and bring it down into the visible realm—and that is called the restoration of all things or the restoration of dominion. He is going to work with us to restore us to our primordial position, the position that He created for us to function in since the beginning.

Because the Lamb of God was slain before the earth was created, in essence, the completed work of God has already been done. We, as human beings, are merely "walking out" in the visible earth realm the things that have already been done in the invisible spirit realm.

You see, to everything there is time and season (Ecclesiastes 3).

> *That in the dispensation of the fulness of times he might gather together in one all things in Christ, both which are in heaven, and which are on earth; even in him...* (Ephesians 1:10 KJV)

> *For I have come down from heaven, not to do My own will, but the will of Him who sent Me. This is the will of the Father who sent Me, that of all He has given Me I should lose nothing but should raise it up at the last day. And this is the will of Him who sent Me, that everyone who sees Son and believes in Him may have everlasting life; and I will raise him up at the last day.* (John 6:38–40 NKJV)

Who is it that shall see Him?

- *And to make all men see what is the fellowship of the mystery, which from the beginning of the world hath been hid in God, who created all things by Jesus Christ...* (Ephesians 3:9 KJV)

- *Behold, he cometh with clouds; and every eye shall see him, and they also which pierced him.* (Revelation 1:7 KJV)

Even those have long been dead and in the grave will see Him. And all who see Him will be raised up in that last day. This has to do with the second resurrection.

There is a time in which the manifestation of the restoration of all things will occur. We just have not yet seen it. It has been hidden. At this moment, Jesus is in the heavens—as well as in us—waiting for the time for restoration to come. As it says in Acts: *"(Jesus) whom heaven must receive until the times of restoration of all things, which God has spoken by the mouth of all His holy prophets since the world began"* (Acts 3:21)

The consummation of God's sovereign plan for mankind is not a new doctrine. It is plainly written and alluded to many times by the Old Testament prophets: *"But this I confess unto thee, that after the way which they call heresy, so worship I the God of my fathers, believing all things which are which are written in the law and prophets"* (Acts 24:14). We know *"He who descended is also the One who ascended far above all the heavens, that He might fill all things"* (Ephesians 4:10).

In the Age of the Church, we were taught that Jesus was going to split the clouds, ride down on His white horse, catch us up into the heavens and carry us away to have a wonderful party in the sky, while the whole earth was burning and going to hell in tribulation. This is an anti-Christ spirited mindset.

If we are going to follow His pattern, we must look at what He did. He left the unending worship of the angels, the glory of Heaven, and came down into tribulation to be rejected, taunted, falsely accused, beaten, crowned with thorns, hung on a cross, stabbed, and died, so that we could be one with our heavenly Father.

We want to do exactly the opposite. We want to be raptured into Heaven and stay in a glorious place of beauty until the whole tribulation is over. This belief system opposes and exalts itself against everything Jesus did for us. If we are going to be His disciples, we must follow Him all the way into hell if necessary, to secure His ultimate goal of bringing all things back into Him.

The theory that Jesus is coming back in order to restore all things opposes what He said. In Matthew 17, Jesus is revealed in His transfigured estate. He clearly says He will not come back to the earth until the Spirit of Elijah first comes to restore all things.

> *And Jesus answered and said unto them, Elias truly shall first come, and restore all things.* (Matthew 17:11 KJV)

> *And all things are of God, who hath reconciled us to himself by Jesus Christ, and hath given to us the ministry of reconciliation.* (2 Corinthians 5:18 KJV)

At this very moment in history, the Lord is raising up a corporate spirit of Elijah, *"And he shall go before him in the spirit and power of Elias, to turn the hearts of the fathers to the children, and the disobedient to the wisdom of the just; to make ready a people prepared for the Lord"* (Luke 1:17 KJV).

We are the ones being called by God to restore all things. We have been anxiously looking for His return for generations now, and all the while He has been waiting for us to step up to the plate and become what He is by following His pattern and being conformed to His image.

We are called to be co-workers and co-creators together with Him for the establishment of His Kingdom and His righteousness in all the earth (1 Corinthians 3:9). He has given us the ministry of reconciliation, to reconcile all things back to Him. Only then will He return from the heavens and manifest in the earth, bringing all of the heavens with Him to build the New Jerusalem right here. Then, everything shall be in earth, as it is in Heaven. What a glorious day that will be!

- *He that spared not his own Son, but delivered him up for us all, how shall he not with him also freely give us all things?* (Romans 8:32 KJV)
- *In whom also we have obtained an inheritance, being predestinated according to the purpose of him who worketh all things after the counsel of his own will.* (Ephesians 1:11 KJV)

- *For of him, and through him, and to him, are all things: to whom be glory forever. Amen.* (Romans 11:36 KJV)
- *And he that sat upon the throne said, Behold, I make all things new. And he said unto me, Write: for these words are true and faithful.* (Revelation 21:5)

Jesus is coming again, but not:

1. until we are totally conformed to His image and His nature, (which is love)
2. until we arise and shine (when the transfiguration takes place),
3. until the mystery of God that has been hidden in Christ is revealed (that is Christ in us, the hope of glory),
4. until we learn to respond to all creation groaning (with the frequency of Heaven, which is love.)

Until those things happen, we will still be waiting.

I believe we are living in the greatest hour of human history. We are entering a time of preparation so that we can ultimately be used by God to be the people in the earth who will develop such an intense desire for union with the divine nature, that, when the time comes, we will be totally, completely prepared to be used by Him to bring about the restoration of all things.

- *Who shall change our vile body, that it may be fashioned like unto his glorious body, according to the working whereby he is able even to subdue all things unto himself.* (Philippians 3:21 KJV)
- *For we are his workmanship, created in Christ Jesus unto good works, which God hath before ordained that we should walk in them.* (Ephesians 2:10 KJV)
- *…[P]ut on the new man, which was created according to God, in true righteousness and holiness.* (Ephesians 4:24 NKJV)
- *For by Him were all things created, that are in heaven and that are on earth, visible and invisible, whether thrones, or dominions, or principalities, or powers. All things were created through Him and for Him.* (Colossians 1:16 NKJV)

- *...[P]ut on the new man, which is renewed in knowledge after the image of him that created him.* (Colossians 3:10 KJV)
- *Thou art worthy, O Lord, to receive glory and honor and power: for thou hast created all things, and for thy pleasure they are and were created.* (Revelation 4:11 KJV)

Do we really believe all that?

> *...[H]e prophesied that Jesus would die for the nation, and not for that nation only, but also that He would gather together in one the children of God who were scattered abroad.* (John 11:51–52 NKJV)

God has given us permission to gather those who have been scattered to the uttermost parts of the earth (Deuteronomy 30:4). *"And if anyone hears My words and does not believe, I do not judge him; for I did not come to judge the world but to save the world"* (John 12:47 NKJV). That is quite an interesting statement. In the King James, it reads, *"If any man hears My words and does not believe, I judge him not."* The Word goes on to say that except a man esteems a thing to be unclean, it is not unclean, but once it is revealed to him as being unclean, then there is no covering for it (Romans 14:14, Hebrews 10:26, James 4:17). So, Jesus says out of His own mouth, *"if any man hears My words and does not believe, I do not judge him; for I did not come to judge the world but to save the world"* (John 12:47).

Death Row Testimony

I once ministered to a man on death row. In a heinous crime, he had killed seven people. He was about ready to go to his death when I was sitting there speaking with him. I told him: "If you would confess with your mouth and believe in your heart Jesus is Lord, you will be saved."

He looked right in my face and he said, "Old lady, you have no idea what I have done."

I looked at him and said, "What you have done is probably less than what I have done."

"What do you mean?"

"Well, I believe the Word teaches us that unless a man esteems a thing to be sin it is not sin.[27] Once it is revealed to him as being sin, then there is no covering for that sin. So, basically, I am more guilty than you are. If I sin against my neighbor, if I look at another man with any kind of lust in my eye, I am more sinful than you are because I know it is sin. The thing you did was a crime of passion and you did not recognize it as sin. Therefore, my sin is greater than your sin. The Bible says, '...*For everyone to whom much is given, from him much will be required...*'"

The man broke into profuse weeping. "I have never heard anything like this before." Right there on the spot, he gave his life to Jesus.

It says a man that hears my word and does not believe I judge him not. So, unless a man esteems a thing as sin, it is not accounted to him as sin.

Jesus spoke these words, lifted up His eyes to heaven, and said: *"Father, the hour has come. Glorify Your Son, that Your Son also may glorify You as You have given Him authority over all flesh, that He should give eternal life to as many as You have given Him"* (John 17:1–2 NKJV). How many has He given Him? All flesh, all things that were ever created were commended into Jesus' hands by his Father. So, Jesus says, *"This is the will of the Father who sent Me, that of all He has given Me I should lose nothing but should raise it up at the last day"* (John 6:39 NKJV).

There is a day coming called the second resurrection. I have been a co-participant with God Almighty in the second resurrection and the restoration of all things. Many people come to me and say, "What you are teaching is heresy. What you are teaching is in total opposition to what the Word of the Lord says." I respond that I did not get this out of a book. I got it straight from the mouth of God Almighty Himself and have participated with Him in the restoration of all things. Nobody on this earth can steal this message from me, because

---

[27] See Romans 14:14.

it is the purpose for which I was birthed in the earth, to teach that all things were commended into His hands. Jesus Christ lost nothing.

> *Then he said to them, "You know how unlawful it is for a Jewish man to keep company with or go to one of another nation. But God has shown me that I should not call any man common or unclean."* (Acts 10:28 NKJV)

In 1997, the Lord sent me to the seven mountains of scripture and told me to prophesy to the continents. I thought, "Who am I, Lord, to do something like that?" I was on Mount Sinai, and the word of the Lord was: "The greatest revival in the history of mankind is going to spring straight out of the seats of satan. The corporate son of man is binding the strong man of the earth, so that Christ might restore the world. The places of greatest darkness, deepest wickedness and grossest depravity will become the linchpins of life for global revival to spread and it is going to begin in Islam." God is about to fulfill some promises to the sons of Ishmael.

When that word went out, all hell broke loose against my ministry. Those still in the Age of the Church got so mad at me saying, "How dare you say the greatest revival is going to spring straight out of the seats of satan?" I said, "First, I did not say it. He said it. If you want to argue, go argue with Him."

The Age of the Church asked, "How dare you say that it's going to be the sons of Ishmael? Don't you know sons of Ishmael are the enemies of the church and the Jews?" I said, "I said it because God made covenantal promises to the sons of Ishmael. He said He would bless them. The book of Genesis shows this is the hour of the unfolding of that blessing." (See Genesis 17:20.)

Immediately after, I turned my attention to the places of greatest darkness, deepest wickedness, and grossest depravity. I have been to some of the worst hellholes you could imagine. Wherever I go, I release the light inside of me and those who are in gross, despicable, ugly, hideous evil, and I see them fall on their faces and give their lives to Jesus Christ. Why? It is because the unfolding of His sovereign plan has begun. God showed me I cannot call any man common or unclean.

The purpose of a redemptive prophet is to lead those in darkness to the light. Because I am a redemptive prophet, Acts 17:18-31 is one of my favorite scriptures. In Paul's discourse on Mars Hill, they were having an annual meeting of all the psalmists and philosophers of the empire. Every year the philosophers came together on Mars Hill to discuss the real meaning of man. Paul joined that discussion. Pay close attention to what he said, because it is a key in the restoration of all things.

> ...*I perceive that in all things you are very religious; for as I was passing through and considering the objects of your worship, I even found an altar with this inscription: to the unknown God. Therefore, the One whom you worship without knowing, Him I proclaim to you.... For in Him we live and move and have our being... 'for we are also His offspring.'"* (Acts 17:22-23, 28 NKJV)

After his discourse, they came to Paul and said, "Could you please come and tell us more about this living God?" As a result of being willing to identify with those in deep evil, those who were the idol worshippers of the whole earth, by identifying himself with them, he was in essence saying we are all the sons of the living God. The fruit of Paul's willingness to identify with them and shine God's light was that the entirety of empire gave their lives to the Lord Jesus Christ. All the idols were cast down. The silversmiths and goldsmiths had to shut down their businesses because nobody would buy their idols anymore. The people brought all their idols and burned them in the middle of the stadium because they had now given their lives to the Lord Jesus Christ.

In the Age of the Church, it was uncommon to have friends who were not saved. But Jesus himself identified himself with sinners. That is one of the reasons why the religious structures of his day came against Him. *"And when the Pharisees saw it, they said to His disciples, 'Why does your Teacher eat with tax collectors and sinners?'* (Matthew 9:11). They had no comprehension that Jesus came not to condemn the world but to save the world (John 3:17).

We need to come to the place where we look at those in great levels of darkness. We need to recognize that a woman in Guatemala, ripping the heads off chickens, drinking their blood so she can fall down on the floor in a demonic manifestation is not just somebody "out there," she is part of us. We need to look at her and see her from the eyesight of Jesus. She is eternally and forever, passionately, and unconditionally loved by Him.

CHAPTER 8

Going on to Perfection

I KEEP SAYING IT because I know it is true. We are living in the greatest day ever. I call it the cross-point between the seventh day of God creating the divine nature and the third day of the church. In God's calendar, a thousand years is like one day. There were two thousand years from Adam to Abraham, two thousand years from Abraham to Jesus, and two thousand years since Jesus' earthly ministry. That adds up to six thousand years, or in God's calendar, six days. Near the year 2000, we stepped out of the sixth day into the seventh day, which scripture refers to as the day of transfiguration, the day of perfection, and the day of rest. That is good news for us: we are stepping out of the minimal level of functionality we had in the Age of the Church into a new age: the Age of the Kingdom.

The church is not ending. God passionately loves His church and His church will go on forever. But the manner and the level in which we function has dramatically shifted. Many who have come out of the Age of the Church find the things that used to thrill them now leave them disappointed and frustrated. They think: "There has got to be more." God has given those called out of the sixty-fold into the hundred-fold a divine dissatisfaction. What used to be exciting is no longer tolerable. Those in the hundred-fold are stepping up and out of a ten-percent level of functionality into the measure that God has called and created us to function in, which is the fullness of the measure of the stature of Christ Jesus.

This new age represents the third day of the church. In scripture, the third day stands for ascension and resurrection power. The church is entering a new level of function We are soon going to take back our primordial position and resume God's original intention for us, which was to have dominion over all things.

The Age of Israel functioned under the law. The Age of the Church functioned under grace. The Age of the Kingdom functions under perfection. Therefore, we must reevaluate much of we thought we knew. In this new age, our level of functionality will change us so much that we will not pray the same, preach the same, or prophesy the same. We will not do altar ministry the same. Every new level of authority we are called into requires a shift in our mentality to a much higher level of and capacity for advancing the Kingdom into all of the earth.

We are preparing to take back the primordial position that we had with God in the garden before the fall of man. Scripture says,

> *Now I say that the heir, as long as he is a child, does not differ at all from a slave, though he is master of all, but is under guardians and stewards until the time appointed by the father. Even so we, when we were children, were in bondage under the elements of the world. But when the fullness of the time had come, God sent forth His Son, born of a woman, born under the law, to redeem those who were under the law, that we might receive the adoption as sons. And because you are sons, God has sent forth the Spirit of His Son into your hearts, crying out, 'Abba, Father!' Therefore you are no longer a slave but a son, and if a son, then an heir of God through Christ.* (Galatians 4:1–5 NKJV)

In the Age of the Church, our teachers, tutors and guides came in the form of the five-fold ministry. We needed them then because we were functioning in an immature state. The Word says as long as we function in immaturity, we need those to come teach us. But as we migrate out of the Age of the Church into the Age of the Kingdom, our teachers, tutors and guides become the Seven Spirits before the throne.

For the last two thousand years, the church has operated in the parameters which were set by God to last until an appointed time. He could not yet reveal how much power He had invested in us. If He had, we would have destroyed the earth several times over because our hearts had not yet been truly dealt with by the cross. Jesus alluded to this when He told His disciples: *"I still have many things to say to you, but you cannot bear them now"* (John 16:12 NKJV). Then, when He was preparing them for His departure, He said:

> *Nevertheless I tell you the truth; It is expedient for you that I go away: for if I go not away, the Comforter will not come unto you; but if I depart, I will send him unto you.* (John 16:7 KJV)

For the past two thousand years, the body of Christ has only been functioning in ten percent of the fullness of what God has created us for, evidenced in the way we prayed: "Lord I want…," "Lord I need…," "Lord please give me…." Our prayers were self-centered, directed toward protecting our comfort zones. In the year 2000, we stepped into what Galatians 4:2 calls *the appointed time of the Father*. So, it is time for us to set aside childish things and begin to grow up into the fullness of the measure of the stature of Christ Jesus—which is perfection. It is not about Him giving us good gifts, or supplying all our needs or taking care of all our problems. It's less about what He is going to do for us and more about what we are going to do together in Him. As we go on to perfection, prayer will become less of an activity and more of a state of being.

Dominion in Healing

In a foreign country under heavy jihadist control where merely whispering the name *Jesus Christ* was a crime punishable by death, I won a national leader to the Lord. He gave me permission to do street ministry. Knowing that it was quite possible that I could be killed while holding such meetings, he sent guards to surround me. I want you to hear the principles contained in this story because they lead us in the direction of perfection.

On the first day, we had a small crowd. It was mostly women, children, and a few non-religious, brave curiosity seekers. I say *brave* because the men knew if they showed up to a Christian meeting, they would probably lose their jobs. It was an average type of meeting: We had good praise and worship; we had a nice message; we had an altar call and people came forward and got saved. Some even got healed and delivered. That night the people who gave their lives to Jesus and those who were healed went home to tell their families and friends what happened.

On the second day, the crowd doubled. Again, we had good praise and worship. We had an anointed message. We had a great altar call. More people responded, more people got saved, and more people got healed. But it was still just another average meeting.

On the third day, the entire spiritual atmosphere shifted. A couple of mullahs came in carrying a dead little boy who was stretched out on a board covered by a sheet. They came and threw this little boy down at my feet, turned around and cried in their native language: "The church of Jesus Christ has no power!"

When I looked down at the little boy, something happened. The Lord drew the veil away from my face. Instead of seeing the little boy, I saw my grandson. My grandson was the light of my life.

When I saw him lying there, dead on the floor, I picked him up, embraced him and began to rock back and forth. I made a deep, groaning, crying, screaming sound. It went on for nearly two hours. I completely forgot I was in the middle of a meeting.

I had the ushers take the little boy and stand him up on his feet. I poured a whole quart of water and a whole jar of oil over his head. I slapped him in the face several times, back and forth. I forced his mouth open and I thrust my breath into it. Lo and behold, the Lord raised the little boy from the dead! When that happened, the entire spiritual atmosphere shifted.

The two mullahs who brought him in to prove that the church of Jesus had no power ran to the altar, threw themselves down and gave their lives to Jesus Christ. All of the people jumped up, ran into the streets and began to shout, "Come and see! Come and see! The little boy who was dead is living again!"

People began to flood in from everywhere. Our little meeting of a few hundred turned quickly into thousands. People came because of the word going out about a little boy raised from the dead.

Miracles like that of the little boy being raised from the dead are going to happen as we come into an understanding of what it means for all things to be made one in Christ Jesus. What does the Word say? *"For the earnest expectation of the creation eagerly waits for the revealing of the sons of God… For we know that the whole creation groans and labors with birth pangs together until now"* (Romans 8:19,22 NKJV). All creation is groaning for the manifestation of the Sons of the living God, which we are.

Romans 8:23 says, *"And not only they, but ourselves also, which have the firstfruits of the Spirit, even we ourselves groan within ourselves, waiting for the adoption, to wit, the redemption of our body"* (KJV). Jesus, Himself, groaned at the tomb of Lazarus. The Word says that He groaned three times (see John 11). What was the outcome? It was the redemption of the body.

That night when the dead little boy was thrown at my feet was the first time I experienced the effects of this groaning. We had tapped into dominion in the area of healing. Every person who came to that meeting got healed. When I talk about healing, I'm not talking about healing from a migraine headache or a stomach ulcer. I am talking about healing from catastrophic diseases that disfigure people. One woman had keloids growing out of her neck that looked like the exposed roots of a tree. They fell off on the floor with a thud. There were men who came in who were not just blind but had no eyes. The Lord formed new eyes in their eye sockets, and they left the meeting seeing 20/20.

Many parents rolled in children who were in beds with all kinds of wiring hooked up to them. Their children had been born brain damaged. Many of them had never spoken, walked, talked, or ever been out of their beds since the day they were born. Their muscles were completely atrophied from lack of exercise. But the children were fully healed. They jumped up out of their beds and ran around. Their muscles, previously nearly non-existent, became suddenly fully formed. These children made amazing joyful sounds, because remember, they had never spoken any words.

There was a little girl whom I will never forget. She had been a victim of an attack against the Christian community. In her particular city, there was a section set aside for only Christians. All Christians were relegated to living in that section of the city in order to keep them from proselytizing Muslim believers and winning them to Jesus Christ.

One night, the army in that city fell into a drunken stupor. They surrounded the Christian section, doused it with petrol and set the entire area on fire. That night, 16,000 Christians were burned to death. (It is interesting that we almost never read any articles about tragedies like this in any newspaper.)

The little girl escaped the police cordon and ran to the home of her grandmother. Her elderly grandmother had never been allowed an education. During her youth, it was against the law for women to even attend school. It was also against the law for any Islamic doctor to administer medical assistance to a Christian.

The little girl's body was covered with both blood blisters and water blisters. The poor grandmother had no idea what to do. She took a bed sheet and wrapped the little girl's body so tightly that all the blisters broke. Eventually during her recovery process, the little girl's arms grafted to the sides of her body. Eight of her fingers had been burned all the way down to the first joint. They became necrotic, dried up and fell off.

So, when I saw her, the little girl only had two fingers she could wiggle, and those only a little bit, because her arms were attached to the sides of her body.

The Lord did a supernatural surgery on her. He separated her arms from her body, grew back all of her fingers which had burned off, and He gave her new skin from her chin all the way down to her knees. The manifestation was so profound that the little girl raced around with her hands lifted. She sang, danced and exulted the Lord Jesus Christ. It was a tremendous, moving healing to witness.

When I say we tapped into dominion in the area of healing, you can see what I mean when I say we saw not just normal, everyday miracles. We were witnessing re-creative miracles occurring in the midst of a previously unbelieving people.

Leaving the First Principles Behind

When the meetings were over, I went home exhausted. I dropped down on my bed at the hotel and I began to praise the Lord: "Oh My God, this is so great, this is so wonderful, this is so magnificent! The little boy was raised from the dead. The mullahs gave their lives to the Lord, and every single person that came was healed." I was thinking, "This is the greatest thing ever!"

All of a sudden, I heard laughter from Heaven.

To tell you the truth, when I first heard Him laughing, I was a little bit offended. I thought, "Lord, don't you get it? The little boy was raised from the dead. The mullahs gave their lives to the Lord. Every single person who came got healed."

Again, laughter resounded from the heavens.

Then the Lord thrust me into what I call a living vision. In a living vision, you see yourself as a third person looking down on yourself as part of the vision. In this vision, I was like a three-year-old child. Nearly every little girl wants to dress up to be big like her mom. In my vision, I had on a great big floppy hat complete with a floppy flower. I wore my mother's silky organza dress. There were pearls draped around my neck, make-up all over my face and lipstick smeared everywhere. On my teeny, tiny three-year-old feet were adult-sized six-inch stiletto heels. My ankles wobbled. Trying hard to be so big, I was tripping all over the shoes and dress.

I said to myself: "What does this vision have to do with the little boy being raised from the dead?"

Going On to Perfection

This is the word that the Lord gave me. It is not just a word for me, but a word for you also, because we are one. The Lord quoted verses from Hebrews chapter 6. He said:

> *Therefore, leaving the discussion of the elementary principles of Christ, let us go on to perfection, not laying again the foundation of repentance from dead works and of faith toward God, of the doctrine of baptisms, of laying on of hands, of resurrection of the dead, and of eternal judgment. And this we will do if God permits.* (Hebrews 6:1–3 NKJV)

There is coming a time, and it has now come, when He is requiring of those who have the high calling into the hundred-fold to set aside all of the first principles of the doctrines of Christ. What are those things?

1. *Repentance from dead works*

   Why? Because we are not going to do any more dead works.

2. *Laying on of hands*

   Why? Because we are going to receive ministry directly from His throne. In the Age of the Church, our focus was on ministry being received from those in leadership in the church. But now our viewpoint has to be redirected from the pulpit to the throne.

3. *Resurrection from the dead*

   I do not know about you, but I would think if people are raising the dead, they must be fairly mature in their faith. But the Lord says, "No: resurrection from the dead is child's play!"

4. *Faith toward God*

   "Faith toward God?" I said to myself. "But Lord, Your Word says, '...Without faith it is impossible to please [You]' (Hebrews 11:6). So, how can we set aside faith towards God if without faith, it is impossible to please You?" He asked me, "What is faith?" I responded: "'*Faith is the substance of things hoped for and the evidence of things not seen.*'" So why do you have to hope for the things you have already seen? When we learn how to ascend and descend on a daily basis, there is no limit to what He will allow us to see. He will show us the things that were, the things that are, and the things that are yet to come. Therefore, having already seen it, we will no longer need to *hope* for the substance or the evidence, because we have already seen the substance and the evidence.

5. *The doctrine of eternal judgment*
See Chapter 7, "Restoration," where I address that issue.

Entering the Third Day/Coming Up to Perfection

I refer frequently to the first day, second day, and third day. We are entering the third day of the Church. In the first day of the Age of the Church, we had a little response to the Gospel. In the second day, the response increased by word of mouth coming forth from those whose lives had been affected. But in the third day (the third thousand-year period since Christ), suddenly we are going to begin to function in the area of dominion, which will change the spiritual atmosphere such that huge numbers of people will respond because they will see, at long last, what all creation has been longing for.

The current word of the Father for us is to "set aside the first principles and come up to perfection." In order for us to accomplish this, we must leave this earthly realm, elevate our sight, come up into the heavenly realms and begin to function from the fullness of the level of Christ Jesus and in the authority that we have from Him from the throne. The Word says we are exalted to the right hand of the Father Almighty. We are joint heirs to the Kingdom of Heaven with Jesus Christ. Everything He has is ours through our adoption as sons.

When we leave that which is behind (those things that are childish), and begin to grow up into the fullness of the measure of the stature of Christ Jesus, the Lord says that then He can impute to us the fullness of our inheritance. What is the fullness of our inheritance? Jesus told us it was all rule and all reign. I come to this conclusion based partly on the following verses. Jesus said:

> *All authority has been given to Me in heaven and on earth.* (Matthew 28:18 NKJV)

> *As the Father has sent Me, I also send you.* (John 20:21 NKJV)

If we are joint heirs with Christ (Romans 8:17), and if we can really do everything that He did and more (John 14:12), then we can assume that which the Father gave Him, He now gives us. Therefore, our inheritance is all rule, all reign, all power and all authority. The Word tells us, *"Jesus knew that the Father had given him power over everything [placed everything into his hands] ..."* (John 13:3 EXP). If we are exalted to the right-hand side of God the Father and are joint heirs together with Him, part of our inheritance is all things that have ever been created. Therefore, it is now time for us to put aside all the first principles and the childlike levels of function we participated in during the Age of the Church. Then we can begin to mature, and the Lord can give us the responsibility of performing and perfecting His sovereign design and will in the earth.

How do we go about coming up to perfection? The answer to that is to practice ascending and descending into the Heavenly realms daily. In preparation for that time, we have to get ready. The pattern for getting ready for the overpowering presence of our Lord is found in Exodus.

> *Then the Lord said to Moses, "Go to the people and consecrate them today and tomorrow, and let them wash their clothes. And let them be ready for the third day. For on the third day the Lord will come down upon Mount Sinai in the sight of all the people."* (Exodus 19:10–11 KJV)

To follow that pattern, there are several things we need to shift and rearrange in our own internal kingdom. The Lord says that the Kingdom of God is within us. Therefore, before we can effectively be used by Him to prosper the Kingdom without, we must first deal with the kingdom within.

Take Off Religious Masks

For the first part of our preparation, we must cleanse ourselves. Cleansing requires us to enter into true understanding of the separation of flesh and spirit. We have to take off our religious masks. Our religious masks are so firmly fixed that we have a difficult time giving up the idea of who we think we ought to be in the body of Christ.

When I served as a greeter in our church years ago, I noticed a profound thing. As families would drive into the parking lot, their kids were fighting, punching, pulling one another's hair, and hitting each other. The parents in the front seat were screaming and yelling at one another. They would park their cars, hold one another's hands, and walk up to the front door.

I would reach out my hand and ask, "Hey, how are you doing today?"

Full of smiles, they would say, "Oh, we're blessed and prospering in all things."

As soon as the time came for them to leave church, they would jump into their car, and immediately the kids would start fighting and the adults would start screaming at one another again.

The two different versions of the same families came from this: they had fixed inside of themselves what was needed—at least outwardly—to be seen as acceptable in the realms of the religious. Thus, they would put on a mask to show themselves to be something that they really were not.

In one way or another, we all have masks we wear to protect our self-image. What is interesting is that while we are trying to protect ourselves, God is trying to kill our selves. Our self-life prevents us from entering into the fullness of what He has for us. We have to take off our masks and be who we really are. In the Age of the Kingdom, our talk must become our walk. In order for us to be qualified as those who would establish the Kingdom of God in the earth. the message and the messenger must be the same.

Confront Anger, Bitterness and Resentment

The second part of our preparation is to confront any anger, bitterness or resentment that we might have in our lives. Often, we do not realize we harbor anger. Consider the following example.

A woman I knew came for deliverance. When she sat down, she said, "I feel like my prayers are just bouncing off of the ceiling. It's like God's not even hearing my prayers at all."

"Well, who do you have anger against?"

"Oh, no one of course. I have forgiven everyone from my heart," she replied.

"Really?" I asked. "So, if your ex-husband walked into this deliverance session and sat down right now to pray with us, you wouldn't get a hard knot in the pit of your stomach?"

She flew into a rage. "That S.O.B.? You have no idea what he did to me!"

I thought to myself: "Yes, out of the abundance of the heart, the mouth speaks."

Her response to my first question was a mask that had to be ripped off. We often do not understand that we have to give up our right to be right. We have to give up our right to be angry, bitter or resentful, even if those feelings go back to terrible rejections or betrayals. The truth of the matter is that the one thing—more than any other single thing—preventing people from entering into higher levels of Kingdom mentality, is the triad of anger, bitterness and resentment.

The Word says this about anger: *"Whoever is angry with his brother... shall be in danger of the judgment"* (Matthew 5:22 NKJV). It does not say you can be, or you might be, but *"...You will be turned over to torment"* (Matthew 18:34, emphasis mine). The Word goes on to say, *"But if you withhold forgiveness from others, your Father withholds forgiveness from you"* (Matthew 6:15 TPT).

I don't know about you, but I need His forgiveness. I cannot afford to hang on to bitterness or resentment—not even that which may have come from rejection. The truth of the matter is, the Word says, *"If I regard iniquity in my heart, the Lord will not hear"* (Psalm 66:18 NKJV). That is one reason the Lord tells us,

> *Therefore, if you bring your gift to the altar, and there remember that your brother has something against you, leave your gift there before the altar, and go your way. First be reconciled to your brother, and then come and offer your gift.* (Matthew 5:23–24 NKJV)

As a result of dealing with that issue first, you will gain open access to His throne.

Anger, bitterness and resentment keep us separated from God's fullness. More than witchcraft or homosexuality, anger and bitterness prevent us from entering into the fullness of what God has for us.

The Word says, *"...The flesh lusts against the Spirit, and the Spirit against the flesh; and these are contrary to one another, so that you do not do the things that you wish"* (Galatians 5:17 NKJV). Therefore, we must wholeheartedly *"[cast] down arguments and every high thing that exalts itself against the knowledge of God, [and bring] every thought into captivity to the obedience of Christ"* (2 Corinthians 10:5 NKJV). Scripture also says, *"Assuredly, I say to you, whatever you bind on earth will be bound in heaven, and whatever you loose on earth will be loosed in heaven"* (Matthew 18:18 NKJV). Nothing we do in the realms of the Spirit can be done without making a decision. If we don't make a decision, we cannot get saved. Without a decision, we cannot get filled with the Holy Spirit. It takes a conscious decision on our part. We have to make that decision.

Therefore, we must make a decision to confront anger and loose the peace of God over our lives. God comes to give us peace not as the world gives it. Only He can give us the peace that surpasses all understanding and that keeps our hearts and minds in Christ Jesus.

The same goes for confronting internal rage that brings sin and destruction into our lives. A woman once came to me for deliverance. Her whole life had been lived in torment. She grew up as a migrant farmer. Every night from the day that she was five to the day that she was fifteen, her father turned her out for the male farm workers. Every night she was systematically raped by at least two or three men —every single night. Because of all that she had endured, she had reason to be enraged.

When she was fifteen, she left home and ran off with a man even worse than her father. An alcoholic and a drug addict, he would enter alcoholic fits of rage and brutally beat her. She was hospitalized many times with her nose and cheekbones broken, crushed sinuses, broken clavicles and broken ribs. The abuse went on for most of their life together. One night, in a drunken rage, he came and set the house on fire. Seven of their children were burned to death. If anyone ever had a reason to be enraged, it was her.

When she came for deliverance, I told her, "Today, you have to make a choice. You can hang onto your rage, anger, bitterness, and resentment, and spend the rest of your life in a state of torment. You can continue wrestling with the feelings of loss, or you can make your own determined decision to begin to bind the rage inside of you and loose the love of God towards those who have hurt and wounded you. The Word says that we have the power to remit sin, and that whosoever's sins we remit, they will be remitted; and whosoever's sins we retain, they will be retained. Today you have a choice. You can hang onto rage and spend the rest of your life in misery, or you can make the choice to release love in place of the rage."

That day she made a decision to remit the sins of all of those who had hurt, wounded or abused her. She could not remember the names of the men who had raped her, because she was only five years old when it all began. So I encouraged her, "Let's take our time, because the deliverance will not be complete until we deal with the anger and the rage inside of you." We spent the next three or four hours asking the Holy Spirit to gently bring the faces of those men before her. One by one, she remitted their sins and asked the Lord to forgive them, help them, save them, deliver them, fill them with the Holy Spirit and cause them to stand upright and walk according to the plan of God.

It took several hours, partly because she had to forgive her own father who had put her into such a horrendous situation. She had to make the decision to forgive her husband who had systematically abused her and killed seven of her children. But, when she had finished, she became one of the most sincerely joyful Christians I have ever known.

Only a few months later, her father showed up on her doorstep and with the news that he had cancer. He did not have money, health insurance, or any way to get medical help. So, she opened her door and invited the very man who had turned her over to rape every night for ten years to come into her home. For the rest of his life, she ministered to him.

This is true forgiveness. She showed the unconditional love of God Almighty to the man who abused her for her whole life. Today, totally and absolutely free, she is an instrument of joy and peace, working in one of the most desperate areas in a region in Africa as a missionary to children.

Remove Confusion and Double-Mindedness

The third part of our preparation for ascending and descending into the heavenly realm is to get rid of all confusion and double-mindedness. We have been very double-minded. During the Age of the Church, we were tossed to and fro with every kind of doctrine. We have to reset our mindsets to get rid of confusion, double-mindedness and oppression.

Depression comes whenever we make a volitional decision to hang on to anger, bitterness and rage. Our emotions carry a frequency which makes an impact on every system of our body. One of the reasons so many people are sick stems from their decision to hang onto anger and bitterness.

A woman came down to the office at the church, and she asked if I could pray for her. She had just been diagnosed with cancer. I said, "Of course, honey."

We knelt down to pray at the altar. I began to pray a normal healing prayer, when all of a sudden, the Lord stopped me.

He said, "Tell her if she wants healing from cancer to go home and forgive her husband."

I looked up at her and I asked, "Do you have a problem in your relationship with your husband?"

She became enraged. Her face turned red as she announced, "As a matter of fact, we are in the middle of a very ugly divorce."

I said, "I don't know how to tell you this, but the Lord said if you want healing from cancer, go home and forgive your husband. Then come back and request healing from cancer again and He will respond."

She was so mad she jumped up from the altar and stormed out.

I later approached her and gave her a card. I said, "I am sorry if I offended you, but I cannot do anything if the Holy Spirit doesn't give me permission. Take this card. If you make the decision to forgive your husband, call me back and I will pray for your healing at that time."

About six months later, I got a telephone call at home. The woman had not only forgiven her husband, because she had made the decision to forgive, but she had also reconciled with him. She had chosen to bind her anger and bitterness and loose the love of God over her life. Their marriage had been completely reconciled.

I said, "Okay, then. The Lord said that if you would go home and forgive your husband, He would heal you from cancer. So, in the name of Jesus, receive your healing."

Instantly, the woman was healed of many tumors. They disappeared. The next day, she went to the doctor, and sure enough, she got the confirmation that all her tumors had disappeared. They had no idea how it had happened—but I can tell you that the whole healing hinged upon her forgiving her husband and giving up her anger and bitterness of all the past sins that she felt had been committed against her.

There was once a village in the middle of the jungle where a horrible bloodbath occurred when 6,000 men in that village were decapitated and disemboweled for no other reason than that they were Christians in the middle of an Islamic state. During the massacre, all the women and children had run away in fear to hide in the forest, because they thought they would be next. I was commissioned by the president of that nation to go into the jungle and minister to the wives and the children of the victims.

It took a few days to round them all up and regather them together in the village gathering place. I asked the Lord what to share with them. His response was: "Teach them about the power of forgiveness."

I responded, "Lord, they saw with their own eyes the beheading of their husbands and fathers. The bodies are piled up in mounds right outside the place we are meeting! The children are still so traumatized their eyes are clouded over. The disemboweled bodies are laying all around the *honai*. The land itself cries out for the shedding of their innocent blood… and You want me to tell them about the power of forgiveness?"

There was silence in response. I thought about it more, and I said, "Yes, Lord."

"Then just DO IT!"

For the next few hours, rather than focusing on meeting the needs of the wives and children, I told them about the scriptural principles of forgiveness.

On the second day, we were met again. I saw the face of a man peering into the building from the left side of the back wall. He was the only man there, so I was curious about who he was. I asked him to come to the front. At first, he refused. Finally, my invitation was too hard for him to deny, and he came forward.

The man was the chief of the tribe who had cut the heads off of all the men. When I realized who he was, I told the widows and orphans that the Lord had given us the opportunity to activate and manifest His forgiveness for this man. They went and got a bowl of water and came forward to wash the man's feet. The chief broke down right there and gave his life to the Lord.

After our service to him was done, I directed him to go into the jungle and call his whole tribe to come and visit us in the morning. The following day, the majority of the tribal members came. The widows and orphans held a foot-washing ceremony. To the last man, with much weeping and many tears, all gave their lives to Jesus.

Today, because of the depth of the forgiveness and reconciliation they received, the men who chopped off the heads and mutilated the bodies of the husbands and fathers have now become the chief financial supporters for the widows and orphans whose husbands and fathers they killed. This power of true forgiveness can only come when people are confronted by those who accurately represent the depth of forgiveness that Jesus has for all mankind.

Give Up the Right to be Right

In going onward to perfection, one of the hardest things to do in our hearts is to give up our right to be right. We all want to prove that our position or stance on a particular subject is right. We will go out of our way, even using Scripture, to justify our right to be right. But if we want to go on to perfection, we have to realize that our right to be right is simply not important.

The instant that we are offended, we are already in sin because offense is really self-defense. We are trying to defend ourselves while God is trying to bring us to the point of death to self. Any offense we carry is instantaneously sin in our lives. In order to go on toward perfection, we must violently confront everything inside of us that would oppose or exalt itself against all that is God or godly.

Cast Out Fear

The Word says that perfect love casts out all fear (1 John 4:18), yet I find many Christians who live under deep levels of fear. We must confront fear if we are to go on to perfection.

I once had a business partnership with a woman. She and I would travel quite a bit to do shows in different locations. She had a fear of flying so intense it became phobic in nature. She became practically petrified when she boarded a plane. I had to pray for her all the way up and all the way down on our flights together to help release her from her fear.

We were in New York at a trade show when she got a phone call that she needed to fly home immediately: her father had had a heart attack. Because our booth was already set up, I could not leave and fly with her. When she went to the airport and boarded the plane, she sat down in her seat, petrified. She started to pray deep from within her heart: "Please Lord, please send someone who can pray for me so I won't be afraid to fly."

After a few minutes, a woman with a great big broad hat came and sat down. She took out a black book, sat it on her lap, bowed her head and began to pray. Linda began thanking the Lord for sending someone to pray for her.

She waited and waited for a chance to speak to the woman who was deep in prayer. The plane started to taxi out of the runway when Linda reached over and grabbed her. Linda said, "Excuse me, I don't want to interrupt you, but I want you to know that you are an answer to my prayer. I was asking the Lord to please send someone to pray for me so that I would not be afraid of flying."

The woman turned to her with cold, icy eyes and said, "I'm not a Christian. What a disgusting thought. I am a witch. I have just come from the International Witch's Convention in Salem where we spent forty days praying and fasting for the destruction of American Christian leaders through greed and lust."

Linda looked at her and thought, "Oh my God!" She jumped up, ran down the aisle, locked herself in the bathroom and stayed there the whole time. She explained later, "I can tell you the truth, I did not care if we were going up, if we were flying or if we were coming down. I was so stricken by what that woman said, I could not go back to my seat!"

Not long after Linda told me about her experience, I became grieved in my spirit when I began to see the fall of many, many great men of God who carried huge levels of anointing. Many were powerful in healing. They were powerful evangelists, powerful pastors and teachers. And they fell, one after another, because of greed or lust. Greed and lust have destroyed more Christian leaders—great, anointed men and women of God—more than any other force under the sun. destroy. I want you to understand that you really do not know what is inside of you. The Word says if we judge ourselves, we are going to find ourselves far better off than we really are. So I encourage you to ask the Holy Spirit to begin to reveal the things in you that would prevent you from entering into the fullness God has for you.

A fearful mindset keeps us down, holds us back, and defers and delays the plan of Jesus Christ in our lives. There are many different kinds of fear that will trouble our minds: fear of rejection, fear of betrayal, fear of the words of men, fear of sickness, fear of loneliness, fear of calamity, fear of exposure. These are only a few of the types of fear that plague Christians on a widescale basis.

We have to take authority and confront every arena inside of us that would keep us from entering into the fullness of what God has for us. We must come to a place where we see no evil, hear no evil, and speak no evil.

I laugh every time I dwell upon this, because I think, "If only we could follow that example, we would have already entered into a place of preparation for perfection in ascension." I encourage you to sincerely seek the Holy Spirit and ask Him to reveal everything that has been concealed from you. Ask Him to bring to light every hidden thing of darkness inside of you.

I frequently tell the story of how I tried for years to enter into a third level of anointing. When I was nearly at my breaking point, I asked the Lord what terrible sin I must have for Him to prevent me from progressing. He told me: "Everything that you have done in the past twenty-five years of ministry has been carnally initiated. Ninety percent of all the works that you have done were done with a carnal mindset."

He might as well have taken a sword and run it straight through my heart.

"But Lord," I argued, "Your Word says that a man is known by his fruit. What about all the people who have been saved? What about all the people who have been healed? What about all the people who have received the baptism of the Holy Spirit? What about all the people who have gone through deliverance in my ministry? That is fruit."

"Yes, that is fruit, but what I want you to consider are these questions: What was your internal motivation? Was your motivation a desire to be indispensable to the body of Christ? Was your internal motivation to build your own name or ministry? Was your internal motivation to make people dependent upon you or dependent upon Me?"

This was the word of the Lord for me, and it is the same message for many other people who are trying to get into that third level of anointing.

The Lord began to lay out many things that I did not even know were in me. If you were to look back at my ministry from the outside in, you would say that it was an extremely prosperous ministry, but the Lord put His finger on my internal motivation. Ninety percent of everything that I had done in the previous twenty-five years of ministry was carnally initiated.

I asked, "Okay, what do I need to do to change this?"

He answered, "Until you are prepared to give up your name, give up your reputation, give up your ministry, give up the anointing, gifts and the fruit of the Spirit in pursuit of nothing more than My presence, then you cannot have this level of anointing. You must go through a time of preparation before you can step into it, because you cannot receive it by the laying on of hands of another man. You can only receive it directly from Me."

I share this story with you because I want you to understand that there is a way that *seems* right in the eyes of men, but that way is death. Therefore, we must yield ourselves to the revelation of the Holy Spirit so that we can accurately judge our internal motivation according to the plans of God and not according to our own level of understanding or our own mindsets.

As we prepare to go on to perfection, as we prepare for ascension experience, and as we prepare to stand in the manifest presence of God Almighty and face-to-face with Jesus Christ, we must violently cast down everything inside of us that would oppose or exalt itself against Him or His honor. This is the way of preparation.

A Note on Suffering

If you are going to rule and reign with Jesus, you will also suffer with Him. Our suffering is for our sanctification, but His suffering was for our purification. To be identified with Him in His suffering means we must yield to being rejected, wounded and bruised by others, even by the very ones whom we have given ourselves for.

If you have experienced wounding and bruising from the body of Christ when you dared to step out of infantile functionality and come into the fullness of the measure of the stature of Jesus Christ, I encourage you to press on. As the Word says,

> *Not that I have already attained, or am already perfected; but I press on, that I may lay hold of that for which Christ Jesus has also laid hold of me. Brethren, I do not count myself to have apprehended; but one thing I do, forgetting those things which are behind and reaching forward to those things which are ahead, I press toward the goal for the prize of the upward call of God in Christ Jesus.* (Philippians 3:12–14 NKJV)

Prayer

Father, in the name of Jesus, I thank You that the seed of this word has fallen on good ground and that it will bear fruit and be multiplied as You prepare us to arise to perfection as we set aside the first principles of Christ Jesus. I ask that You reveal every hidden thing of darkness inside of us that we might arise and shine. I ask that Your light may come, and the glory of the Lord rise upon us.

> *Arise, shine; for thy light is come, and the glory of Jehovah is risen upon thee.*
>
> *For, behold, darkness shall cover the earth, and gross darkness the peoples; but Jehovah will arise upon thee, and his glory shall be seen upon thee.*
>
> *And nations shall come to thy light, and kings to the brightness of thy rising.*
>
> *Lift up thine eyes round about, and see: they all gather themselves together, they come to thee; thy sons shall come from far, and thy daughters shall be carried in the arms.*
>
> *Then thou shalt see and be radiant, and thy heart shall thrill and be enlarged; because the abundance of the sea shall be turned unto thee, the wealth of the nations shall come unto thee.* (Isaiah 60:1–5 DARBY)

Why will they come?

- Because we preach a good sermon? No.

- Because we heal the sick? No.
- Because we raise the dead? No.

Why? Because Your light shall be seen upon us!

We promise that when it happens, we will give You all the praise, all the honor and all the blessing. In Jesus' name we pray. Amen!

CHAPTER 9

THE POWER OF UNLIMITED VISION

THE LORD MAKES PROMISES TO US in scripture, and some of these promises come with limitless power. Unlimited vision means we have a limitless capacity to see the things that were, the things that are and the things that are yet to come. With unlimited vision, we can see into the angelic realm, into the earth realm and into the demonic realm. We can see into the past, the present and the future.

The body of Christ has come to a place of leaving behind all childish things. When that which is perfect (Christ) comes, that which is in part passes away. In the Age of the Church we knew in part, we saw in part, and we prophesied in part. But, now in the Age of the Kingdom, when Christ is formed in us, all of the "in part" passes away and everything in our pursuit becomes unlimited. So it is with our vision. In other words, partial knowledge is going to become a thing of the past for those who seek Him with all of their heart, all of their mind, all of their soul and all of their strength. *"Nevertheless when one turns to the Lord, the veil is taken away. Now the Lord is the Spirit; and where the Spirit of the Lord is, there is liberty"* (2 Corinthians 3:16–17 NKJV).

The first time that I read the verse in 1 Corinthians which states, *"For now we see in a mirror, dimly, but then face to face. Now I know in part, but then I shall know just as I also am known"* (1 Corinthians 13:12 NKJV), I thought to myself: "How is it even possible that we could know Jesus as well as He knows us?" He knows everything about us! He knows every thought we have, every word we speak, every deed we do, how many cells are in our body and how many hairs are on our heads. But the Word says in that time, we will know Him as well as He knows us. That is mind-boggling. Now, a lot of times people say, "Well, you cannot think the thoughts of God." I respond, "We did not used to be able to think the thoughts of God, but now we can because the Lord is downloading the technology for that capacity to us in this hour." When we see the glory of the Lord, it changes us from one image to another image and from one glory to another glory, even as by the Spirit of the Lord.

Every time we have an ascension experience, every time we go into the heavens and gaze into the character of Jesus Christ, we are changed. We are changed from one image to another image again and again, going ever higher and higher. Every time we ascend, and every time we gaze into His eyes, we are changed.

He is so multi-faceted and multi-dimensional. Every time we ascend into His presence, He releases into us one more aspect of His multi-dimensional character. After an ascension experience, we can return to the earthly environment and manifest the aspect of His character that He has revealed to us.

One day, I ascended into Heaven and was standing there gazing into the eyes of Jesus. I could see the entire universe inside of His eyes. Suddenly, He grabbed me and turned me around. He drew me into His body, and my eyes were looking out of His eyes. When that happened, everything changed. Nothing looked the same; everything looked radically different. Heavenly reality is so different than we have been taught to think. When we gaze into His glorious eyes, when we feel His breath upon our cheeks, when we hear His whispers in our ears, "the things of earth grow strangely dim."

Unlimited Knowledge

It is God's desire and stated purpose that we have clear and unlimited vision, but also that we should function in unlimited knowledge so that the enemy cannot gain an advantage over us. An example of this is seen when the King of Syria was making war against Israel, but

The Power of Unlimited Vision

every single move was made known to Elisha. The king asked his servants,

> *"Will you not show me which of us is for the King of Israel?"*
>
> *And one of his servants said, "None, my lord, O king; but Elisha, the prophet who is in Israel, tells the king of Israel the words that you speak in your bedroom."* (2 Kings 6:11–12 NKJV)

How did Elisha know the moves that were going to be made before they were made? Elisha had unlimited vision into the activities and plans of the enemy. Do you know we can know exactly what the enemy is doing? When we ascend into the heavens and look down and see into the second realm, we can know where he is going, what he is doing, and what his plans, strategies and directives are.

When we come into that level of unlimited vision and knowledge, the enemy has no authority over us at all. It is interesting that Elisha could know what was being said in the king's bedchamber. That is unlimited knowledge: he knew what the king was planning to do before he did it.

When the king sent his army to catch Elisha, his servant, Gehazi, saw the army and was afraid, but Elisha was totally undisturbed because he had unlimited vision and knowledge. His eyes were opened, and he saw the spiritual forces that were around about. He saw the angelic hosts camped round about him, and that completely alleviated all fear. He looked into the realms of the unseen and saw the number of angels were greater than that of the soldiers on the field. That knowledge came from his measure of unlimited vision. He prayed that Gehazi would have the veil removed from his eyes, so that he could see into the angelic realm. This set him free from fear also (2 Kings 6).

What was the result of his unlimited vision and knowledge? Without fear, and single-handedly, he went down and smote them with blindness. Elisha brought the entire army captive into Samaria. So, we see that when we begin to operate in that level of unlimited vision, the enemy can have no power over us whatsoever.

When we can see into the unseen, we can stand with courage and boldness before any enemy and say—just as Jesus did to Pontius Pilot when asked whether He knew that Pilot had the power of life and death over him—*"You could have no power at all against Me unless it had been given you from above"* (John 19:11 NKJV). Having unlimited vision into and knowledge of unseen mysteries gives us great confidence. In our battles against darkness and our battles within ourselves, unlimited vision and knowledge further releases us from fear. Once we can see and understand the plan of our heavenly Father, we will realize we have absolutely nothing to fear. The words of man, the barriers that would hold us down, delay, or defer the plans and cause of Christ in our life, will no longer have any control over us whatsoever.

In the Age of the Church, we could work according to the gift of prophecy, but the gift of prophecy and the spirit of prophecy are two totally different operations. Jesus, knowing the thoughts of those He faced, asked, "Why are you thinking evil in your hearts?" The thoughts and intentions of their hearts were revealed as clearly if they had been spoken aloud. This is the level of knowledge that the Lord wants to bring us into.

> *And at once some of the scribes said within themselves, "This Man blasphemes!"*
>
> *But Jesus, knowing their thoughts, said, "Why do you think evil in your hearts? For which is easier, to say, 'Your sins are forgiven you,' or to say, 'Arise and walk?'"* (Matthew 9:3–5 NKJV)

In a story with a similar message, in Luke 7:49, we learn *"they that were with [them] at table began to say within themselves, Who is this who forgives also sins?"* (Darby), after Jesus explained to that the woman who anointed his feet with oil was forgiven because she loved much. Jesus answers their questions before their questions were even asked because He had unlimited knowledge. He knew their thoughts; He knew what they were saying within themselves. This is the Spirit of Knowledge: it is not the gift of knowledge nor the word of knowledge. Jesus did not operate by the word of knowledge. The gift operates in the "in part" realm. Jesus operated by the Spirit of Knowledge.

Remember, before the throne are the seven spirits: the Spirit of Wisdom, the Spirit of Knowledge, the Spirit of Understanding, Spirit of Counsel, Spirit of Might, and the Spirit of the Fear of the Lord and the Spirit of the Lord. I used to think that they were just stationed there, but then the Lord showed me that in order for us to gain access to our governmental rulership with Him in His throne, we would have to encounter those specific spirits. We have to learn how to walk in the level that the seven spirits extend to us. When we learn how to walk through them, then we access the power to rule in His throne.

Knowledge which is divinely inspired without measure is in the unlimited realm. This is the realm that God is calling us to right now—the unlimited knowledge realm. So, let this mind be in you which is also in Christ Jesus. You know that we can have the mind of Christ; we can think the thoughts of Christ; we can lay hold of the thoughts of Christ. This is the level that He is calling us to as manifested sons of God, as overcoming victorious sons. He is allowing us to tap into unlimited knowledge because we have the unlimited mind of Christ.

Unlimited Anointing

Jesus had unlimited anointing. He could cast out demons. He could heal the sick. He could raise the dead. He explained it in this way:

> *The Spirit of the Lord is upon Me,*
> *Because He has anointed Me*
> *To preach the gospel to the poor;*
> *He has sent Me to heal the brokenhearted,*
> *To proclaim liberty to the captives*
> *And recovery of sight to the blind,*
> *To set at liberty those who are oppressed;*
> *To proclaim the acceptable year of the Lord.* (Luke 4:18–21 **NKJV**)

We share in that unlimited anointing:

> *But the anointing which you have received from Him abides in you, and you do not need that anyone teach you; but as the same anointing teaches you concerning all things, and is true, and is not a lie, and just as it has taught you, you will abide in Him.* (1 John 2:27 **NKJV**)

UNLIMITED RESOURCES

For years, we have been taught in the Age of the Church that all the wealth of the wicked will soon be poured into the bosom of the righteous (see Proverbs 13:22). We have always assumed that the "wealth of the wicked" would be their money. But may I suggest that this wealth may not be monetary wealth. Perhaps the correct interpretation is that the "wealth of the wicked" is really their immortal souls. Isaiah 45:3 tells us *"And I will give thee the treasures of darkness, and hidden riches of secret places, that thou mayest know that I, the* LORD, *which call thee by thy name, am the God of Israel"* (KJV). Perhaps the "treasures of darkness" refer to the infinitely priceless spirit within them (covered over with darkness though it be), rather than their earthly wealth.

Once we successfully capture the hearts of the wicked, they will give liberally and generously of all they have out of thankfulness for their release from the dark chains of their worldly captivity. I have met and won the hearts of many people of great substance. Once their release is accomplished, they give generously to any good cause that can be proven to be of God. What's more, they do it—unlike the church—with no strings of control attached.

God has proven to me that He is more than capable of heaping unlimited resources upon us when He finds us in submission to His divine design and when He hears the *yes* in our hearts.

UNLIMITED TRANSPORTATION (TELEPORTATION)

Jesus could move from one dimension into another. He could even disappear before the eyes of the people. He teleported and bi-located all the time. *"No one has gone up into heaven, but there is One who came down from heaven, the Son of Man [Himself—whose home is in heaven]"* (John 3:13 AMP). Jesus lived on the earth and in the heavens, both at the same time. If He did it, so can we. Jesus told His disciples:

> *Most assuredly, I say to you, he who believes in Me, the works that I do he will do also; and greater works than these he will do, because I go to My Father. And whatever you ask in My name, that I will do, that the Father may be glorified in the Son.* (John 14:12–13 NKJV)

I have had many teleportation experiences. A favorite teleportation experience of mine occurred when I received an email from an underground home cell pastor in China. She was thanking me for coming to her church, and she declared that all of her people had been totally shifted by my visit there. I had been to China several times, but I had never been to her particular province.

Because there is another woman by the name of Nancy who also ministers in China, I naturally assumed that this pastor had sent the email to me by mistake. I responded to her, thanking her for all of her accolades, but I told her that though I had been to China several times, I had never been to her town before. Perhaps, I wrote, she had mixed me up with the other minister.

Within a few minutes, she sent me back a picture of *me* preaching in her pulpit in a city where I had never knowingly been. Now, I had been travelling in the spirit for many years and I understood that. But my question was, if I had only been there in the spirit, how did she take a picture of my body?

I teach that we frequently travel into the realms of the spirit while our body and our soul are sound asleep in our beds. When our body and our soul—which contains our mind, our will, our emotions, and our memory—go to sleep, our spirit, which does not require sleep, is caught up into the heavens to see the things that were, the things that are, and the things that are yet to be. So, I am quite familiar with the fact that we travel frequently through the spirit realms while our body is in REM sleep. I'd had many experiences of translocation. But the question remained: "How did she take a picture of my spirit?" If it was a true picture, that meant my body had to be there, too, and not just my spirit. I was confused. So, I enquired of the Lord.

He immediately took me back to the day after His resurrection when all the disciples were gathered in a house with all the doors and windows closed. Jesus appeared and walked straight through the walls, which meant that He was there in spirit. But then, He held out his hands and said, "Put your fingers into the nail holes in my hands and thrust your hand into the sword wound in my side," which meant that His body was there, too.

If Jesus did it, that means we can do it too, because He said so in John 14:12. I still don't fully understand how she took a picture of my body in China at the time I was home asleep in bed, but His answer put my heart at rest.

Unlimited transportation is a present reality in my life and in the lives of many other Christians I have met. I once told the Lord it would be much more fun to translocate if only He could find a way for me to take my suitcases and my computer.

Unlimited Authority

Jesus had unlimited authority. The Word says: *"And Jesus came and spoke to them, saying, 'All authority has been given to Me in heaven and on earth'"* (Matthew 28:18 NKJV). Jesus even had authority in the eyes of those outside the household of faith.

> *Now when Jesus had entered Capernaum, a centurion came to Him, pleading with Him, saying, "Lord, my servant is lying at home paralyzed, dreadfully tormented."*
>
> *And Jesus said to him, "I will come and heal him."*
>
> *The centurion answered and said, "Lord, I am not worthy that You should come under my roof. But only speak a word, and my servant will be healed. For I also am a man under authority, having soldiers under me. And I say to this one, 'Go,' and he goes; and to another, 'Come,' and he comes; and to my servant, 'Do this,' and he does it."*
>
> *When Jesus heard it, He marveled, and said to those who followed, "Assuredly, I say to you, I have not found such great faith, not even in Israel! And I say to you that many will come from east and west, and sit down with Abraham, Isaac, and Jacob in the kingdom of heaven."* (Matthew 8:5–11 NKJV)

Jesus does not look at men the same way we do. When we look, we try to determine whether a man is a Christian or not. Jesus can see into the heart and judge the Gentile unbeliever to be more worthy to sit in His courts than many who are of the household of faith.

I have Buddhist and Muslim friends who exhibit much more of the spirit of Christ than many Christians I know. One has built millions of dollars of high-rise apartments for the poverty-stricken and homeless people of his nation. He has built medical schools, nursing schools, computer schools, athletic stadiums, and the largest single hospital facility in his nation. He has done all this without any desire for recognition. Not one award has been given for his generosity. Not one newspaper article has been written regarding the billions of dollars he has given for the relief of human suffering and the betterment of education all over Asia. He does it all with only one aim in mind. His intention is to be a source for the betterment of humanity, to release people all over Asia from the spirit of poverty, to minimize human suffering, and to better educate and train his people to equip them to become better citizens. I wonder how Jesus would judge His heart? Would he be considered a "Good Samaritan?"

Mother Theresa is another example of someone whose heart of compassion for the poor was exemplary. Yet, she was criticized by many Christian magazines for having said: "There are many ways to get to God." She gave tirelessly for the betterment of the poorest people in her nation, without regard to their personal, spiritual beliefs. She thought nothing of holding a dying patient in her own arms for hours as they were crossing over to the other side. She openly embraced the dirtiest, smelliest, sickest, most desperate people, giving her whole life and all of her love to those who could repay her nothing. I wonder how Jesus would have judged her faith?

Jesus has full authority to judge people as He sees fit, whether it meshes with our traditional understanding or not. He created them, and He will ultimately judge them.

> *For by Him all things were created that are in heaven and that are on earth, visible and invisible, whether thrones or dominions or principalities or powers. All things were created through Him and for Him.* (Colossians 1:16 NKJV)

> *Having disarmed principalities and powers, He made a public spectacle of them, triumphing over them in it.* (Colossians 2:15 NKJV)

Jesus openly triumphed over the principalities and powers, because even they were created by Him and for Him. Does that mean that they are ultimately subject to Him?

> *And they were astonished at His teaching, for He taught them as one having authority, and not as the scribes.* (Mark 1:22 NKJV)

> *Then they were all amazed, so that they questioned among themselves, saying, "What is this? What new doctrine is this? For with authority He commands even the unclean spirits, and they obey Him."* (Mark 1:27 NKJV)

Even the demons were subject to Him. Why? Because they were actually created by Him and for Him. He has also given us the same authority: *"And when He had called His twelve disciples to Him, He gave them power over unclean spirits, to cast them out, and to heal all kinds of sickness and all kinds of disease"* (Matthew 10:1 NKJV).

I spent many of my last forty years casting out demons and healing the sick. While I have only gained total dominion in the area of healing once, I believe that increased levels of authority will soon fall upon all the sons of God who have manifested the overcomer life. When the day of our revealing comes, all the earth will recognize and yield to the power granted to us on His behalf.

At one time in my life, I spent several years casting out demons five to six days a week, eight hours a day. During all that time, I only had two people who were not totally delivered. They ultimately turned out to be infiltrators, commissioned by darkness to invade the ranks of believers in order to sap the strength of the saints. They had contracts with Satan signed in their own blood; they had agreed to devote themselves to wearing down believers by invoking their sympathy and causing the saints to spend hour upon hour trying to set them free.

During these deliverance sessions, the demons would leave. But then, after lengthy deliverance sessions, the person who had the demons would go right out and invite demons seven times stronger to re-inhabit them. This made their strength increase. I learned much from these encounters.

One of the women whom we spent weeks of hard labor on had passed herself off as trying to escape her high priestess status in the ranks of the Satanists. Unsanctified mercy led us to spend weeks of time trying to get her free.

One night, I had a dream that she was placing curses under the carpet and carving hexes on the closet walls of the place where she was staying. In my dream, I saw her raising an ax over the heads of the children in that home. After the dream, the Lord led me to contact the FBI to find out whether or not she might be an infiltrator. She was ultimately found to be wanted by the FBI for murder in seven states.

Jesus has given us His authority and His power. But He can only release us to operate in them according to the intensity of our desire for union with Him. If He had shown us from the beginning of our walk just how much power He intended for us to manifest, we would have destroyed the earth many times over. Until our hearts are ultimately dealt with by the cross, until we have totally surrendered our lives in pursuit of His purposes, the measure of rule we are given will still be slightly limited.

Unlimited Dominion

Jesus has dominion forever over all things. He wants us to know that we have that same power.

> *And what is the exceeding greatness of His power toward us who believe, according to the working of His mighty power which He worked in Christ when He raised Him from the dead and seated Him at His right hand in the heavenly places, far above all principality and power and might and dominion, and every name that is named, not only in this age but also in that which is to come.* (Ephesians 1:19–21 NKJV)

We have been seated with Him in heavenly places. Therefore, if we are in Him, and He is in us, we are also seated above all principality, power and dominion.

His desire is that we should recognize the exceeding greatness of His power to us that believe, according to the working of His mighty power. When Jesus said, *"The things I do, you shall do also, and greater things than these shall you do"* (John 14:12), He really meant it. We shall have unlimited dominion even as He had it.

When Jesus said in Matthew 5:48, *"Therefore you shall be perfect, just as your Father in heaven is perfect,"* He really meant that we would be perfect. And not just perfect, but perfect as our Father in heaven is perfect! *"For sin shall not have dominion over you, for you are not under law but under grace"* (Romans 6:14 NKJV). A time is coming when sin will no longer have dominion over us, and we shall be perfect in all our ways. We shall have dominion even as He had dominion.

The time of our perfection is near. We are about to set behind us all the first principles of Christ Jesus. Consider the following verses:

> *I in them, and You in Me; that they may be made perfect in one, and that the world may know that You have sent Me, and have loved them as You have loved Me.* (John 17:23 NKJV)

> *But let patience have its perfect work, that you may be perfect and complete, lacking nothing.* (James 1:4 NKJV)

> *Therefore, leaving the discussion of the elementary principles of Christ, let us go on to perfection, not laying again the foundation of repentance from dead works and of faith toward God, of the doctrine of baptisms, of laying on of hands, of resurrection of the dead, and of eternal judgment. And this we will do if God permits.* (Hebrews 6:1–3 NKJV)

The Lord is beginning to open up our understanding and is elevating our level of functionality in this hour.

This is a current word for those who are called to the overcomer life and the Melchizedek order:

> *For though by this time you ought to be teachers, you need someone to teach you again the first principles of the oracles of God; and you have come to need milk and not solid food. For everyone who partakes only of milk is unskilled in the word of righteousness, for he is a babe. But solid food belongs to those who are of full age, that is, those who by reason of use have their senses exercised to discern both good and evil.* (Hebrews 5:12–14 NKJV)

The Power of Unlimited Vision

Therefore, leaving the discussion of the elementary principles of Christ, let us go on to perfection, not laying again the foundation of repentance from dead works and of faith toward God, of the doctrine of baptisms, of laying on of hands, of resurrection of the dead, and of eternal judgment. And this we will do if God permits. (Hebrews 6:1–3 NKJV)

Resurrection from the dead is in the first principles. It is kindergarten stuff compared to what He wants to do in us. How can we leave behind first principles if our eyes are still on the signs, wonders and miracles? They are important, but they are not the most important thing. Jesus told his own disciples: "If you cannot believe me simply for my namesake, then please at least believe me for the miracles." He said: *"Believe Me that I am in the Father and the Father in Me, or else believe Me for the sake of the works themselves"* (John 14:11 NKJV).

Our first pursuit must always be to develop intimacy with the Divine nature. Miracles will come, but they derive from the level of intimacy that we have with Him and in Him. If we focus on the miracles themselves, we will eventually be led astray, thinking that those miracles were a demonstration of our power, not of His. I must confess, I have never seen such a magnificent manifestation of God's power since the day in 1998 when I saw a little boy raised from the dead. But I do believe with all my heart that it was just intended to be a foretaste of the unlimited dominion we will function in the day of our full revealing as sons of God.

I am nothing more than a forerunner and a catalyst. I am not even my own voice. I am the voice of the One. I don't have one ounce more anointing than you. We all have the same Jesus. What I do have is forty years of experience exercising the gift of God that is in me. *"But solid food belongs to those who are of full age, that is, those who by reason of use have their senses exercised to discern both good and evil"* (Hebrews 5:14 NKJV).

As an oracle of God, the testimonies that I share are not because I want recognition or admiration. These experiences are given to me purely out of the love of God, to encourage you and to prepare you, that one day we will all perform these types of miracles, almost without effort. As we set our sights on developing unity with the Father, all these things that were once rare will become common in our daily lives.

Prayer

Father, I thank you and praise You that you are touching the hearts and minds of Your people. You are changing and rearranging our thought processes and our paradigms. I praise You, Lord that You are changing the structures of our thinking patterns to bring us into unlimited knowledge, unlimited vision, unlimited anointing, unlimited resources, unlimited authority, and unlimited dominion. Lord, I thank You and praise You that You are downloading these from the heavens right now. We give You all honor and glory for all the things You have done, all the things You are doing, and all the things that are yet to come, for You are the God that was, is, and ever shall be all at the same time. In the glorious, strong and mighty name of Jesus we pray. Amen.

LIMITED EDITION - Chapter 10

The New Mystical Move

THE COMING MYSTICAL MOVE OF GOD is a controversial subject that breaks a lot of church-age mindsets. As we move out of the Age of the Church and into the Age of the Kingdom, many former mindsets have to be completely dismantled. If you read things here that you do not understand, take those things and put them on a back shelf. Wait for the Lord's timing for you to be able to operate in and manifest these mystical principles in all of the earth. I promise you they are making their appearance. Many saints are already openly practicing and operating in Kingdom mystical principles.

Part of the secret of the mystery of operating in the mystical is learning to live from the inside out. The kingdom within is a mystical principle few of us have laid hold of. We ascend into the heavens and see all kinds of things in heavenly realms, but the most practical and pressing application of becoming co-workers together with Him for the establishment of His Kingdom is dealing with the kingdom within. Before we establish His Kingdom, we must first appropriately establish the kingdom within. As we do this, we will realize that the further we go within ourselves, the further we evacuate from the control of the creature. In other words, the further inward we go, the closer we get to the Creator.

The revealing of the sons of God is beginning to unfold in the earth. Jesus said, *"Most assuredly, I say to you, he who believes in Me, the works that I do he will do also; and greater works than these he will do, because I go to My Father"* (John 14:12 NKJV). The first time I read that verse, it blew every circuit in my entire mind. I thought to myself, "How is it even conceivable that anybody could do greater things than Jesus did?" I thought He had made a mistake here. Surely He did not mean to say that we are supposed to do *greater* things than He did. But it is in His Word: not only are we going to do the things He did, we are going to do *greater* things than He did. We need to begin to declare this to the heavens as being a state that we are currently migrating into as the corporate body of Christ.

The Word says, *"Beloved, now we are children of God; and it has not yet been revealed what we shall be, but we know that when He is revealed [through ascension], we shall be like Him, for we shall see Him as He is"* (1 John 3:2 NKJV, bracketed addition, mine).

I love that this word was given during the beginning of the laying of the foundations of the Age of the Church. *"It has not yet been revealed what we shall be..."* means there is something that we shall be that has not yet been revealed in the earth. *"As it has been written, 'Eye has not seen, nor ear heard, nor have entered into the heart of man the things which God has prepared for those who love Him'"* (1 Corinthians 2:9 KJV). There is something futuristic that our eyes have not yet seen, and our ears have not yet heard.

I declare to you today that we are entering the Age of the Kingdom when those things that have not yet been seen and heard are suddenly going to be seen and heard. Billions of people who went before us desired to see the things that we are going to see, but they did not see them. They desired to hear the things that we are going to hear, but they did not hear them. Abraham, Enoch, and Moses desired to see them, as did Peter, James, and John. They all desired to see the things that we are going to see, but they did not get to see them. We are going to see them.

Part of our movement, or spiritual progression, means that we are no longer going to be identified by our culture, skin color, gender, religion, nationality, or our parents' DNA. There are things we will longer be identified with just because they are found in our natural

DNA and were given to us according to our birth. In the coming move of God, we are going to be fully identified with the new creation, renewed in the knowledge according to the pattern of the exact image of our Creator.

> ...[We] have put on the new man who is renewed in knowledge according to the image of Him who created him... (Colossians 3:10 NKJV)

> We stand fully identified in the new creation renewed in knowledge according to the pattern of the exact image of our Creator. (Colossians 3:10 MIR)

Jesus came to do a whole lot more than save us from our sins. He came to be the pattern of how we are to walk in holiness, righteousness, perfection, and truth before a perfect God. Some of what the Lord is about to do will shock a whole lot of people. It will stretch them way out of their comfort zones.

God is going will do things in this coming move have never been done before. In Jesus' day, the people said, *"We have seen strange things today"* (Luke 5:26 NKJV). When Jesus showed up on the scene, they saw things that they had never seen before. Yet we are living in a much better day, and we will do even greater things than Jesus did. He taught: *"Most assuredly, I say to you, he who believes in Me, the works that I do he will do also; and greater works than these he will do, because I go to My Father"* (John 14:12 NKJV).

The day when it was possible to take a neutral stance to the supernatural is drawing to an end. We must open our capacity to dream bigger. We must engage our hearts to experience the things of God, not just read about them in the Bible. We must awaken our desire for maximized fulfilment in our own lifetime.

How do we do that? What kind of spiritual migration is that going to demand on our part?

BEING A MYSTIC

Before I answer those questions, I want to explain what it means to be a mystic. In the Age of the Church, God began to release me to preach about the coming mystical move. The accusations that came against me were violent.

I was being accused of teaching "New Age." I have told this story before, but let me share it again. I went to the Father weeping and crying, telling the Lord what they were saying I was teaching New Age. "Am I really teaching New Age?" I asked.

He laughed and said, "Well after all, my darling, it is a new age!"

After that answer, when people came after me with that accusation, I would say, "Oh thank you! It is true that we are entering into an entirely new age."

The second round of accusations was, "Well, you are nothing but a darned mystic."

I would go crying to the Father, "Father, they are saying that I'm nothing but a mystic. Am I really a mystic?"

He laughed. "Well, do you know what a mystic is?"

I said, "I do not know, but I know it is not good." I felt the accusation against me was that I was teaching an Eastern cult religion or something like that.

He said, "Go look up the term mystic."

When I looked it up in *Webster's Expanded Reference Dictionary*, there were multiple definitions of what a mystic is. Only two had anything to do with Eastern cult religions. I adopted one of the first definitions for myself. I'll paraphrase it here: "A mystic is someone who receives supernaturally derived information from unseen sources through communion with the divine nature." I said, "Glory to God! I really *am* a mystic!"

At that time, I had no knowledge or understanding of what a mystic was. I have since learned that Kingdom mystics are those who are co-redeemers with Christ, and their mission is to lead souls to God. While Jesus obtained for us the possibility of our salvation, the work of our conversion and redemption is ongoing. Mystics are the great lovers of God, who offer and give themselves completely to the Lord.

> *I now rejoice in my sufferings for you, and fill up in my flesh what is lacking in the afflictions of Christ, for the sake of His body, which is the church...* (Colossians 1:24 NKJV)

Although mystics are often submerged in a sea of pain and loneliness as willed by God, they are at the same time full of love, joy and happiness; they are totally ravaged by the love of God in joyful union with Jesus.

Bodily Pain

> *Remember the prisoners as if chained with them—those who are mistreated—since you yourselves are in the body also.* (Hebrews 13:3 **NKJV**)

Many old-time mystics experienced deep pains in their bodies as they entered into sympathetic intercession for people who were in bonds.

Once I was called by the Lord to get out of bed in the middle of the night and go pray. I had been up for several nights already praying. I said, "Lord, I am so tired. Can I just pray in the morning?"

He was insistent, "Get up right now!"

Two or three times I belabored the fact that I was really tired and hadn't had any sleep: but His insistence overwhelmed me. I got up and went out into my living room.

In the living room, I knelt down by the side of the sofa and began to pray in a totally new prayer language. As well as I can remember, the words in that prayer language had to do with Miguel, with Belshazzar and with Nieta Melankova.

I thought, "Well that is wonderful the Lord has given me a new prayer language." So, my spirit picked up a little bit. All of a sudden, a pain ripped through my lower body. I grabbed my legs. I started to scream and roll around on the floor.

When I did this, my husband jumped out of bed to see what the matter was. At that time, my husband was not yet saved. Even though he had never heard me pray in tongues, he already thought I was a wild Jesus freak. So, with everything in me I tried to regain what little composure I could gather, and I said to him, "I'm okay, honey. Just go back to bed. I'll be there shortly."

I grabbed a pillow and began to scream into it so that I would not keep him up all night wondering what in Heaven's name was going on.

The pain that ripped through my legs was so bad that I felt like my legs were being crushed. All night long I rolled about on the floor until about half-past four in the morning. Suddenly, the pain lifted. I was unemotional after the whole thing stopped. I thought to myself how it was an interesting thing that happened, I got up, I went to bed and rapidly went to sleep with no more pain in my legs at all.

I had no idea what had been accomplished until several weeks later when I received a letter from a missionary friend of mine with the headline: "Nieta Melankova goes free. Legs healed." I grabbed the article and began to read. A woman in Eastern Europe had been accused of preaching the gospel to the children in a communist country where Christianity was forbidden. She had been incarcerated in several different institutions, but this particular time, they had put her in a sanatorium. But she was well loved by all the people in that nation, and their cry arose for her to be released.

Because of the power she functioned in, she had a positive international reputation as well. People from the United States, from London and all over Europe wrote to that nation demanding she be released. Due to global demand, the authorities felt like they were pushed into a corner and had release her. But to stop her from preaching the gospel, one night they brought her into the middle of the cobblestone courtyard of the sanatorium and ran over her legs with a road grader. Her legs were totally crushed.

They gave her no medical assistance. Her legs became necrotic and gangrenous. On the day of her release, they strapped her into a wheelchair and rolled her out into the cobblestone covered courtyard . When she saw the crowd of people waiting outside of the gates to greet her, her face lit up. She stopped the man pushing her, took off all the belts were holding her in the chair, got up and walked out of the sanatorium. Many of the guards fell down on their faces and gave their life to Jesus, right there, because they knew this was a miracle from God and there was no way she should have been able to walk out of that sanatorium.

There have been many other times I have felt physical pain in my own body only to find out later that the pain was related to somebody receiving a dynamic healing. Isn't this in fact what Jesus endured for us? The Lord said He endured the suffering and the pain in His body for the joy set before Him.

Some of the practices we will discuss as we consider mystical life are dependent upon the depth of your desire to develop radical intimacy with God Himself. Your journey depends upon the level of your devotion to Him. What it can produce is a release from human limitations. Below, I will outline the manifestations and explain some of them briefly.

Manifestations of the Mystical Move

Dreams and Visions

A great increase in revelation comes through dreams and visions. The Word says God speaks to a man in the night while his soul is sound asleep (Job 33:15). The Lord can speak to us so accurately during the middle of the night because our soul, which is the part of us that exalts itself against all that is God or Godly, is asleep. Therefore, at night, the Lord can speak to us directly, spirit to spirit, without argument or interruption from our soul.

Supernatural Knowledge

Supernatural knowledge is that which you have not gained through earthly pursuit, but which comes only from encounters with the Seven Spirits that are before the throne. In the Age of the Church, our teachers, tutors, and guides were the five-fold ministry, but in the Age of the Kingdom, they are the Seven Spirits that are before the throne of God. This mystical knowledge that comes will come through an encounter with the Spirit of Knowledge.

Ascension Prayer

The Global Ascension Network has been put together for people around the world to enter into global ascension. When we practice ascension prayer, we go up into the heavens and see what the Father is doing. This prayer follows the pattern of Jesus, who said,

> ... *Verily, verily, I say unto you, The Son can do nothing of himself, but what he seeth the Father do: for what things soever he doeth, these also doeth the Son likewise.* (John 5:19 KJV)

If Jesus, the Son of God, could do nothing except what He saw the Father doing, how do we think we can accomplish anything of eternal purpose if we cannot see what the Father is doing?

Bi-location and/or Translation

Bilocation is a state of being in which you learn to walk with your feet in two different realms at the same time. Perhaps it is more accurately defined as living in the Spirit realm while walking in the earth without conflict between the two. It can also refer to the concept of *translation*, which refers to being active in two different locations at the same time or being seen in two different places simultaneously.

Mental Telepathy or Cardiognosis

Mental telepathy is emerging as an increasingly familiar Kingdom function. People who are closely connected either by prayer or relationally are beginning to hear the thoughts of the people around them and know exactly what they are thinking. This leads to cardiognosis. In cardiognosis, you have such a close, heart-to-heart connection with people that you can actually know, understand and perceive what they are going through at the same moment they are going through it.

Automatic Writing

In the Age of the Church we were taught that automatic writing was straight from the pit of hell; but the truth of the matter is everything the enemy does is only a slightly twisted counterfeit of its righteous counterpart. The devil cannot create. He can only copy or slightly twist something God Himself has created. Therefore, automatic writing is the same. As we move into the Age of the Kingdom, we must redeem the way that we perceived it in the Age of the Church which was only according to the twisted counterfeit. The way that we are going to do it in the Age of the Kingdom is the righteous real.

STIGMATA

Stigmata, the physical appearance of blood on your body related to Jesus' suffering, are a dramatic manifestation and little spoken of in the Age of the Church (at least in Protestant circles). (I am developing a teaching concerning stigmata which will be available at a future date.)

MEDITATION, OR QUIETISM

Many of the old mystics from the 16th, 17th, and 18th centuries embraced and adopted the practice of meditation, which can be simply defined as silent prayer. In my estimation, silent prayer is the most powerful prayer that we can offer at this time. When we enter the manifest presence of God Almighty, we do not have very much to say. In the Age of the Church, we spent too much time talking and too little time listening.

FLIGHT

Have you ever dreamed that you could fly, and seen yourself flying all night long? Or perhaps you've dreamed of breathing underwater? Actually: we can fly. I remember when I was about two or three years old, and Superman first came out, I thought, "Oh, wouldn't it just be awesome if I could fly?" After my younger sister was born, my mother nursed her on a frequent basis. To entertain myself, I would grab a little tea towel, take two diaper pins to pin that little tea towel to my shoulders, and I would run next door.

There was a vacant lot to the left of our house, and a three-story Presbyterian church on the corner. Every time my mother would pick up my baby sister to nurse her, I would run over to the church, climb up the stairs to the second story balcony, throw my arms out and throw my little, tiny body off of the second story of that church building, truly believing with everything in me that I could fly.

My mother would come with a flyswatter ready to crack me on the backside. She would say, "Get down off of there! You are going to kill yourself! You are going to break your back!"

I would reply, "No, Mom! I can fly. Really, I know that I can fly!"

She would swat my little heinie all the way back home.

The very next day, as soon as she picked up my sister to nurse her, I would grab that little tea towel, the diaper pins and off I would run to the church again. Again, my Mother would chase me down. "What are you doing? You are going to break your leg!"

"Mom, I can fly! I really can fly!"

"No, you cannot. You are going to kill yourself!"

The Lord showed me one time that today I *can* fly because I prophesied over myself that I could really fly. Flight is a reality today and we can do it. Many of you have been doing it all along. Many of you fly at night but do not remember what you have been doing because at night your mind, your will, your emotions and your memory go to sleep. Your spirit, however, never sleeps. Your spirit can fly all over the earth and do all kinds of overcoming, conquering exploits in the invisible realm all while your body is sound asleep.

Governing

In governing, we step into the reality of our sonship, and know our place to govern the universe or the multiverse. People will claim, "That is heresy to say we can do that." My reply is this: Jesus said the things that He did we can do and greater things than He did we can do (John 14:12). We can not only govern our cities, we can govern galaxies, and we can govern the multiverse.

Angelic Encounters

We will have encounters with the angelic, the great cloud of witnesses, and the men in white linen. Ultimately these encounters will lead us into what I call the seventh day transfiguration of the corporate Son of Man.

Other manifestations will include the following:

ECSTASIES AND TRANCES

PRECOGNITION

CONTROLLING THE ELEMENTS

So, you may wonder, if all of these manifestations are going to occur, how do we get to that state? How do we begin to function in it? How do we begin to operate in higher levels of mystical application and manifestations in the earth?

> *By faith Enoch was taken away so that he did not see death, and was not found, because God had taken him; for before he was taken he had this testimony, that he pleased God.* (Hebrews 11:5 NKJV)

By faith Enoch was caught up into the heavens. The whole book of Hebrews is "by faith." We can have encounters with Enoch. I have encountered Enoch many times during the last six-year period. The things that he has downloaded to me during those encounters are so powerful that if I open them up to teach them right now, I would be branded an international heretic. Enoch has much to say about this new age that we are entering into. (I would like to add that I never pursued relationship with him. It was not even on my mind. But he appeared to me one day and that relationship has changed my life forever.)

I have been developing a new teaching, "Walking in the Shoes of Enoch," but every time I get ready to release it, the Lord says, "No: wait. There is something still missing." So, I am waiting, praying and believing that the thing that is missing will one day, in a *suddenly* moment, make its appearance. The day will come when I'll be able to stand up and declare the purposes of the sovereign unfolding of God's divine purposes for all of the earth through the voice of Enoch.

But to everything there is a time and a season. Until the day comes when I gain permission from Yahweh, I must be patient and not succumb to the temptation to release things before their time. Some people pressure me to do so, but if I were to release mysteries out of season, literally every person hearing my voice would internally erupt into fire. Enoch is not one to be tampered with. He is lightning, fire, thunder, and electrically-infused presence all combined. His mysteries cannot be released lightly.

My friend, Justin Abraham, says it this way: "Faith is taking that first step into the heavenly realm, even when you do not see the whole staircase." The mystics are great lovers of God who offer and give of themselves completely to the Lord. *"I now rejoice in my sufferings for you, and fill up in my flesh what is lacking in the afflictions of Christ, for the sake of His body, which is the church…"* (Colossians 1:24 NKJV)

Although mystics sometimes suffer a great deal of pain, they operate in one hundred percent love. Identifying with people in their pain through the joy and happiness set before them as they are consistently and daily ravished by the love of God in joyful union with Jesus Christ.

A mystic pursues union with the divine nature. Do you want to have total complete, unfettered union with the divine nature? We can have it, and it is available today! It comes through the frequency of our ascending and descending experiences. When you ascend into the heavens and stand face to face with Jesus Christ, when you feel His breath on your cheek, when you hear His whispers in your ear, when you can reach out and touch His hair and gaze into His eyes, when you can enter into His body, look out of His eyes and see the earth from His perspective rather than from earth's perspective, I would say that you have begun the journey towards union with the divine nature.

The Bible says, *"Therefore, if anyone is in Christ, he is a new creation; old things have passed away; behold, all things have become new"* (2 Corinthians 5:17 NKJV). The phrase *new creation* literally translated in Hebrew is the word *kainos*.

I have taken this revelation from Justin Abraham's *Beyond Human*.[28] I love Hebrew words and their interpretations which give us a greater

---

[28] Justin Abraham. *Beyond Human: Fully Identified in the New Creation.* Seraph Creative, 2016. The quotations which follow are from Abraham's chapter, "The Kainos Sons." For simplicity, citations are marked (*BH*).

level of understanding and a depth of wisdom. The Hebrew letters themselves are living beings that live in the heavenly realms. Understanding the original Hebrew in scripture will shift, change and rearrange many of your thought patterns. They will be dynamically stretched when you go back to the Hebrew and find out the Hebrew interpretation of a word such as *kainos*.

Kainos, according to *Vine's Bible Dictionary,* means something totally, completely "new as to form or quality, of different nature from what is contrasted as old." It means "unlike anything like that was old." It means "without previous instance; never before known or experienced; unexampled, or unparalleled." (That definition, as Justin Abraham points out, comes from dictionary.com.)

It doesn't mean the reformation of something already in existence. It means unprecedented, totally novel, uncommon, and unheard of, as a definition of an immortal and ever living metamorphosis. I love that statement because it refers to our primordial position as being immortal. We are taking back our primary position, going back to the way we were established and created in the garden, which in its greatest essence means immortality. Our immortality is about ready to swallow up our mortality.

"You have been regenerated (born again) not from a mortal origin (seed, sperm), but from one that is immortal by the ever living and lasting word of God" (1 Peter 1:23 AMPC, qtd. in *BH*). Kainos means then that we have been "seeded by the DNA of God" (see *Beyond Human*). I love that because we have two types of DNA. We have our natural DNA—that which defines what color our eyes are going to be, what color our hair is going to be, or how tall we are going to be.

But we also have the DNA of God. This represents an entirely new type of creation, superseding and eclipsing what has been seen before. It is an order above and beyond earthly life. This goes back all the way to the teaching about the seventh day transfiguration of the corporate son of man. It means a new creation life. Therefore our nationality, our ethnicity, our skin color, our education, and our economic status mean absolutely nothing as we enter into the new kainos reflection of God's spirit, for we are now being totally identified with

Jesus Christ Himself. He is in us, we are in Him. This means being entirely "immersed in the burning layers" (*BH*) in union with the divine nature. *"The exact life of Christ is now repeated in us. We are being co-revealed in the same bliss; we are joined in oneness with him, just as His life reveals you, your life reveals Him"* (qtd. in *BH*, based on Colossians 3:4 MIR).

Kainos means we are now living in a "co-world with Christ" (*BH*), which has to do with bi-location. This co-world that we are living in with Christ is "filled with ever-living saints, numerous angels and indescribable wonders. [It is a] reality of time-bending possibilities and many dimensional planes of existence" (*BH*).

There are multitudes and multitudes of dimensions that we have not even tapped into yet. In fact, in every particular arena of the Kingdom there are three hundred and sixty different dimensions to be excavated by us as we ascend and descend from our position at the right hand of God the Father Almighty. We are infused with supernatural powers—with wisdom, knowledge and a whole lot more.

This creates for us an entirely huge, expansive, unexplored world beyond our wildest dreams. If our dreams could reveal to us how expansive our arena of authority is, it would totally blow our minds.

The good news for us is now as we leave the Age of the Church and enter the Age of the Kingdom is that the glass ceiling under which we have been walking is now being shattered and we are entering into the fullness of our inheritance. The Bible says, *"Since we are co-laboring, we also urge you not to receive God's grace in vain"* (2 Corinthians 6:1 TLV). We are called to be co-workers and co-creators together with Him for the establishment of His Kingdom and His righteousness in all the earth.

If we are called to be co-creators, that means inside each and every one of us there is enough power to create an entire universe. Not because we are powerful but because the One who created it all lives inside of us. We have worlds to explore above and beyond our wildest dreams. We are now co-workers and co-creators together with Him; therefore, everything that Jesus did we can do also. According to John

14:12 we are now entering the age of the "greater things." The greater things are about ready to be unfolded. The Word says,

> *With all wisdom and understanding, he made known to us the mystery of his will according to his good pleasure, which he purposed in Christ.* (Ephesians 1:8–9 NIV)

> *And to make all men see what is the fellowship of the mystery, which from the beginning of the ages has been hid in God, who created all things by Jesus Christ…* (Ephesians 3:9 NKJV)

There is a mystery of God that has been hidden in Christ since the very beginning. I introduced this concept in Chapter 3, "Overcoming." Part of the mystery (and the mystery itself is multifaceted) is that the all-knowing, all seeing, all powerful, almighty God, who is so big, so huge, so magnificent that everything that has been created can live in Him, would fold Himself up so small that He could put Himself inside of us. Much of the mystery that has been hidden, however, is about to be revealed. Our God, who is so big and so huge, who folded Himself up so small and put Himself inside of us, is about ready to unfold. As He begins to unfold, we are going to find ourselves doing exploits above and beyond anything we could imagine in our wildest dreams.

BI-LOCATION: FROM JESUS' PATTERN

Regarding bi-location, let me share how to live in two different realms simultaneously. First I want to call upon the pattern of Jesus who is our forerunner. Jesus was often found in bi-location. He lived from two different realms at the same time. He told Nicodemus,

> *If I have told you earthly things and you do not believe, how then will you believe if I tell you heavenly things? No one has ascended into heaven but He who came down from heaven, that is, the Son of Man who is in heaven.* (John 3:12–13 NKJV)

Because He uses present tense, He is saying: "Not only am I on the earth now, but I am also in Heaven now. The Son of Man who was in the earth was also present in Heaven at the same time. No one has ever gone up to Heaven, but there's one who has come down from Heaven, the Son of Man who dwells in and has His home in Heaven."

Jesus lived on the earth and in Heaven, both at the same time. If Jesus did it, we can do it because He said so (John 14:12). He said, essentially, "I am going in advance, I am opening a door, I am preparing the way for you that wherever I am you may be also." Jesus does not live in time: rather, time lives in Him. Time is an earthly paradigm. In the realms of the spirit, there is no such thing as time, space, or distance. Jesus is not confined to time. If He made room for us to be wherever He is, we can be wherever He is at all times—whether past, present, future; whether in Heaven or whether on earth because He made a way for us to be with Him wherever He is. He said, *"And if I go and prepare a place for you, I will come again and receive you to Myself; that where I am, there you may be also"* (John 14:3 NKJV).

So, following His pattern, note what Jesus says:

> *Most assuredly, I say to you, the Son can do nothing of Himself, but what He sees the Father do; for whatever He does, the Son also does in like manner.* (John 5:19 NKJV)

> *I speak what I have seen with My Father...* (John 8:38 NKJV)

Notice, too, what John says here: *"Jesus spoke these words, lifted up His eyes to heaven, and said: 'Father, the hour has come'"* (John 17:1 NKJV). When John uses the phrases "lifted up His eyes," or "lift up your eyes," he refers to elevated sight. The phrase "lifted up His eyes" literally means Jesus was raised up on high (*epairó*, from *Strong's* G1869, which comes from *airó*, G142, which means to raise, take up, lift) to where God dwells, that is *ouranos* (G3772). Jesus shifted upward in dimension in order to pray. He was in Heaven and on earth at the same time. It was natural for Jesus to shift up dimensions in order to engage the heavenly realms. As a mature son, He had free access there.

"Let us therefore come boldly to the throne of grace, that we may obtain mercy and find grace to help in time of need" (Hebrews 4:16 NKJV): This is not just a poetic statement. It clearly infers we have direct access to the throne. Jesus has given us this access. He says, *"I am the door. If anyone*

enters by Me, he will be saved, and will go in and out and find pasture" (John 10:9 NKJV). The entrance here does not necessarily refer to the day that you were born again. Every day is the day of salvation: that is why the Word says, "This is the day of salvation."

> *...Look up and lift up your heads, because your redemption draws near.* (Luke 21:28 NKJV)

> *For He says, "In an acceptable time I have heard you, And in the day of salvation I have helped you." Behold, now is the accepted time; behold, now is the day of salvation.* (2 Corinthians 6:2 NKJV)

So, every day is the day of salvation. Notice particularly He said those who enter in by Me will go in and out, up and down, and they will find pasture there (John 10:9). This refers to the dynamic of Jesus' life of ascending and descending, going in and out. Jesus says,

> *Father, I want those you gave me to be with me, right where I am, so they can see my glory, the splendor you gave me, having loved me long before there ever was a world.* (John 17:24 MSG)

What Jesus prays here is that we would see Him as He was in the fullness of His glory, the glory He had with the Father before the earth ever was. He was saying, "I want those You gave Me to be with Me wherever I am." That means no matter where He is, whether He is on earth, whether He is in Heaven, whether he is *in* us, whether He is in the past, present, or future, His desire and His petition to the Father is that we should be with Him wherever He is that we might see him in the splendor of His glory. Again we see an allusion to ascension experience.

Jesus has given us access to the throne. The Bible tells us to set our sight on things above and not on things on the earth (Colossians 3:2). That is why we do not look to those things that we see here for they are temporal and they are going to pass away, but rather we look to those things are eternal that will last forever. You died in Him and your life is hidden with Christ in God.

> *If then you were raised with Christ, seek those things which are above, where Christ is, sitting at the right hand of God. Set your mind on things above, not on things on the earth.* (Colossians 3:1–2 NKJV)

For this reason:

> *While we look not at the things which are seen, but at the things which are not seen: for the things which are seen are temporal; but the things which are not seen are eternal.* (2 Corinthians 4:18)

We can both translate or bi-locate. We can go to Heaven now to see Jesus. We don't have to wait until we die to see that glorious realm. We can know the Father's will. We can hear the Father's voice whenever we are in ascension experience. We can do the works of Jesus, and greater works than He did we can do now, because we are entering into the spiritual migration period in which we will begin to manifest as co-workers and co-creators together with Him.

The next thing that I want to discuss is telepathic thought or *cardiognosis* which is heart-to-heart knowledge. *Webster's* definition for telepathy is a communication between people of thoughts, feelings, desires involving mechanisms that cannot be understood in terms of known scientific laws.

You have been practicing telepathic thought already; you just do not think of it in that manner. Have you ever been thinking of somebody that you had not seen in twenty years, wondering where they were and what they are doing, and the very next day you got a telephone call from them or you bumped into them in a grocery store? A lot of that has to do with the low-level function of telepathic thought.

Cardiognosis is the heart-to-heart transfer of communication from one person to another. This is a common event in the lives of people who are quite close in relationship, such as a husband wife for instance. They begin to know one another so well, that they can almost read one another's thoughts and know intuitively what is in their heart.

Tele- means over a distance. *-Pathy* means perception, or empathy. *Cardiognosis* means heart to heart knowledge. Jesus is our pattern here so let's look up some things regarding Jesus in His capacity for telepathic thought.

> *And He (Jesus) was casting out a demon, and it was mute. So it was, when the demon had gone out, that the mute spoke; and the multitudes marveled. But some of them said, "He casts out demons by Beelzebub, the ruler of the demons." Others, testing Him, sought from Him a sign from heaven. But He, knowing their thoughts, said to them: "Every kingdom divided against itself is brought to desolation, and a house divided against a house falls."* (Luke 11:11–17 NKJV)

> *But Jesus knew their thoughts and said to them: "Every kingdom divided against itself is brought to desolation, and every city or house divided against itself will not stand."* (Matthew 12:25 NKJV)

> *And at once some of the scribes said within themselves, "This Man blasphemes!" But Jesus, knowing their thoughts, said, "Why do you think evil in your hearts? For which is easier, to say, 'Your sins are forgiven you,' or to say, 'Arise and walk?'"* (Matthew 9:3–5 NKJV)

Notice it says, "Jesus, knowing their thoughts, said, 'Why do you think evil in your hearts?'" So, He not only knew their thoughts, He knew their hearts. This also has to do with cardiognosis.

> *"But that you may know that the Son of Man has power on earth to forgive sins"—then He said to the paralytic, 'Arise, take up your bed, and go to your house." And he arose and departed to his house. Now when the multitudes saw it, they marveled and glorified God, who had given such power to men."* (Matthew 9:6–8 NKJV)

The word *men* is plural. *Power* was being given to men, not only to Jesus.

"But Jesus did not yet entrust himself to them, because he knew how fickle human hearts can be" (John 2:24 TPT). Therefore, He, by telepathic thought or cardiognosis, refused to entrust Himself to any man because He understood that their hearts and their thoughts were evil. How did He know that? Because he could read the frequencies of their thoughts and the intents of their hearts—He operated in telepathy and cardiognosis. The Word says, *"...I am the one who thoroughly searches the most secret thoughts and the innermost being..."* (Revelation 2:23

TPT). Basically, Jesus is saying, "I know everyone's thoughts and feelings, I examine every motive of a man's heart." In John 2:24, we learn Jesus did not entrust His life to them because He knew them inside and out and knew how untrustworthy they were. He did not need any help in seeing right through them and their thoughts: *"For the Lord searches all hearts and understands all the intent of the thoughts"* (1 Chronicles 28:9 NKJV).

If Jesus did it, we can do it (John 14:12)! In fact, the inner capacity we have for doing this is part of the reason for the prosperity of the prophetic movement in the church today. Prophets have been actively communicating with the people they have been prophesying over by reading the frequencies of their minds and hearts. Yet as the church, we haven't yet realized the power of this principle of entering into oneness of mind and heart with others.

> *The exact life on exhibit in Christ is now repeated in us. We are being co-revealed in the same bliss; we are joined in oneness with him, just as his life reveals you, your life reveals him.* (Colossians 3:4 The Mirror)

We were created to be the reflection of his glory. Do we really believe that? The Bible says that is what we were created for: to be the reflection of His glory. Do we really believe that the things that Jesus did we can do also, and indeed greater things than Jesus did we can do? This is one of the ways that the prophetic operates.

Here are a few examples from my own experience. I was in Jakarta, Indonesia, winding up my stay there. I was getting a little fretful about making my plane because when I am there, my appointments run every half hour, all day, every day, for eighteen hours at a time.

A friend of mine called and she said, "Nancy there's somebody here that you really need to meet before you leave Jakarta."

I said, "Nat, I really need to leave right now or I am going to end up missing my plane."

She pressed on: "He is a very important government official. He is a descendant of Sukarno, who was the founder of our nation. I feel like it is really critical, or I would not even ask you."

She brought him to the place where I was closing up my other appointments. When he and his business partner came in, the word of the Lord that came out over him was that he was going to be raised up and used by God in Myanmar to shift, change and rearrange the educational structures in the whole of the nation.

The word went on to say that he had had a problem in his relationship with his father. When he was growing up, his father was quite a harsh man. As long as he performed according to his father's desires, he felt embraced and accepted. But when he did not perform according to his father's desires, he felt the sting of rejection like a whip coming out of his father's mouth. When I said that, he fell over on the table and began to weep.

Immediately after I was done with that prophetic word, I jumped in the car and ran to the airport headed for Singapore. I made it just in time to catch my plane before the door closed.

In Singapore that evening, I got a telephone call from the same girl again.

She said, "Nancy, I do not know if you knew this or not, but he and his business partner were headed to Myanmar to go and impact on their educational systems."

I said, "Well I didn't have any idea, but of course God knew what His plan was for him."

She then said, "He wants to fly to Singapore before he leaves for Myanmar tomorrow. Would you be able to see him in Singapore?"

"Nat, I do not have time. Honestly, my appointments are stacked up back-to-back already in Singapore."

"Well, if he would be willing to fly there just for five minutes, could you squeeze out five minutes?"

"Well… okay. Just bring him and I will try and squeeze him in between two appointments."

She came and brought this young, high-level government official to the room where I was ministering. He had been mightily impacted by the prophetic word. While he was there, I led him to the Lord Jesus Christ.

(Prophetic words, by the way, are one of the strongest instruments for evangelism—especially amongst Muslims. If you go to a Muslim leader and quote scripture, a concrete wall will be drawn down between you and him. But if you can take his hand and tell him what the word, the way, and the will of the Lord is for his life, it is like his heart will suddenly melt. I have won many Islamic leaders to the Lord through that very prophetic evangelistic path.)

I did not have any time to talk with him about all his salvation meant, but I saw question marks floating all around his head as if they were in a great big huge bubble. I told the man, "I see that you have many questions."

He came from a generations' long line of leaders. To be Hajj teachers means that they actually went to the Middle East to study Arabic so that they could teach from the Quran directly.

His family was strongly Islamic, and he had all these questions floating around his head. So, I repeated, "I see that you have many questions you want to ask. Unfortunately, I don't have time to answer them now. All I can tell you is if you have any questions, Jesus is the answer to every question you can ask. If you have a question, you just ask Jesus and He will give you the answers." I only had maybe five to ten minutes with this young man.

The following week I went back through Jakarta once again and he met me at the airport. He said: "I want to show you what God has done." He had a Samsung Note that he had just bought and as soon as he left Singapore, he had begun to write down all of his questions. Before he could even put the question mark on the questions, the answers came. He wrote down all the answers. He had page after page of questions he had asked Jesus. Every one of them was answered, one hundred percent of the time, in scripture, though he had never read the Bible before.

Telepathic Experience

I was in a heavily jihadist-controlled area. The church there was very small because the persecution Christians faced was extreme. Many of the believers had had their family members beheaded; many of the churches had been burned down. Christians frequently had their cars bombed. We were meeting in a small room in a motel when in ran a man wildly swinging a machete. Several men followed along behind.

When he entered that room, it was like the breath got sucked out of it. Everybody drew in their breath with a gasp. Many had lost family members to the violence of this one particular man. He ran down the aisle, wagging his machete wildly in the air. He was coming down to cut my head off, shouting: "Kill the American infidel!"

The Lord told me to spin round immediately and begin to prophecy over him.

I looked right at him and I said, "Sir, I am so thankful that you are here today! You think that you came in here to do damage to all of these people, but actually you are here by invitation of God almighty, the creator and maker of the whole universe. He has invited you here today because He wants to speak to you spirit to spirit and person to person."

The man stopped dead in his tracks. He turned and told all of his men: "STOP!"

He then turned around to me.

I, caught up into the heavens to see the things that were, the things that are, and the things that were yet to come, began to read what was in his mind. I said, "I see that you are a very spiritual man. You have been looking for God all of your life. You simply have not found him yet. The Lord is showing me that when you were about eight years old you investigated the possibility that Jesus Christ might be the Son of God, but you denied Jesus Christ as being the Son of God, because if you accepted Him as being the Son of God, then you must also accept the Father.

"In your vocabulary, the word *father* is a dirty word because your father and your uncles sexually abused you when you were a young boy. When you left your home to escape their violence, your father took all of your legal inheritance as the firstborn, divided it up amongst your seven brothers and left you without a single cent. The Lord is showing me that to this day there is an open, gaping, bloody wound in your heart because of the word *father*.

"But I tell you today, you have another Father in heaven, who loves you totally, completely, and absolutely, in spite of all the things you have done, and He wants to invite you today to hear His heart for your people."[29]

With that, the man fell over on the floor and began crying. He stopped the meeting, motioning all of his men to come to the front. The funny thing was that the people hosting the meeting, assuming I was going to do altar ministry, had left a huge open area in the front of the room. So, all of these Islamic jihadists came down and sat down next to their leader and for the next four and a half hours the Lord told me to teach them about the restoration of the Islamic people.

I taught as the Lord commanded me. For four and a half hours this young man and all of his little army sat there with their mouths open, listening, hardly able to believe what it was that they were hearing. One of the pastors who was there had a video camera. He videoed one man's face and it seemed he did not even blink an eyelash for over four and a half hours.

Afterwards, the man came up to me and said, "Lady, you probably do not know who I am."

I sort of giggled in my heart and I thought, "Well, I bet I could take a good guess at it."

He said, "I am the head of all of the pasantrans in this nation."

A *pasantran* is a place where they teach Islamic Jihad terrorism. In this land, pasantrans are formed to teach and train kindergarten children how to strap bombs on themselves and go into restaurants and schools and blow people up. I actually had video of the second graders taking apart and putting together M16 rifles blindfolded. So,

---

[29] This is an example of seeing into the past, the present, and the future of all things relating to this man's life.

when I say they are Jihad terroristic minded I mean it. Many jihadists in the Middle East send their children to school there to learn jihadist principles.

He continued, "Do you think that it would be at all possible for you to come to the pasantran tomorrow and teach what you have been teaching here?"

I just laughed. If you had any idea how absolutely impossible such an invitation was, you would be in total amazement. I am five things they hate: (1) I am an American; (2) I am Caucasian; (3) I am Christian; (4) I am a woman; (5) I'm a female prophet.

Such an invitation should have been a cultural impossibility. But, the Word says whatever door God opens, no man can shut (see Isaiah 22:22 and Revelation 3:8). So, when he asked me to come to the pasantran, I said, "I do not even need to pray about that. I will be there tomorrow morning."

The next day this man, whom I found out later had cut the heads off five hundred Christians and burned down six hundred churches, that same man on that day gave his life to Jesus Christ. Because he was then "born in Zion," inside of the next three and a half years, he made a million and a half converts straight out of Jihad terrorism.

When the Lord speaks to us about us exhibiting the mystical, supernatural moving of the Spirit in order to win people, He means it.

I went to a strategic planning meeting for the upcoming presidential election while we were in Jakarta. We had been meeting all morning and there was a team of young men that were going to come to it, but they had heard that I was a Christian and that the people who were hosting this meeting were also Christians, they really did not want to come. Amongst the five of them, one was Buddhist, one was Confucian, one was an atheist, one was a gnostic, and there was a lukewarm denominational Christian.

They were talking about the fact that if they came to this meeting, this crazy Christian woman would probably throw them down on the ground and hold them down until they finally came up speaking in tongues. But then it was really funny: they called the head of the household and said, "We have been driving out here for an hour and a half and we cannot find your home, so I guess we are not going to be able to make it to the meeting."

About that time, the hired driver of that household opened up the gate and there they were, sitting right in front of her house making that telephone call. So, the driver motioned them to come in. They were sitting in the car almost sweating, thinking they were going to have to go meet with all of these Christians. One of them said, "Well, we don't have to worry too much because we know this strong Muslim leader will be in the meeting, so it can't get too crazy."

What they did not know was I had already led that strong Muslim leader to Jesus. He was filled with the Holy Spirit, following God and seeking radical union with the Divine Nature.

They walked in the door carrying their briefcases. I said, "I do not know who you are, but before you sit down at this table I would just like the opportunity to pray with you."

They looked at one another and rolled their eyes like, "Oh my. Here we go. She is going to throw us down on the ground and make us speak in tongues."

I invited them to sit across the table from where we were. I went and laid hands on each one of their backs. The word of God that came out of me was mind boggling.

These five had such an imperative destiny from the Lord that I could go on for a solid hour telling you what the Lord said, but I want to get back to the telepathic part of what happened. By the time I got done, they were all down on the floor weeping and giving their lives to Jesus. I was reading their thoughts telepathically and I said, "You are thinking right now that this woman made all of this up. That none of this could possibly be real. It is too big, it is too huge! There is no way that it could ever happen. So the Lord says: 'To prove to you that this is not her speaking, but this is Me (The Lord), I am going to cause you to win an international award that would be theoretically impossible for you to win except by My hand and by My favor.'"

By the time they got up off the floor they were amazed. The whole spiritual atmosphere of the room shifted. They opened up their briefcases to show us what they had done to publicize the one who was running for president, and it was an amazing technology that they had put together.

About two months after that, I was at home one day and I got a video call from the five men. They said, "You are never going to believe what happened."

"What?"

"We just qualified for the I-40 award to be held in London."

The I-40 award is an internationally recognized award given to the most innovative businesses for the year. About 2,800 businesses apply for it and it's narrowed all the way down to the forty most innovative.

I think they said it took Google about fifteen years to get on the I-40 list and it took Facebook about ten years to get on that I-40 list. Every person on that I-40 list was already a multinational, multi-millionaire dollar conglomerate and here were these five young men starting out with a new business, still trying to figure out how to even write their own paychecks, receiving the I-40 award at the Stock Exchange in London.

When the leader of the group got up to receive the reward, they asked him if there was anything that he would like to say. Being only a couple of months in the Lord, he said, "Yes, I want to start off by saying we would not be here were it not for the favor of God Almighty, the creator and maker of the whole universe. Without Him, this award would have been totally impossible!"

Of course, I broke down right in the middle of the stock exchange and started crying. I thought, "How many Christians would get up on national television in an event like that and give all the credit for everything that they had received to God Almighty?"

There are many things that the Lord is doing to bring telepathy to the forefront. It is much stronger in fact when you are in deep states of union with people. In the heavenly realms, our thoughts speak louder than our words. We communicate in colors, in frequency, in sound, and in high-speed beams of living colors—like spiritual fiber optics.[30]

An example of telepathic communication comes from my middle daughter, Jennifer. She has experienced telepathic thought communication with angelic beings. When she was about eight years old and we had a very good friend, Brian, who was a college student. I used to be a college minister at Texas A&M, and the students would come to our house on a regular basis.

Brian had a brother who had cancer. We had been praying for his brother for quite some time, and my younger daughter Jennifer got a word from the Lord that this was not a sickness unto death. She was very excited to tell Brian not to worry his brother was not going to die.

Near Christmas time, we were having an Advent celebration. Brian came to the house and he asked if he could do the scripture reading for our celebration. We handed him the Bible and he read 1 Corinthians 15, which addresses the fact that we have a celestial body and we have a terrestrial body, but the glory of one is not the glory of the other. He then proceeded to tell everybody, "I have some really good news! My brother Chris died today, and he no longer has the natural body but the celestial body."

With that, my daughter Jennifer jumped up, ran to her bedroom, slammed the door and fell on her bed, weeping and crying. We were trying to get her to open her door. She did not want to talk to anybody. When we finally coerced her to come and open up the door, I told her, "Honey, Chris is out of pain and it is actually a good thing."

She said, "But Mom, God told me this was not a sickness unto death!" She couldn't understand because when she received a word from God, it was always on target.

---

[30] Recently, I launched the Global Ascension Network. In order for us to host as many people as we are going to have, we are required by the online network to have fiber optics. When they were installing the fiber optics, I saw all kinds of heavenly principles involving fiber optics.

After Brian left that night, I was tucking Jennifer into bed saying her evening prayers. She looked up at me so intently and she asked, "Mom, God cannot lie right?"

I said, "Right."

"Well I *know* that God told me that this was not a sickness unto death. So, if He cannot lie what we need to pray tonight is that He would show me how He kept His promise."

I thought that was quite a wise prayer for such a young girl, so I prayed that prayer with her.

The next morning, she came running into my bedroom. She said, "Sit down! I want to tell you what happened in my room last night."

I sat on the bed and asked, "What happened?"

She patted my hand. "Now Mom, do not be afraid. Everything is going to be alright."

"Well, what happened?"

She said, "Last night after we said our prayers and we went to bed, I woke up about three o'clock in the morning and she said my whole room was flooded with angelic beings. They were so beautiful," and she said, "by the way they do not look anything like what we think they look. They do not have harps and wings and all that stuff".

I said, "Really? Well how do they look then?"

"It is like they are made of light and you can see straight through their bodies. They have these big silver heads and they do not have ears and eyes and all that. They do not have lips and mouths, but they can talk to you and you can understand what it is that they are saying."

I said, "Is that right?"

She kept on: "They were so brilliant, and so bright! They were singing the most beautiful music I have ever heard in my whole life. I kind of held my pillow up over my face because they were too bright to look at. All of a sudden one that was radically different than the others came over and nudged up against me. He leaned over, and he whispered in my ear.

"Mom, it was Chris."

I said, "It was Chris? Really?"

She replied, "He said in a way not in words" (telepathically) "that God had sent him back here to show me that indeed the Father had kept His promise that he had not died. He was not only alive but probably more alive than he was when he was here in the earth."

So, we can have angelic telepathic messages being sent to us. I think about how many times my children taught me lessons about what a lack of faith I had. Jesus pointed out how children can teach us when the disciples asked if He heard what children were saying: *"Out of the mouth of babes and nursing infants You have perfected praise"* (Matthew 21:6 NKJV). My children had so much faith that many times they would pray the most ridiculous, impossible things, and yet the very next day, it would happen exactly like they prayed it.

Many were the times that I left their rooms trying to figure out how to tell them that God does not always answer our prayers the way that we expect. Sure enough, often the very next day, their prayers would be answered exactly as they had prayed them. It was a constant source of conviction for me—that their simple, child-like faith could produce answers that I thought to be impossible.

Paul wrote: *"Fulfill my joy by being like-minded, having the same love, being of one accord, of one mind"* (Philippians 2:2 NKJV). Once we understand the principles of how to be one with one another we can have the same mind, the same thoughts, the same thought patterns as someone that we are very close to.

> *Finally, brethren, farewell. Become complete. Be of good comfort, be of one mind, live in peace; and the God of love and peace will be with you. Greet one another with a holy kiss. All the saints greet you. The grace of the Lord Jesus Christ, and the love of God, and the communion of the Holy Spirit be with you all.* (2 Corinthians 13:11–14 NKJV)

The Holy Spirit only has one mind, so functioning in the mystical manifestation of telepathic thought should come as no surprise. *"So we, who are many, are [nevertheless just] one body in Christ, and individually [we are] parts one of another [mutually dependent on each other]" (Romans 12:5 AMP).* This verse says each one of us is joined with one another and we become together what we could not be alone. I mention these verses because I want you to understand that when we become one, that is functioning in a unity of spirit of oneness of mind and we can actually think one another's thoughts.

The future, especially as we become co-workers and co-creators together with Him for the establishment of the Kingdom of God, is going to be totally defined by oneness. That means including, but not being limited to, oneness of mind and oneness of thought. That means communications will go from mind to mind because the communications that happened in our thought processes are transmitted through frequency.

Precognition

Another manifestation of mystical life is precognition, the ability to see into future events. The movie *Minority Report* is about a group of people called "precogs." Precogs are able to tell the future and were used to solve crimes or prevent crimes from ever happening. The precogs receive information in advance of crimes that are going to be committed. Their thoughts are communicated via a holographic machine. It tracks the frequencies of their thoughts and police are disseminated to stop crimes before they occur. Thus, the authorities can prevent murder and other major crimes. It is interesting to me how frequently movies reflect the manifestation of mystical ways above and beyond what you would ever hear talked about from a church pulpit.

Precognition is only one aspect of our capacity for completely unlimited vision, of seeing the things that were, the things that are, and the things that are yet to come. When John wrote Revelation, he saw not only those things that were, but those things that are, and those things that are yet to come. Though you may not have used the specific terminology before, many of you have been functioning in precognition since the time you came to earth.

The Word says God speaks to man in the night while his soul is sound asleep. When your body and your soul go sound asleep, your spirit never sleeps. Your spirit is caught up into the heavens to do great exploits from Him and is thrust into a place where, in the spirit, you can see the things that were, the things that are, and the things that are yet to come. We have been operating minimally in precognition, but we have not known how to describe what has happened to us when we come back down.

This manifests in our daily lives when all of a sudden one day we enter into a conversation with people that we have never met before and we have this overwhelming sensation inside that we have been involved in this exact same conversation before. In fact, we know exactly what each person is going to say and when. We know the doorbell is going to ring, the dog is going to bark, the baby is going to cry, and it all happens exactly as we know it should. But our soul, that part of us that exalts itself against all that is God or godly, sits right up in our body and says: "You foolish person. You can't have been in this conversation before, you just met these people today!" Then because we did not understand what just happened, we put the occurrence on a back shelf and we say, "Oh, that was a déjà vu!"

In actuality, what happened was one night, your body and your soul (your mind, your will, your emotions, and your memory) went to sleep. Your spirit, though, was caught up into the heavens, and it was thrust forward to see the things that were yet afar off. Only on that particular day the thing that you saw that was yet afar off was downloaded into earth's present, and your spirit picked remembered it. This is how precognition works.

> ...*We do not look at the things which are seen, but at the things which are not seen. For the things which are seen are temporary, but the things which are not seen are eternal.* (2 Corinthians 4:18 **NKJV**)

There are many scriptural proofs concerning precognition. One appears in this passage:

> *Therefore the heart of the king of Syria was greatly troubled by this thing; and he called his servants and said to them, "Will you not show me which*

of us is for the king of Israel? And one of his servants said, "None, my lord, O king; but Elisha, the prophet who is in Israel, tells the king of Israel the words that you speak in your bedroom." (2 Kings 6:11–12 NKJV)

It said Elisha knew the plans of the king of Syria before he actually invaded Israel. The king thought there was a spy in the land, but his servant said, "No, my king. Elisha the prophet who is in Israel tells the king of Israel the words that you are actually speaking in your bedroom." So, he knew the plans of the king of Syria before Israel was ever even invaded. His spirit was caught up in the night and carried away to the bedroom of the King of Syria, where he heard his plans spoken in the future.

The thing that was once rare is now going to become common. Where before we may have recognized occasionally that we experienced precognition, it is now going to become a way of life. What was once reserved for the single prophet is now going to be common for the whole body.

This is part of the purpose of the five-fold. In the Age of the Church, we thought that the five-fold ministry was called by God to do the work of the ministry, but the Word of God does not say that. It says the apostle, prophet, pastor, teacher, and evangelist are called by God to equip and perfect the saints for the work of the ministry. Therefore, my job is to work myself out of a job. If I can equip and perfect you in the prophetic and in the art of ascending and descending, you will no longer need me. Hallelujah!

The new mystical move of God will bring us into higher levels of consciousness than we have previously experienced. Our activities will include, but not be limited to the following:

- Total devotion to God
- Release from human limitations
- Dreams and visions
- Ecstasies and trances

- Precognition
- Supernatural knowledge
- Ascension prayer
- Groaning
- Bilocation and/or translation
- Mental telepathy or cardiognosis
- Automatic writing
- Stigmata
- Meditation/quietism
- Flight
- Governing the universe or the multiverses
- Governing galaxies
- Governing cities
- Controlling the weather
- Angelic encounters
- Engagements with heavenly creatures
- Encounters with the great cloud of witnesses
- *Ultimate* transfiguration

Many of the manifestations not covered here are covered in detail in other chapters, and I will cover more in future teachings.

The Lord is increasing our levels of functionality in direct proportion to the intensity and depth of our desire to know Him in a higher, deeper, wider, broader way than we have ever conceived possible. He wants this increased intensity of relationship even more than we do. He has been longing for it for all eternity, and now, at long last, a sufficient part of the body is arising to seek that radical intimacy with the Divine Nature that will become our pathway to procuring it.

LIMITED EDITION - Chapter II

The Order of Melchizedek

WE ARE HEADED into the restoration of the Order of Melchizedek. What is the Order of Melchizedek? What does it look like? How does it function? The Order of Melchizedek functions at a completely different level of government than we have seen or experienced in the church age.

Prior to being introduced to Melchizedek, I was a deliverance minister. For six days a week, every week, for twelve to fourteen years, I had people flying in from all over the United States to see me for deliverance. For six days a week from eight in the morning till six at night, all I did was cast out devils. So, I knew the devils and they knew me. They didn't like me very much!

During that time, I met and ministered to people coming out of the occult. One was a young man who was part of a satanic order called the Urania Group, many of whose members formed part of something called the Satanic Order of Melchizedek. In his previous life, the young man had made blood covenants with darkness through eating human organs and drinking human blood. But I had led him through a genuine salvation experience. I knew that he had been saved and had received the baptism of the Holy Spirit. I loved him. He was like a son to me, and he loved me a whole lot, too. Although there are demonic tongues, he was full of the Holy Spirit and spoke in the tongues of the Holy Spirit. Still, there was something contractually inside of him that was disturbing him.

One day he came to me and said that he needed to address the issue. Before I ever walked someone through deliverance, I would share potential situations that could occur and explain how I liked to handle them. I would say, "When I lay hands on you, things are going to begin happening in your body. You may feel like you are going to scream or curse, cry, belch or throw up. You may even slither across the floor like a serpent. I've seen a perfectly put-together woman in a velvet three-piece suit, dripping with gold jewelry, get down on all fours, run around my living room like a dog, lift up her leg and pee in the corner of my living room. I've seen people turn into banshees and werewolves. Whatever it is that you feel like you need to do, I want you to do it. There is nothing you can do that I have not already seen. Trust me, I have seen it all!"

Many will say that is not good advice. They suggest I tell the person who needs deliverance to command the demons to come out quietly without making a sound. While it's true that Jesus told demons to be quiet and come out of a man, the demons threw the man down on the ground and ripped him apart. So, if Jesus had that level of response, we should be prepared for the people we lead through deliverance to respond in like manner. There is something about a person's testimony that changes when demonic forces leave and they see it with their own eyes. I want people being delivered to leave *knowing* that their deliverance was real. When they know it's real, their future testimony intensifies.

I proceeded to tell the young man, "Do whatever you feel like your body needs to do. The first voice you will hear when I lay hands on you is going to tell you, 'Better be careful or you are going to kill this lady. You are going to overcome her and overpower her.'" I told him not to listen to that voice. He could not kill me because it was not me that he would be wrestling with: it was the Holy Spirit. I told him not to worry about what he would look like or what he would say. I had seen it all at one time at one time or another. Little did I know that I would soon have to eat those words.

I laid hands on his shoulders. When I began to pray, the Holy Spirit took over. My voice switched and shifted into huge levels of authority.

Suddenly, the young man's whole countenance changed. His facial features pulled back and he began to look like a wolf. He got down and put his nose right on the end of my nose. He said: "Lady, you do not have any idea who you are dealing with."

I looked back at him and said, "Honey, you do not have any idea who you are dealing with."

He let out a hideous laugh, spun around, and completely disappeared from sight. Not only did his visage disappear (I am not talking about an illusion), but his entire substance disappeared. I had my hand on his shoulder. Suddenly there was no shoulder, and my hand dropped. He disappeared, substance and all.

My first thought was "Hmm… I just got done telling him there was nothing he could do that I had not seen before!"

I lifted up my head and said, "Okay, Father. You better show me what to do about this because I do not know." I stood there praying in tongues, and suddenly the young man turned around and reappeared, facing me again.

He got in my face, let out a hideous, demonic laugh and said, "I told you, you do not know what you are dealing with."

I said, "And I told you, you do not know who you are dealing with!"

He laughed, spun around, and disappeared from my sight yet again.

My legs were starting to shake, my knees were getting a bit weak, and I was thinking, "Okay, what do I do with this? I have no idea what to do with this, Lord. How do I handle it?"

In his invisible state, the man began to throw books from the fireplace mantle at me. He hit me from behind. I couldn't respond because I couldn't see him. He had stepped into another dimension.

He spun around and appeared again. He put his nose right on the end of my nose, and his eyes were demonized. He said, "I told you…"

I responded, "And I told you…"

I grabbed him around his neck and threw him down on the floor. We wrestled for about six hours. Eventually, the man was delivered.

That deliverance did something inside of me because I knew the young man was a member of the Satanic Order of Melchizedek. I went into my bedroom after he left and threw myself on my bed. I began to weep. I cried out, "Lord, if the Satanic Order of Melchizedek has so much power that they can just disappear from sight, how are we supposed to combat that as the body of Christ?"

I heard the Lord say, "It is a twisted counterfeit of a righteous reality. When you plug into the righteous reality, you will have a thousand times more power than that!"

I thought, "Okay, Lord." But what He told me was more than I could handle at that time, so I put it on a back shelf. I tried to stop thinking about it, because I did not really understand or know what to do with it.

A few years went by. During a prophetic conference at my church, a man walked down the aisle. I leapt off the stage and jumped on top of his chest, then began speaking over him. The word that came out of me was this: "The Spirit of the Lord says you are one who is going to be a spearhead and forerunner of the restoration of the Order of Melchizedek in the earth. You will go back into previous generations to recapture unused portions of lost anointings that are still emanating in the spiritual atmosphere."

Today, he is a mighty man of God, and the things that I prophesied over him have come to pass. However, I still did not understand. I did not understand who Melchizedek was and what his purpose was on earth. Once again, I set it on a back shelf. I do that sometimes when I do not understand or do not yet want to press into new revelation that the Lord has for me.

Another year went by. I was at a conference when another man walked in. I ran out, grabbed his head and declared, "The Spirit of the Lord says you are one that is going to be a restorer of the Order of Melchizedek. You are going to go back in the generations, and you are going to recapture lost anointings that are still emanating in the earth's atmosphere. You are going to activate those things and shift and change things in the spiritual world."

I thought to myself, "Lord, what does that mean? I do not know what that means!"

Most of what has happened to me in the spiritual realm started out of ignorance. I just did not have any idea. One of the hardest things for us is to realize and acknowledge that we just do not know what we do not know. In this case, I figured I was going to have to study Melchizedek.

I went into the desert like I usually do. There I spent the first day reading the Word of God and engaging in praise and worship. On the second day, the Lord began to download some things from the heavenly realms. On the third day, all of a sudden, I was thrust up into the Spirit. The Lord took me back through my life and revealed everything from the time I was two years old to the current day. He showed me things that had been done or said in my life that were preparations for what was coming.

When I was little, my mother was what they then called mentally ill. She was in and out of several different mental hospitals. As I migrated through my own spiritual life, I thought it was too bad that she had been in a denominational church. No one ever told her how much joy there was in getting saved: too bad she did not know about that.

When I received the baptism of the Holy Spirit, I thought how sad it was that nobody had ever told my mother about the baptism of the Holy Spirit. I thought about how baptism in the Holy Spirit would have allowed her to overcome her oppression and depression. Later, when I got into deliverance ministry, I thought how it was so sad that nobody knew about casting out demons back then, because my mother could have been delivered of a whole life full of misery in three or four hours.

As the Lord took me back through my life from the time I was two until the present day, I came to a place when I was eight years old. In the Spirit, I was sitting at the table with my mother. I could always tell when she was sick because the sound of her voice changed. She was in one of those moments.

She said, "I saw it again today."

I asked, "What mother?"

She said, "You know: those triple concentric circles."

"What are you talking about? I do not understand."

"Yes, you do!" she demanded. "I'm talking about the triple concentric circles that happen when you throw a stone in a pond and the ripples go out like ever-expanding circles."

I explained again that I still did not know what she was talking about. She was so agitated. She fully expected me to understand about the triple concentric circles.

Through this ascension experience that took me into my past, I realized that my mother was a seer. But if you saw things nobody else could see and heard things that nobody else could hear in the 1950s, you were deemed crazy. They took her and put her in a mental institution. They fried her brains with daily electroshock therapy treatments.

Suddenly, I realized my mother was a precursor to the priesthood of Melchizedek. She paid the price for everything that has now been downloaded into me regarding triple concentric circles.[31]

Back at my computer, I thought, "Well, Lord, how can I find out about Melchizedek?"

---

[31] I will outline these in a future work. They include the 30, 60, and 100; First Day, Second Day, and Third Day; First Heaven, Second Heaven, and Third Heaven; Faith, Hope, and Love; Salvation, Sanctification, and Purification; Prophet, Priest, and King: and many more! Picture three concentric rings, with the first listed on the outside circle, the second sandwiched in between, and the third at the very center.

I was reminded of this verse: Jesus was *"designated by God as High Priest according to the order of Melchizedek. Concerning this we have much to say, and it is hard to explain, since you have become dull and sluggish in [your spiritual] hearing and disinclined to listen"* (Hebrews 5:10–11 AMP).

Then I thought, "You have so much to say about this, yet Melchizedek is only in the Bible five or six times. How am I going to find out anything about him?" An internet search pulled up what seemed to be millions of references to Melchizedek. But most of those references came out of Satanism or the occult. Then I remembered the Lord saying if we want to see what He is doing, look at the twisted counterfeit because there is a righteous real behind every twisted counterfeit. We are called to spearhead a whole new ministry for the priesthood of Melchizedek, but first we must know what the Order of Melchizedek is, and how or what it does on the earth.

So, the question is this: Who was Melchizedek? The Bible begins to teach about Melchizedek in the book of Genesis: *"Melchizedek king of Salem (ancient Jerusalem) brought out bread and wine [for them]; he was the priest of God Most High"* (Genesis 14:18 AMP). *Salem* means *peace*, and Salem in that day was the precursor for Jerusalem. Melchizedek was the king of Salem, which means king of peace. He was also called the priest of the Most High. The question remains: What was he? Church history reveals that he was a theophany or a Christophany. A theophany is an appearance of God made manifest in mortal flesh; a Christophany is a pre-appearance of Christ Jesus. The Book of Hebrews reveals more about Melchizedek: *"Without father or mother, nor ancestral line, without beginning of days nor ending of time, but having been made like the Son of God, he remains a priest forever without interruption without successor"* (Hebrews 7:3 AMP).

Before Melchizedek could appear at Abram's tent, Abram had to endure fighting and the overthrow of the Babylonian kings of that area. Abram had just come through a time of intense warfare when Melchizedek appeared. Isn't that interesting? In parallel fashion, the Age of the Church has just gone through twenty-five years of a global spiritual warfare movement. Why did we go through that spiritual warfare and what was its purpose?

Melchizedek appeared in Abram's tent at a very important *kairos* time of God. Historically speaking, every thousand years, God has raised up one man to change the way that man communicates with Him. This appearing of Melchizedek happened about two thousand years after creation as we have known it, a time when God's desire was to raise one man to bless the nations of the earth.

Today, we stand at a transition place—a *kairos* moment, if you will—in which God desires to raise humanity's levels of conscious awareness of His sovereignty. We are being raised up by Him to represent the one new man called to bless the nations of the earth.

There were several kings Abram had to conquer before he came into position: "*...Amraphel of Shinar, Arioch of Ellasar, Chedorlaomer of Elam, and Tidal of Goiim, they [invaded the Jordan Valley near the Dead Sea*" (Genesis 14:1–3 AMP). The first was Amraphel, the king of Shinar. His name means "one that speaks of secrets: the speaker of darkness and the communicator of deception." The second was Arioch, King of Ellasar which means "savage and merciless, a lion seeking whom he may destroy." The third was Chedorlaomer, the king of Elam. He was the Babylonian god who was "the servant and communicator of false positions." The fourth was Tidal, which means "one that is cast out of Heaven." He was the maker of an evil seed. An evil seed lives in the tree of the knowledge of good and evil. It reproduces fruit after its own kind and it also reproduces an evil generation.

The purpose of the entire spiritual warfare network movement on the earth was to bring us to the place where we recognize that these four kings have to be destroyed in our own lives. Inside of us, there is that one that speaks out of the tree of the knowledge of good and evil. We must overcome him and put him under our feet. It is called our soul, mind, will, and emotions. That voice inside of us that is the "communicator of false positions."

In the Age of the Church, we were taught: "You are a poor, miserable sinner and you will always be in sin!" That is a "communicator of a false position." We were taught: "You are just a human being having a spiritual experience." That is a communicator of a false position because that is not who we really are. In fact, we are the exact opposite. Who we really are is a spiritual being having a human experience. When we are cast down or oppressed, or when we are depressed, it is hard for us to enter the overcoming life. Ninety percent of that comes because of the communicator of false positions, which is a Babylonian mindset that has kept us from understanding our true governmental positions as sons of the living God.

As we begin to take authority over the Babylonian mindsets that live inside of us, we come to the position where Abram was when he began to receive from the priesthood of Melchizedek. Before he could receive that ministry, he had to conquer the Babylonian kings who controlled his future destiny to become the father of many nations.

Many of you have been overcoming Babylonian mindsets. Those mindsets hold you back; they defer and delay the cause and plan of Christ Jesus in your life until you, by violent force, overcome them. And they must be overcome by violent force: *"And from the days of John the Baptist until now the kingdom of heaven suffereth violence, and the violent take it by force"* (Matthew 11:12 NKJV.)

God is raising up what I refer to as *one new man* to produce an incorporated priesthood of Melchizedek. Everything Jesus did as He walked on the earth in mortal flesh, we are now called to do as a corporate body—and not only the things that He did, but greater things than He did are we called to do (John 14:12) as the Lord raises up the one new man. It is going to happen in the introduction of the priesthood of Melchizedek. If we are going to be part of this whole new movement of God, the first thing we must do is dethrone our own Babylonian mindsets.

Recently, I was having a discussion with a prophetic friend of mine. He explained how everything inside of him had been shaken. He said all the things that he used to think were established in concrete, written in black and white, regarding what God can or cannot do, were actually Babylonian mindsets.

Essentially, his pre-established mindsets have been morphing through the destruction of Babylonian mindsets. The old mindsets appeared to be etched in concrete, but we must shatter and blow them up. For two thousand years, we thought we knew God. But guess what? We have only known ten percent of His power. We have to cast down all Babylonian mindsets. When we do, the process can throw us into tilt because we have to reevaluate everything we thought to be the whole truth. My heart resonated with his as my friend shared what he was experiencing. Everything that he was going through, I had gone through myself.

When we get to the other side of this transformation, all of a sudden those experiences begin to make much more sense. As those habits that we formed in the Age of the Church are being extracted from us, it is hard for us to understand that if what we learned was not the whole truth, or if it was only half-truth, how do we get from half-truths or no truth to all of the truth? It is hard journey. It means dismantling the "in part" teachings and adopting whole new mindsets and parameters regarding our traditional belief system. I had to do exactly what my friend was doing. I had to call into question every doctrine I thought was secured in the heavens. I even had to come to a place of asking myself: What does it really mean to be born again?

....

In early 2005, I was ministering amongst cannibals and headhunters. As I was sharing the love of Jesus with them, there was a man who had a spear in his hand. He was jumping up and down, spinning and twisting, dancing and laughing, and carrying on at the Word that I had given to them. So, I went to my interpreter and asked him If he could ask what I had said that made the man respond that way.

The interpreter came back with tears in his eyes. He said, "Oh, that man said from the time he was eight to the time he was fifty, the Spirit of Light and Revelation walked with him through the jungle every day. That spirit told him all the things you just said, but he never knew his name. Today you told him his name."

I looked at the cannibalistic warrior. He was all painted up and mostly naked. I asked the Lord, "Are you trying to tell me that man knows You?"

The Lord just laughed and said, "Oh yes! He knows Me much better than you do!"

I caught myself wondering, "What church aisle did he walk down? Who did he make a prayer of salvation with?"

Do you see what I am trying to say? As concepts that we were taught in the Age of the Church come under serious challenge, we must acknowledge what God is doing in the earth right now goes above and beyond the normal boundaries of our theology. We have to dethrone many of our minimized concepts in order to be qualified as kings and priests in the order of Melchizedek.

In Genesis 14, Melchizedek is referred to as the "king of Salem" which translates as the "king of peace" and the "king of righteousness." Jesus is called "Prince of Peace" and "Prince of Righteousness." This was extremely puzzling to me. I asked, "Lord, how is it possible that Jesus is called 'Prince of Peace' and 'Prince of Righteousness' and Melchizedek is called 'king of peace' and 'king of righteousness?'" I could not understand that. After all, there is no one greater in the whole universe than Jesus. He is and always has been King of kings, and Lord of lords. So, why would Melchizedek be called "king of peace" and Jesus be called "Prince of Peace," and why would Melchizedek be called "king of righteousness" and Jesus be called "Prince of Righteousness?"

In the late 1990s I was in Jordan in the courts of King Abdullah. I was there with friends to bid on the purchase of King Hussein's plane for the Global Peace Initiative. While I was there, I got a word for one of the princes. I went to my translator and I said, "The Lord gave me a word for one of the princes in the middle of the night last night."

He was very excited. "That is really great! What prince was it?"

And I said, "Well, I do not really know." I told him the name of the prince that I thought it was.

His countenance fell, and he said, "Oh, *that one*. Well he Is a prince, but he is not the crown prince. Even the crown prince though he is the crown prince has no real authority until he is crowned the king!"

The statement hit me like a bolt of lightning. I realized (from the Lord), that Jesus is called Prince of Peace and Prince of Righteousness because His people have not yet crowned Him King. If we had indeed crowned Him King, we would have dethroned ourselves to the point that His sovereignty could manifest in our mortal flesh.

So, Melchizedek is called the king of peace and the king of righteousness. What did Melchizedek do when he first showed up at the tent of Abram? He did something that we all are going to begin to do following the patterns established in the Word of God.

Melchizedek was not limited to time, space or distance. He went into the future and he grabbed a technology that would not be introduced for two thousand years. Yet he brought it back from the future, and he set it down in Abram's tent. He broke the bread and he poured the wine. That is called *communion*. When Jesus first instituted communion, He did not say, "Take and eat. This is a symbol of My body and blood." He said, *"This is My body and My blood."* Present inside the body and blood of Jesus was our spiritual DNA, fully manifested in the earth realm. (By the way, communion rightly understood has the capacity to restore our longevity.)

When Melchizedek delivered that communion to Abram (which literally translated means "high father"), Abram's name was changed to *Abraham* (which means "exalted father of many multitudes"). In other words, by the breaking of bread and the pouring of wine, he was transformed from the natural man into the spiritual man.

Whenever the Lord changes somebody's name, He is changing their nature. Abram's nature really did change. The adding of the simple letter *h* meant he was totally endorsed by God. The letter *hey* in early Hebrew was a pictograph of a man with his arms raised and praising God. It literally means "great and glorious.".

The Hebrew word for *name* is essentially the same as the word *nature*. Every time the Lord wanted to raise up a man to change the way the earth related to him, He changed his name. That's why Abram became Abraham. That's why Sarai became Sarah. That's why Jacob became Israel. That's why Saul became Paul. When we enter the ranks of the overcomers, we also will be given new names, which means we will move out of our natural DNA and into the full demonstration of our spiritual DNA.

> *He who has an ear, let him hear what the Spirit says to the churches. To him who overcomes I will give some of the hidden manna to eat. And I will give him a white stone, and on the stone a new name written which no one knows except him who receives it.* (Revelation 2:17 NKJV)

Melchizedek was the priest of the Most High God. This is an interesting concept. How could he be a priest of the Most High God? The priesthood had not yet been ordered on the earth because Aaron and Levi were still in the loins of their father. They had not even been born yet and the priesthood had not yet been established. But, even if it had been established, Melchizedek could not be a priest. Why? The priesthood was established by generational descendants. Since Melchizedek had no mother and no father, he would be disqualified from being a priest because he had no generational antecedents.

I want you to hear that with your spirit ears: he had no generational antecedents. No mother, no father, no beginning of time, and no end of days: therefore, he would be disqualified for the priesthood. How did he then become a priest of the Most High God? The priesthood is an ancient priesthood. Actually, it predates the earliest priesthood and is more superior to the priesthood of man. Melchizedek blessed Abram and said, *"Blessed (joyful, favored) be Abram by God Most High, Creator and Possessor of heaven and earth; And blessed, praised, and glorified be God Most High, Who has given your enemies into your hand"* (Genesis 14:19–20 AMP).

We learn the following: *"And Abram gave him a tenth of all [the treasure he had taken in battle]"* (Genesis 14:20 AMP). This *tenth* probably reminds you of the tithe that Christians give to the church. What is the tithe? The church has twisted the meaning of the word *tithe* so that we think it only refers to money. It does mean money in the one sense, but it also implies ten percent of everything. It is ten percent of your labor; it is ten percent of your creativity, your gifts and your time. Can you imagine the difference it would make in all our lives and in the life of the church if everyone gave 2.4 hours (ten percent of our time) every day toward developing union with the Divine Nature? All of that is part of the tithe.

Keep in mind that what Abraham gave was a tithe: ten percent. I am here to tell you that what you represent is a tithe. The Order of Melchizedek represents God's tithe to the earth. You represent ten percent of those being extracted from the Age of the Church to establish a whole new foundation for God's forward move in the earth.

> *The Lord said to my Lord, "Sit at My right hand, Till I make Your enemies Your footstool." The Lord shall send the rod of Your strength out of Zion. Rule in the midst of Your enemies! Your people shall be volunteers in the day of Your power; In the beauties of holiness, from the womb of the morning, you have the dew of your youth. The Lord has sworn and will not relent, 'You are a priest forever According to the order of Melchizedek'"* (Psalms 110:1–4 NKJV)

Jesus said everything that He had was ours by the adoption of sons, that whatever He did, we could do and greater things. This is a prophetic word for you: You are a priest forever according to the order of Melchizedek! Inside of you, there is a part that had no beginning of time and no end of days. Inside of you, there is a part that had no earthly mother or father. It is called your spirit.

You are to rule in the middle of your enemies. God is giving you absolute authority to put every enemy under your foot. "That thy people will be volunteers in the day of Your power in the beauties of holiness from the womb of the morning, you have the dew of your youth. The Lord has sworn, that thou art a priest forever in the order of Melchizedek." You just have to receive it. I am saying, "the Lord has sworn, that thou are a priest forever in the order of Melchizedek." Get that down in your spirit. You cannot receive it if you receive it in the natural.

Every high priest is selected from among men, and is appointed to represent man in matters related to God, to offer gifts and sacrifices for sin. (Hebrews 5:1 NKJV)

According to Genesis 14, Melchizedek was a priest unto God, not a priest unto man. There is a radical difference. A priest unto God represents God to man, not man to God.

He the high priest ordained of man is able to deal gently with those who are ignorant and going astray. Since he himself is subject to weakness. (Hebrews 5:2–3 NKJV)

This is an application to the earth-ordained priesthood: the Aaronic, the Zadok, the Levitical priesthoods. Why? Melchizedek or Jesus was perfect and not subject to sin. That is why the Aaronic or the Levitical priesthood had to offer sacrifices. When they went in to offer sacrifices into the holy of holies, they were offering sacrifices for themselves, too, because they themselves were still in their sin.

This is the difference between these two types of priesthood. The early priesthood were men—called of men, ordained of men—to serve men and be the voice of men to God. That was the earthbound priesthood. Melchizedek, on the other hand, was not called by man or ordained by man. He was called by God and ordained by God to serve God, to minister to God, and to be the voice of God from the heavens down to the earth. This is what is now known as the emerging ministry of the oracle, who represents the voice of God in the earth.

So, there are two radically different priesthoods. One is ordained by man to serve man and to be the voice of man to God. The priesthood ordained by man functions from the earth upwards. The other is ordained and called by God to serve God and be the voice of God from God in Heaven down to earth. One functions from the earth upwards, and the second functions from Heaven downward. Eventually, these two will meet and come together in order for the fullness of everything that God has prepared to manifest in the earth realm.

I want you to receive this in your spirit. The reason why you are reading this book is that you are called by God: you are ordained by

God to serve God, to minister to God and be the voice of God for mankind. That is your purpose; that is your function. No one takes this honor of becoming a high priest upon themselves: they must be called by God. Christ also did not take upon Himself the glory of becoming a high priest. In other words, you cannot just get up in the morning and say, "Okay, I am a Melchizedek priest." We cannot take that on ourselves. It must be given by God. What does the Word of the Lord say? *"...Whom He predestined, these He also called; whom He called, these He also justified; and whom He justified, these He also glorified"* (Romans 8:30 NKJV).

The total, absolute and complete plan of God is going to go out into the nations of the earth. You did not choose it: He chose you! Actually, it is only through our ignorance that we could even step into it. Sometimes I tell people we are living in the greatest, most exciting time ever in the history of humanity. Even so, there is greater excitement ahead. The things happening in the earth right now are so great, so huge, and so powerful that we are shifting into a new move of God that has never before been seen or witnessed on the earth.

Our levels of function are being heightened in preparation of the mystery of God that has been hidden in Christ since the very beginning (Ephesians 3:9) which will be finally revealed. What will be revealed? Christ in you, the hope of glory. *"It has not yet been revealed what we shall be..."* (1 John 3:2 NKJV), and

> *Eye has not seen, nor ear heard,*
> *Nor have entered into the heart of man*
> *The things which God has prepared for those who love Him.* (1 Corinthians 2:9 NKJV)

God said to Jesus, "You are My Son, I have begotten You." As the order of Melchizedek in Christ, we are designated by God to walk as sons and to operate as priests to the Most High God.

> *...You are a priest forever*
> *According to the order of Melchizedek.* (Psalms 110:4 NKJV)

How can we have been priests forever in the order of Melchizedek? The answer is that we are now becoming in the earth realm what we have always been in the spirit realm. We were in Him in the beginning; we will be in Him in the end. From time immortal all the way back to the beginning, we have been in Him, called to be priests after the order of Melchizedek. We were predestined and foreordained to walk as sons of the living God.

It's not a new thing. You actually have been functioning in it, you just did not know and are not yet aware of what it is you have been doing. You were predestined and foreordained by God to live in the most dynamic time in all human history, in order to manifest Yahweh's glory in all the earth.

> *...He chose us in Him before the foundation of the world, that we should be holy and without blame before Him in love.* (Ephesians 1:4 NKJV)

> *Having predestined us to adoption as sons by Jesus Christ to Himself, according to the good pleasure of His will.* (Ephesians 1:5 NKJV)

> *But we are bound to give thanks to God always for you, brethren beloved by the Lord, because God from the beginning chose you for salvation through sanctification by the Spirit and belief in the truth.* (2 Thessalonians 2:13 NKJV)

> *To which He called you by our gospel, for the obtaining of the glory of our Lord Jesus Christ.* (2 Thessalonians 2:14 NKJV)

> *Let your light so shine before men, that they may see your good works and glorify your Father in heaven.* (Matthew 5:16 NKJV)

Our light is about to be made manifest in the earth. We are in a state of preparation for the seventh day transfiguration of the corporate son of man. If we are following His pattern, those who have qualified for the overcomer life are about to follow Yeshua right into His transfiguration.

The priesthood, therefore, is not a temporal priesthood, but an eternal priesthood. It lasts forever and it never ever passes away. During the days of Jesus' life in the flesh, the Bible says:

> ...[I]n the days of His flesh, when He had offered up prayers and supplications, with vehement cries and tears to Him who was able to save Him from death, [He] was heard because of His godly fear. (Hebrews 5:7 NKJV)

In the preparation of the body of Christ for stepping into the order of Melchizedek, there are lots of cries and lots of tears. We, too, will be heard because of our reverent submission. One of the things sadly lacking today in the body of Christ is reverence and submission. As we have face-to-face encounters with Christ, both reverence and submission will return in great proportions.

We are called because the Lord knew from the beginning of the foundation of the earth that we would be those who would offer Him our reverent submission. That means submitting everything that is in our lives. That means giving up our own hopes, giving up our own ministries, giving up our own ideals, giving up our own dreams, giving up our doctrines and our theology, giving up our right to be right. We give up and sacrifice everything that is inside of us so that we can be prepared for this priesthood. This produces ultimate death to self and surrender to His sovereignty.

The desire for radical yieldedness is increasing in us all to levels above and beyond our capacity to control. If I would have told you a year ago that you would be where you are today, you would have thought it impossible. The Lord is preparing you for reverent submission, in which you give up anything and everything that opposes or exalts itself against the glory of the Father.

> *Though He was a Son, yet He learned obedience by the things which He suffered. And having been perfected, He became the author of eternal salvation to all who obey Him, called by God as High Priest "according to the order of Melchizedek."* (Hebrews 5:8–10 NKJV)

In the body of Christ, especially in the Age of the Church, we have been taught that name-it, claim-it, grab-it, blab-it, theology that says if you are in the direct will of God, you will never suffer. When I first heard that message, I almost threw up. I thought to myself, "Well, goodness gracious, I wish somebody would have told the disciples that they would never have to suffer if they followed Christ. They were ripped apart, torn asunder, boiled in hot oil, crucified upside down, whipped with many lashes, and drawn and quartered by the chariots of Rome. I guess maybe they just didn't have enough faith. I wish somebody would have told that to Jesus. If He was doing the will of the Father, He would never have suffered."

Can you see how the enemy uses those messages, those that have the sound of goodness and give the appearance of goodness, but have as their purpose death? The Lord says there is that thing that seems right in the eyes of men, but the way thereof is death (Proverbs 16:25). The wrong message produces death in the realms of the spirit: if people think they are suffering because there is something wrong with them, they cannot go on.

Jesus said that before He comes again, first the Spirit of Elijah must come again to restore all things: *"Indeed, Elijah is coming first and will restore all things"* (Matthew 17:11 NKJV). He explains, *"But I say to you, I will not drink of this fruit of the vine from now on until that day when I drink it new with you in My Father's kingdom"* (Matthew 26:29 NKJV).

We are in a state of preparation to manifest the transfiguration of the corporate son of man in the earth. (See the chapter on the Corporate Transfiguration). During this time of preparation, we will find that we align ourselves either with the Spirit of Moses or the Spirit of Elijah which were present with Yeshua at his transfiguration. If the purpose of the coming of the Spirit of Elijah is to restore all things, it might be expedient for us to understand his preparation for his first prophetic call, as well as in the person of John the Baptist, in whom he manifested himself as the spirit of reformation.

In the preparation of the spirit of Elijah, Elijah was sent to sit between the Brook Cherith and the River Jordan. I digress, but there is a principle here that needs to be expressed if we are truly to understand our calling to the Order of Melchizedek.

I am a word person. I do not just read the Bible; I look up every single word and find out what it really means in Hebrew. Why would the Lord send Elijah to *sit*—that means *rest*—between the Brook Cherith and the River Jordan? The hardest thing for a Christian to do is just sit. We feel that we must always be doing something in order to be productive. But we are entering the seventh day, which is the day of rest.

Cherith means to be ripped apart, to be torn asunder, to be severed bone from marrow, to be utterly circumcised in every area of the flesh. Doesn't that sound like so much fun?! This represents the preparation of the Spirit of Elijah, whom the Lord will call to arise in the body of Christ in order to restore all things before He returns.

I used to think, "Well, Lord, if I could just get to the Jordan, I could charge right on over to the Promised Land." Then I found out what *Jordan* means. *Jordan* means to be pushed down, forced down, kicked down, cast down, cut down, pressed down, to utterly "descend into the lower regions." Now, what do we know about utterly descending into the lower regions?

Elijah was in a place where the brook had dried up and there was famine in the land. The Lord sent ravens to feed him. I used to think, "Isn't God so good. He just sends those ravens out of the sky to feed the great prophet and take care of all his needs." In further search for the truth about Elijah, I looked up the word *raven*. *Raven* comes from the root word *rahweh*, which literally translated means to be sold off, mortgaged, occupied, and turned over to the blackened fowls of the air. Doesn't that sound like so much fun?!

I am trying to get to something here. It was not enough that Elijah, as part of his preparation, was ripped apart, torn asunder, severed bone and marrow, utterly circumcised in every area of the flesh. It was not enough that he was pushed down, forced down, kicked down, cut down, cast down, pressed down, and had to utterly descend into the lower regions. He also had to be mortgaged, occupied, and turned over to the blackened fowls of the air. Does that sound like the God you know?

Maybe you have been through trials and suffered rejection; you may have even been ripped apart and torn asunder. If you have been enduring this kind of conflict, you are in a good place because you are being prepared for an Elijah move of God.

For Elijah, it was not enough that he endured all this preparation: next the Lord has the audacity to send him to Zarephath. *Zarephath* literally means "the all-consuming fire." Elijah had to go through the all-consuming fire to get through his preparation. There is a coming baptism of fire that will bring us to the culmination of our preparation for ruling and reigning.

Not only did the Lord send him to Zarephath, He sent him to the home of a widow woman who was considered by the existing religious structure as worse than a dog. She was one of the Hebrew refugees who had been carried off in the Babylonian captivity and had intermarried with idol worshippers. She was considered unclean and unworthy of fellowship with the faithful Jews. (By the way, she is the counterpart of the Samaritan woman at the well to whom Jesus ministered and who was ultimately responsible for bringing a whole village to know Him. None of His disciples counted her worthy of receiving ministry from Him, either.)

Elijah and Moses were precursors of what we are becoming. Elijah could call down fire from heaven. He could control the weather. He could raise the dead and heal the sick. He had power to overthrow all the religious prophets of Baal of his day. So, why would God send this promising, budding prophet to the home of an unacceptable widow woman?

While he did many signs and miracles, the one least talked about was the one that manifested in the home of the widow woman. She came to him, saying: *"What [problem] is there between you and me, O man of God? Have you come to me to bring my sin to mind and to put my son to death?"* (1 Kings 17:18 AMP). Elijah took her son up to his own bed. He spread himself over the son's dead body three times and called forth life from death (1 Kings 17:19–22).

What does this miracle have to do with us today? The Word teaches us that many more are the sons of the widow woman than the sons of she who has the bridegroom (see Isaiah 54:1). Today, there are 5.8 billion dead sons in the earth. Part of our purpose as the emerging, corporate Spirit of Elijah is to spread ourselves over them and call forth the power of God to bring those sons from death into life.

A prerequisite of the priesthood of obedience is achieved through suffering. Many of you have suffered—though not to the shedding of innocent blood. But you have suffered accusations, betrayals, rejection. I want you to internalize this now: You are being ripped apart, you are being torn asunder, and you are being severed bone from marrow. You are being utterly circumcised in every area of your flesh. There is a huge tectonic shift going on right now. It is essentially a quantum shift. It is a global shifting of mindsets.

Jesus *"learned obedience by the things which He suffered"* (Hebrews 5:8 NKJV). Once made perfect, Jesus became the source of eternal salvation for all who obeyed Him. He was designed by God to be a priest after the order of Melchizedek. Does that mean "after" as in literal time? Does it mean he was called to be a priest "after" (as in "like unto") the order of Melchizedek? What does that mean? And, if Melchizedek is so important, why isn't there more told about him in the scriptures?

> *For though by this time you ought to be teachers, you need someone to teach you again the first principles of the oracles of God; and you have come to need milk and not solid food. For everyone who partakes only of milk is unskilled in the word of righteousness, for he is a babe. But solid food belongs to those who are of full age, that is, those who by reason of use have their senses exercised to discern both good and evil.* (Hebrews 5:12–14 NKJV)

> *Therefore, leaving the discussion of the elementary principles of Christ, let us go on to perfection, not laying again the foundation of repentance from dead works and of faith toward God, Of the doctrine of baptisms, and of laying on of hands, and of resurrection of the dead, and of eternal judgment. And this will we do, if God permits.* (Hebrews 6:1–3 NKJV)

There are people in the body of Christ who are not being permitted to see the things that you are seeing or to hear the things that you are hearing. This can only be done *"if God permits."* That should cause us to explode inside, because God *has* given us permission to become the beginning of the final outpouring on the earth. We have to come to this position by election; we cannot work ourselves into it. You cannot simply decide that you are going to be a part of it. You can only come if God permits.

Do you have any idea what that means? I know people in the Age of the Church who are such good people. They love God with all their hearts. They serve the Lord in missions overseas. They were the spearheads and the road pavers for the baptism of the Holy Spirit. But they are not learning and understanding the same things we are.

Melchizedek broke the bread, poured the wine and blessed Abram. The result was that Abram became Abraham. At that time, God struck a unilateral, unconditional, eternal, irrevocable covenant with Abraham—all while Abraham was still asleep: *"For when God made a promise to Abraham, because He could swear by no one greater, He swore by Himself, saying, 'Surely blessing I will bless you, and multiplying I will multiply you'"* (Hebrews 6:13–14 **NKJV**). This covenant was unilateral and unconditional because it did not require Abraham's volitional acceptance. Abraham was sound asleep when the covenant was spoken by God over him. This covenant did not say *if* you keep my commandments, or *if* you obey my precepts. It said *"I will..."* That is an unconditional promise.

> *And so, after he had patiently endured, he obtained the promise. For men indeed swear by the greater, and an oath for confirmation is for them an end of all dispute.* (Hebrews 6:15–16 **NKJV**)

Once you truly understand in the depths of your being what the covenant with Abraham was all about, it will answer every question that you have had concerning the move of God that is occurring right now. When God, having no name greater than His own name, *swears* by His own name, I believe He intends to keep the promise He made. After all, it is impossible for God to lie.

There are many promises and prophecies in both the Old and New Testaments which declare that every descendant of Abraham will know Him, from the greatest to the least. I had a hard time understanding how all of Israel could be saved when ninety percent of them have gone to the grave without confessing Jesus as Messiah. When I enquired of the Lord, He caught me up in the spirit and took me far into the future to show me how He will keep His promise. When we can access future events, it is easy to see how things will work out in the long run.

During that ascension experience, I actively became a co-worker and co-creator together with God for the fulfilment of His promise and for the restoration of all things, which has to do with what happens in the earth during the second resurrection.

> *These heroes all died still clinging to their faith, not even receiving all that had been promised them. But they saw beyond the horizon the fulfillment of their promises and gladly embraced it from afar. They all lived their lives on earth as those who belonged to another realm.* (Hebrews 11:13 TPT)

> *Abraham believed God, and it was accounted to him for righteousness.* (Romans 4:3 NKJV)

This is not the first time that the unfolding of God's sovereign plan for mankind has been seen—it has been seen before. The difference between them and us is they did not live long enough to see the thing they hungered for, longed for, waited for and desired. But we are going to see it.

Prayer

Father, we thank you that we have been predestined and foreordained to walk as the sons of the living God. We ask you to bring to completion the good work you have begun in us, so that we can *"become the thing we behold."*

As we continue to pursue You into the heavenly realms, may You prepare us totally to enter into the hundred-fold order of Melchizedek, that we may be qualified to rule and reign with You in Your throne. Turn us into effective ministers and oracles, according to your divine design. We believe You to do abundantly above all we can hope or expect in bringing us into *"the fullness of the measure of the stature of Christ."*

We love You totally. We ask You to show us how to love You the way You love us, and further show us how to love those outside the ranks of our faith with same measure of love You have for them—total, complete, unconditional love, because You are love!

About the Author

Nancy Coen is a globally-recognized conference speaker and teacher. Her journey has taken her to over 130 nations. She ministers to the poorest of the poor and the richest of the rich, being "no respecter of persons." Her ministry extends beyond the four walls of the church to touch the lives of bankers, billionaires, businessmen, and government officials, as well as the poor and poverty stricken.

Nancy has raised up corporate ascension groups in over thirty nations to do the business of mandating and legislating from the heavenly realms to produce changes in the earth. Many of these groups have been functioning for up to twenty years and have seen massive changes as a result of initiating prayer from divine positioning.

She has been married to Bob Coen for over fifty years. They currently reside in the beautiful Colorado Rockies. They have three children, twenty-one grandchildren, and as of this writing, seven great-grandchildren.

Nancy's next book will be *Living the Limitless Life*. Be sure to watch for it!

www.ingramcontent.com/pod-product-compliance
Lightning Source LLC
Chambersburg PA
CBHW060048230426
43661CB00004B/699